Object-Oriented Database Systems

Concepts and Architectures

Object-Oriented Database Systems

Concepts and Architectures

Elisa Bertino

University of Genoa

Lorenzo Martino

TECSIEL S.p.A

ADDISON-WESLEY
PUBLISHING
COMPANY

Wokingham, England · Reading, Massachusetts · Menlo Park, California · New York
Don Mills, Ontario · Amsterdam · Bonn · Sydney · Singapore
Tokyo · Madrid · San Juan · Milan · Paris · Mexico City · Seoul · Taipei

The programs in this book have been included for their instructional value. They have been tested with care but are not guaranteed for any particular purpose. The publisher does not offer any warranties or representations nor does it accept any liabilities with respect to the programs.

Many of the designations used by manufacturers and sellers to distinguish their products are claimed as trademarks. Addison-Wesley has made every attempt to supply trademark information about manufacturers and their products mentioned in this book.

Cover designed by Chris Eley
incorporating illustration © Galleria dell'Accademia, Venice/The Bridgeman Art Library, London
and printed by The Riverside Printing Co. (Reading) Ltd.
Translated and typeset by Logotechnics C.P.C. Ltd., Sheffield
Printed in Great Britain by T.J. Press (Padstow) Ltd., Cornwall

First printed 1993.

ISBN 0–201–62439–7

British Library Cataloguing-in-Publication Data
A catalogue record for this book is available from the British Library.

Library of Congress Cataloging-in-Publication Data is available

Contents

Preface

Of all currently available database systems, object-oriented database systems represent some of the most promising ways of meeting the demands of the most advanced applications, in those situations where conventional systems have proved inadequate. This book deals systematically with object-oriented systems and looks at their data models and languages, and their architecture.

A description is given of the models and languages of some specific systems, to put into context the various features which characterize an object-oriented data model.

The book is aimed both at university students reading computer or information sciences, engineering and mathematics and at researchers working in the field of databases. It is also directed towards those involved in databases and information systems in an industrial and applications context who are interested in being introduced to the various aspects of this new information technology.

Guide to the Reader

The text is divided into ten chapters. Chapter 1 is a general introduction to recent trends in the field of databases. Chapter 2 describes object-oriented data models, various semantic extensions to these and the models of a number of systems. Chapter 3 covers query languages. Chapters 4 and 5 describe versions and evolution, respectively. Chapter 6 deals with authorization models. Chapters 7 and 8 discuss optimization of queries and implementation and access strategies, respectively. Chapter 9 describes the architectures of certain systems. Finally, the Summary is a conclusion and covers future trends in research and development.

Each chapter is largely self-contained although the concepts presented in Chapter 2 are used in all subsequent chapters. It is therefore advisable to read Chapter 2 before reading any of the later chapters. Also, Chapters 7 and 8 deal with concepts related to query languages and therefore it would be advisable to read Chapter 3 before reading them.

Acknowledgement

Part of the material contained in this book is covered in articles written by the first author together with other researchers and colleagues, including Won Kim, Mauro Negri, Giuseppe Pelagatti and Licia Sbattella, to whom we owe enormous thanks. We would also like to thank Cristina Borelli and Etnoteam for the information that they kindly supplied us on the GemStone system. Finally, we would like to thank Chiara Faglia and Donatella Pepe of Addison-Wesley Masson for having made this project possible and for having followed it through with us in the various stages of its development.

We dedicate this book to our parents.

1 Introduction

In this chapter we give a brief description of the background to database technology and current trends in order to ascertain the reasons behind the development of object-oriented databases. In particular, we discuss the chief features of advanced applications which require new techniques to be developed to enable the execution of data management tasks.

1.1 Database Management Systems

In any type of organization, considerable resources and activity are dedicated to the gathering, filing, processing and exchange of data based on well-established procedures in order to achieve specific goals. For example, in a bank, data management systems are set up for the purpose of providing financial services, whereas in a hospital, data organization is based on the provision of health services. In recent years, due to marked changes in computer technology and due to the subsequent lowering of costs there has been an increase in the numbers of electronic processors for facilitating and developing data processing possibilities. In particular, the late sixties saw the development of data management technology with the implementation of data base systems which were arranged as a set of persistent data and a set of applications programs which were used to access and update the data.

Over the last thirty years, this technology has continually been upgraded. The first database systems were based on the use of separate files. ISAM and VSAM are examples of file management systems. Starting with this technology, there was a move towards an approach whereby data are integrated into a single collection (Database). Management of these is carried out by DBMS ('Database Management Systems'). DBMS are centralized or distributed software systems which provide facilities for defining databases, for selecting data structures necessary for storing and searching for data, either interactively or by means of a programming language. The first were database management systems – characterized by a hierarchical model – such as the IMS system and the System 2000, while the CODASYL database systems, such as IDS, TOTAL, ADABAS and IDMS, were developed later. The following generation was noted for the advent of relational database technology (Codd, 1970). These relational databases are installed increasingly in all sizes of systems, from large processors to personal computers, since they are straightforward and easy to use. The simple design of the abstraction mechanisms of the relational data model has enabled simple query languages to be developed. Thus these systems have also been made accessible to non-expert users. Examples of languages based on the relational model include SQL (Chamberlin, 1976), the QUEL of the INGRES system (Stonebraker *et al.*, 1976) and the QBE developed at IBM (Zloof, 1978).

Relational DBMS have contributed considerably to the impact of database technology. In particular, these systems have proved to be an effective tool enabling data to be used – also employing procedures not envisaged during the design of the database – by several users simultaneously, incorporating high level and easy to use computer languages. Furthermore these systems afford efficient facilities and a set of functions which ensure confidentiality, security and the integrity of the data they contain. Therefore relational DBMS are one of the basic elements of technology in the development of advanced data systems.

A conventional type of DBMS, for example, a relational DBMS, or an advanced type of DBMS, is characterised by a 'data model'. This is a set of logical structures which allows the user to describe the data which are to be stored on the database together with a set of operations for handling the data. The relational model, for example, is based on a single data structure – the relation. A relation can be seen as a table with rows (tuples) and columns (attributes) which contain a specified type of data, for example, whole integers or character strings. The operations associated with a data model define the data structures which represent the entities of the application domain which one wishes to model in the database, to access it to retrieve data, and to use it in order to carry out updates. In the case of the relational model, access operations can, for example, be used to retrieve the tuples satisfying specific conditions, as well as to select certain attributes of these tuples. Update operations are for inserting and deleting tuples and for changing the values of the attributes of the tuples.

The various operations provided by a DBMS are expressed by means of one or several languages. Normally a DBMS provides a DDL ('Data Definition Language') which defines the database schema. In a relational DBMS, the arrangement is a schema of a set of relations. For each relation, the name and the field (type of data) of each attribute of each relation are given together with any requirements relating to the integrity of semantics – for example the requirement whereby an attribute must assume values other than zero. Furthermore, DBMS provide a DML ('Data Management Language'). Very often, the DML component which allows access operations is known as a 'query language'. In addition to these types of languages, DBMS are provided with a further language for controlling and administering the database. This language, which is often indicated as the DCL ('Data Control Language'), provides functions such as authorization and physical resource management functions (for example the allocation of indices). In addition, a DBMS provides a set of functions whose purpose is to ensure the data quality and integrity, as well as easy and efficient access to data. Thus a DBMS is equipped with mechanisms for concurrency control, and that enables several users to gain access to data at the same time. It also has recovery mechanisms which ensure the consistency of the database if the system crashes or in the case of certain user errors. DBMS contain also auxiliary access structures to ensure efficient access to data, and a sub-system for optimizing query operations. This sub-system, known as the 'query optimizer', is, usually, very sophisticated in relational DBMS.

1.2 Advanced Applications

The first and most important DBMS applications were produced in managerial and administrative areas. This has influenced the principles of the organization and use of data in current DBMS which are characterized by data models with little expressive power. Recently, as a result of hardware innovations, new *data intensive* applications have emerged. For these a number of functions is required on DBMS, only some of which are available on the relational DBMS. For example Engineering applications, such as CAD/CAM, CASE (*Computer Aided Software Engineering*), CIM (*Computer Integrated Manufacturing*), or multimedia systems, such as geographic information systems, environmental and territorial management systems, document and image management systems, medical information systems, and decision support systems. The principal feature which unites these applications and which differentiates them from managerial ones is the need to model and to manage data whose structure and whose relationships with other data cannot be mapped directly back onto the tabular structure of the relational model. For example, representing a complex object in the relational model means the object has to be subdivided into a large number of tuples. Then a considerable number of *join* operations have to be carried out so that the object can be rebuilt when access is necessary.

Objects managed in the applications environments mentioned above are often multimedia ones and they are much more complex than objects managed by conventional DBMS. These are defined as aggregations of other objects. This creates a series of requirements concerning their modelling and management. With regard to modelling, a data model is required which expresses in the most natural and direct way possible both the structure of the individual objects and the existing relations between different objects. Not only must the data model be able to express static (or structural) relations but also the behaviour of the objects and the constraints which they must satisfy. In these applications environments, the structure of the objects as well as the relations between them are subject to change over time.

Finally the model must be extensible, in that the application must be able to define its own types of data, together with the associated operations, and to use them to define other types of data in the same way as the types of data supplied by the system. Extensibility is important since different applications very often need different types of data. For example, CAD applications need geometrical shapes and vector arrays, whereas CAM applications require matrices to describe robotic arm movements. Furthermore, developing a DBMS which provides all the possible types of data necessary for every possible application is not feasible. One solution is to supply a set of base mechanisms – building blocks – which allow the user to define his own types of data.

With regard to management, the nature of the applications, the size of the objects and the duration of the operations on these, the way in which a number of problems is tackled has to be thought out again, if not broadened or changed completely:

- Versions of objects have to be managed so that different states of evolution, validity periods or alternatives or information based on hypotheses can be taken into consideration.

- The transactions can be of long duration (for example, we are thinking of changing an object which represents a plane wing) and the size of data involved can be very large. This requires the crash recovery and consistency control mechanisms to be rethought.

- To retrieve complex objects quickly, appropriate storage techniques have to be developed. For example it must be possible to group together the objects most frequently used by applications (clustering) and to redefine these groupings when access patterns change.

- *Protocols* which efficiently support communications between the system's *clients* have to be provided. This requirement is very important in planning applications which involve groups of users whose cooperation must be made easier by the system. Indeed a lack of coordination between the various designers will very often reduce the possible parallelism in the development of the work and will waste resources. Incorrect or different interpretations of the same design data can also give rise to design errors. In Ahmed *et al.* (1991) various functions were identified which are able to support a higher level of coordination for cooperative activities. These functions include mechanisms for advising users of changes to the state of objects, and notifying the availability of objects.

- The 'evolutionary' nature of applications makes changes to the database schema a rule rather than an exception. It must therefore be ensured that the arrangement can be changed dynamically without having to shut the system down.

- Applications must be provided with both primitives which manipulate the object as a whole, and primitives which manipulate their various components. It is also necessary to provide capabilities for accessing and manipulating sets of objects through declarative query languages. In addition to query languages, one or more programming languages have to be provided. Certain applications, including engineering and scientific ones, require complex mathematical data manipulations which would be difficult to perform in a language such as SQL.

- Protection mechanisms must be based on the notion of the object which is, in this context, the natural unit of access.

- Functions for defining deductive rules and integrity constraints. The system must have efficient mechanisms for evaluating rules and constraints.

Finally, another important requirement concerns new applications for interacting with existing applications and the ability to access the data managed by such applications. This is crucial since the development of computerized information systems often passes through several stages. Very often the choice of one specific data management system is made on the basis of current application requirements and of available technology. Since both of these will change over time, organizations often find that they have to use heterogeneous data management systems which are often different in kind, resulting in problems concerning the interconnection of such systems.

1.3 Current Trends in Database Technology

In order to meet the requirements imposed by new applications, research and development in databases follows different trends (not necessarily diverging ones) which very often involve the integration of database technology with programming language technology, such as object-oriented programming languages or logic languages, or with artificial intelligence technology. Despite the existence of marked differences in such trends, there is a common tendency towards increasing the expressive power of data models and of data management languages. The principal trends can be characterized as follows:

- *Extended relational systems*
  This trend is closest to the relational DBMS. In general, there is a tendency to extend the relational DBMS with various functions, for example, the possibility of directly representing complex objects (DBMS with a nested relational model) (Roth *et al.*, 1988; Schek and Scholl, 1986), or to define *triggers* – actions which are automatically executed by the system when specific conditions concerning data arise (active DBMS) (Ceri, 1992). Almost all relational DBMS producers have extended, or are planning to extend, their products to include these functions (see, for example, the Postgres system (Stonebraker *et al.*, 1990)).

- *Object-oriented database management systems*
  These systems integrate database technology with the object-oriented paradigm which was developed in the area of programming languages and software engineering systems. This trend is, for the most part, driven by industrial developments even though there are not yet any consolidated theoretical foundations for object-oriented languages and models.

- *Deductive database management systems*
  These systems integrate database technology with logic programming. The principal characteristic of these systems is that they provide inference mechanisms, based upon rules, which generate additional information from the data stored in the database. These systems (at least certain aspects of them) are based on sound and well-established theoretical foundations, and they are being intensively researched in academic circles (Bertino and Mondesi,

1992; Cacace *et al.*, 1990). Industrial developments and applications are still very limited.

- *'Intelligent' database management systems*
These systems extend database technology incorporating paradigms and techniques developed in the field of artificial intelligence. Typical examples are represented by natural language interfaces or systems based on knowledge representation, for example, the CLASSIC systems (Borgida *et al.*, 1989) and ADKMS (Bertino *et al.*, 1992b).

In general, although the various trends are based on different approaches, such as the integration of DBMS functions with very diverse programming models, one can quite reasonably foresee that most of the next generation's DBMS will have a set of common characteristics which will include: the ability to define and manipulate complex objects, some form of hierarchy of types, mechanisms for supporting deductive rules and integrity constraints.

1.4   Object-Oriented Database Management Systems

The directions in previous trends outlined above includes OODBMS (*Object-Oriented Database Management Systems*), the most promising technology for the next generation of DBMS and for the development of integrated development environments, although it still lacks a common data model and formal foundations similar to those of the relational model. And their levels of operational efficiency, (in areas such as transaction and security management) and performance have yet to match those of established products. In fact, research has mushroomed and the first products from the various American and European start-up companies (in Europe, Altair comes to mind) have appeared on the market. A number of trends have begun to converge, including the adoption of standard platforms and client/server architectures, and moves towards standardization, such as the Object Management Group, CAD Framework Initiative and the ANSI task group on object-oriented databases. Major hardware manufacturers are involved in these initiatives and in the intense research effort, not only on an academic level. Some hardware manufacturers are involved in joint initiatives with OODBMS producers. OODBMS are perceived by hardware manufacturers and by the leading software companies as an essential component of their strategy (Jeffcoate and Guilfoyle, 1991).

The object-oriented model is one of to-day's most promising approaches in software development (Deutsch, 1991). One can reasonably foresee that using a similar approach for database management and for the development of *data-intensive* applications will bring all the benefits currently available in the field of software engineering. In particular, as discussed in Deutsch (1991), it was stated, both in a recent Usenet report on software manufacturing companies and in certain preliminary data gathered at the ParcPlace Systems research centre, that while the object-oriented approach requires a longer initial analysis phase, most software development projects require fewer people and are shorter. It was also discovered that the amount of code necessary (also of significant factors of scale) is less, when compared with cases in which conventional technology is used. Although data are not yet available on the costs of long-term maintenance of the software developed with the object-oriented approach, one can foresee that the drastic reduction in the amount of code and increased reusability will have the effect of reducing these costs. Some interesting examples of applications of this approach are given in Pinson and Wiener (1990).

With regard to the applications of the OODBMS for end-users, these are still at the experimental stage. Realistically, a number of factors has to be taken into account: it is impossible to abandon, from one day to the next, the 'old' DBMS, due to the obvious effects on a company's operating continuity, the shortage of suitably qualified staff, the lack of real 'guarantees' that it will be possible to reuse new data and applications environments already created, and ultimately to preserve existing investment intact. However, these factors will probably impact less on OODBMS compared with other types of advanced DBMS, such as deductive DBMS. This is because the object-oriented model can integrate different types of systems more easily. Some important experiments have been reported on CAD systems (Bertino *et al.*, 1989), on public data banks and in multimedia systems (Bertino *et al.*, 1992; Woelk and Kim, 1987). In particular, these experiments have shown that non-conventional data management systems, such as image databases, can also be integrated by using an object-oriented approach.

1.5   A Look at the Past

Despite the fact that the first OODBMS appeared not so many years ago, this type of system has undergone intense industrial development. Several generations of OODBMS can be delineated.

The first generation of OODBMS dates back to 1986 when G-Base was launched by the French company, Graphael. In 1987, the American company, Servio Corp., introduced GemStone. In 1988, Ontologic introduced Vbase and Symbolics introduced Statice. The common aim of this group of suppliers was to support persistent languages, in particular, those relating to artificial intelligence such as LISP. The distinguishing feature of these systems was the fact that they were stand-alone systems, and they were based on proprietary languages and did not use standard industrial platforms. In 1990, the total number of systems installed by these companies was estimated at between 400 and 500, and the systems were located, in particular, in the research departments of large companies.

The launch of Ontos in 1989 marked the start of the second stage in the development of OODBMS. Object Design, Objectivity and Versant Object Technology products followed soon after. Compared with the first generation of OODBMS, the second generation all use a client/server architecture and a joint platform: C++, X Window System and UNIX workstations.

The first third generation product, Itasca, was launched in August 1990, only a few months after the second generation OODBMS. Itasca is a commercial version of Orion, a project developed by the Microelectronics and Computer Corporation (MCC), a research institute based in Austin, Texas, and financed by a number of American hardware manufacturers. The other third generation OODBMS are O_2s, produced by the French company Altair, and Zeitgeist, a system developed internally by Texas Instruments.

While the first generation of OODBMS is considered as object-oriented languages with persistence, the third generation ones can be defined as DBMS with advanced characteristics (for example, version support) and with a DDL/DML which is object-oriented and computationally complete. Beyond the technical differences (architecture and functions), third generation OODBMS are the result of long-term research projects run by large organizations seeking to capitalize on their investments. Therefore they are very advanced systems both from the viewpoint of database technology and software development environments. As such, they are essential tools in the development and management of both data and of applications software.

1.6   Organization of the Book

The principal aim of this book is to provide an introduction to object-oriented data models and their corresponding languages, and to certain architectural aspects of data management systems based on these models. The data models and languages of certain systems are also focused upon and described in detail. Thus we are able to demonstrate the differences between the various models of object-oriented data. We should emphasize, at this stage, that there is as yet no established, theoretical definition of the object-oriented data model. We are also able to supply readers who are interested in specific systems with relevant introductory material. Certain aspects more closely related to research are dealt with, introducing some topics of current interest. The reader may find some interesting starting-points on which to base his or her own research.

Chapter 2 is the central chapter of the book, looking at general characteristics of object-oriented data models and certain semantic extensions proposed for such models. It also deals with some OODBMS data models. Chapter 3 discusses query languages which are one of the characteristic features of OODBMS compared with other object-oriented programming languages. Chapters 4 and 5 discuss respectively issues concerning management and evolution of both database schema and instances. Obviously, the management of versions and multi-user development are not functions which belong to an object-oriented data model. However, the type of applications we expect to be developed on an OODBMS require this type of function. Chapter 6 discusses the authorization mechanisms which are crucial in any multi-user data management system ensuring controlled access of data under different access modes for different groups of users. Chapters 7 and 8 cover certain aspects concerning implementation. In particular, Chapter 7 describes query optimization techniques, while Chapter 8 discusses indexing techniques and other aspects of implementing objects. Chapter 9 describes briefly the architectures of various OODBMS, illustrating their main architectural components. Finally, the Summary draws some conclusions, discusses certain problems still unsolved by research on OODBMS and illustrates some possible paths in the development of such systems, such as integration with logic programming.

1.7 Bibliographical Notes

The literature on databases and on systems designed to manage them is very extensive and there are many books and journals which cover the widest range of subjects within this area. Classical texts include Ullman (1989), Korth and Silberschatz (1986), and the more recent book by Vossen (1991); in particular, the latter includes an interesting introductory chapter on the OODBMS covering in detail the GemStone system model. Numerous books have been written on relational systems, including Date (1987, 1990), and Maier (1983) which covers thoroughly all aspects of the theory of the relational model. Finally, with regard to the design of databases we would mention Batini et al. (1991), which appeared recently, and which examines a methodology based on the Entity-Relationship model for database design.

There are currently very few books written on OODBMS – there is a book by Cattell (1991), which is above all an introductory work, and a text by Kim (1990), which mainly covers the ORION system. The book by

Cattell contains an interesting chapter which discusses the principal requirements of advanced applications. Most of the literature on OODBMS is in
the form of articles, or a collection of articles. In particular, introductory
articles include the articles by Bertino and Martino (1991), Joseph *et al.*
(1991), Maier and Zdonik (1989) which illustrate the main aspects of
object-oriented data models and the main architectural aspects of
OODBMS. Finally, the text edited by Kim and Lochovsky (1989) presents
an interesting collection of articles covering aspects and problems of
OODBMS and various applications of them.

2 Object-Oriented Data Models

In this chapter we describe the various distinguishing features of the object-oriented data models and systems. There is no common model to use as a point of reference, no formal foundation for the concepts we will be describing, and, as yet, no standard for object-oriented models, as there was in the case of the relational models in the Codd article (1970).

Many of the underlying ideas of object-oriented programming derive from the Simula language (Dahl and Nygaard, 1966), but this model only later began to be widely used, as a result of the introduction of Smalltalk (Goldberg and Robson, 1983). Other languages were then developed, including C++ (Stroustrup, 1986), CLOS (Moon, 1989) and Eiffel (Meyer, 1988). The key to object-oriented programming is to consider a program as being composed of independent objects, grouped into classes, which communicate with each other by means of messages. These concepts were also developed in other areas, for example, the knowledge-based languages (Fikes and Kehler, 1985), and different interpretations were often adopted. Databases require a proper data model and, in spite of the lack of a standard, certain generally accepted concepts concerning the model can be grouped together into a *core model* or *basic model*. This solution is sufficiently powerful to satisfy many of the requirements of advanced applications, and identifies the main differences compared with conventional models (Kim, 1990). It also serves as a basis for discussing the more important differences among the data models of the various OODBMS.

Obviously the core model, however powerful, does not capture integrity constraints and semantic relationships which are important for many types of applications. Such constraints include, for example, the uniqueness of the values of an attribute, the acceptability of the null value for an attribute, the range of values which an attribute can assume and similar concepts. Semantic relationships which are considered to be essential include the notion of 'part of/between' pairs of objects and object associations. These concepts, which are typical of databases but not of programming languages, shall be discussed after the discussion on the basic concepts.

We will also survey the data models of three systems: GemStone (Breitl *et al.*, 1989), O_2 (Deux *et al.*, 1990), Iris (Fishman *et al.*, 1989). These systems were chosen chiefly because various features of their data models, access and manipulation languages differ. Thus we are able to show specifically the variations of the core model.

2.1   Basic Concepts

The concepts of the core model include:

- Objects and identity – each real-world entity is modelled as an object. Each object is associated with a unique identifier.

- Complex objects – a set of attributes (or *instance variables* or *slots*) is associated to each object; the value of an attribute can be an object or a set of objects. This characteristic enables arbitrarily complex objects to be defined in terms of other objects.

- Encapsulation – each object contains and defines both the procedures (*methods*) and the interface with which it can be accessed and manipulated by other objects. The interface of an object consists of the set of operations which can be invoked on the object. The state of an object (attributes) is manipulated by means of methods invoked by the corresponding operations.

- Classes: all objects which share the same set of attributes and methods are grouped together in classes. Each object belongs to (*is an instance of*) some class.

- Inheritance: a class can be defined as another instance of one or more existing classes and will inherit the attributes and the methods of such classes. The class so defined is often referred to as a *sub-class*, whereas the classes from which it has been defined are referred to as *super-classes*.

- Overloading, overriding and late binding – with these functions, different methods can be associated with a single operation name, leaving the system to determine which method should be used in order to execute a given operation.

2.1.1 Objects and Identity

In object-oriented systems, each real world entity is represented by an object to which is associated a state and a *behaviour*. The state is represented by the values of the object's attributes. The behaviour is defined by the methods acting on the state of the object upon invocation of corresponding operations.

Each object is identified by a single OID (*Object Identifier*). The identity of an object has an existence independent of the values of the object attributes. By using the OID objects can share other objects and general object networks can be built.

Objects and Values

However, there are some models in which both objects and values (often called *literals*) are allowed and in which not all entities are represented as objects. Informally, a value is self-identifying and has no OID associated with it. All primitive entities, such as integers or characters, are represented by values, whereas all non-primitive entities are represented as objects. Other models, such as O_2 (Deux *et al.*, 1990), allow the definition of complex values which cannot, however, be shared by objects. In general, complex values are useful in cases where aggregates (or sets) are defined which are to be used as components of other objects but which will not be used as independent entities. A typical example is that of dates. They are often used as components of other objects; however, it is unlikely that a a user will issue a query on the class of all dates.

Difference Compared with the Key Concept

An important concept of the relational model is the *key* concept, an attribute or set of attributes whose values identify univocally each tuple in the set of all those tuples belonging to the same relation. Let us consider, for example, a relation which contains information such as a social security number, name and surname, address and date of birth, for a set of people in which the key could be represented by the social security number.

Very often a relation can have several alternative keys, called *candidate keys*, and the key which is actually chosen as the key of the relation is known as the *primary key*. In order to maintain correlations between the tuples of different relations *external keys* are used. This approach involves adding the key attributes of one relation into another. For example, to maintain the relationship whereby each employee is associated with the department in which he works, an additional attribute containing a department code for every employee tuple must be added to the Employee relation. For any given employee, the code indicates the department in which that employee works.

A key consists of the value of one or more attributes and can be modified, whereas an OID is independent from the state of the object. Two objects are different if they have different OIDs, even when their attributes have the same values. Moreover, a key is unique within a relation, whereas the OID is unique within the entire database. By using OIDs one can define heterogeneous collections of objects which even belong to different classes. Indeed, a collection consists of a set of OIDs which identify the objects belonging to the collection. These OIDs are independent from the class to which the objects belong.

There are certain advantages of using OIDs over keys as the object identification mechanism. Firstly, since OIDs are implemented by the system, the applications programmer must not concern himself with selecting the appropriate keys for the various classes of objects. Better performance is obtained, in that OIDs are implemented at low level by the system. Furthermore, as discussed in Cattell (1991), although the keys are more significant for the user, they present a difficulty – the short keys, which are more efficient (for example, social security number, part number, customer number, etc.) have little semantic meaning to the user, whereas the longer keys (name and surname, book title, etc.) tend to be extremely inefficient if used as external keys. In most cases, especially when external keys have to be used, users tend to use artificial codes which often have no semantic significance, but which are able efficiently to identify the tuples of a relation. This suffers from the same disadvantage as OIDs – minimal semantic significance – but has none of the latter's disadvantages.

Identity and Equality

Object identity introduces at least two different notions of equality between objects:

- the first, denoted by '=', is *identity equality*: two objects are *identical* if they are the same object, that is, if they have the same identifier;

- the second, denoted by '==', is *value equality*: two objects are *equal* if the values of all their attributes are recursively equal.

Therefore two *identical* objects are also *equal* whereas the reverse is not true. Certain data models also support a third type of equality often referred to as *shallow* equality where two objects are shallow-equal, although they are not identical, if all their attributes share the same values and the same references.

Approaches to the Construction of the OIDs

For the purpose of understanding the problems discussed in this book, it is interesting to analyze the different approaches to constructing OIDs used in the current systems. In the ORION system (Kim *et al.*, 1989a), an OID consists of a pair – 'class identifier, instance identifier' – where the first is the identifier of the class to which the object belongs and the second identifies the object within the class. When an operation is invoked on an object the system extracts the class identifier from the OID and determines the method for executing the operation. This approach has the disadvantage of making the migration of an object from one class to another, as in the case of reclassifications, difficult. This is because it involves modifying all the OIDs of the migrated objects. In such situations, each reference to migrated objects is invalidated.

In another approach, used, for example, in Smalltalk (Goldberg and Robson, 1983), and in the Iris system, the class identifier to which the object belongs is generally stored as control information in the object itself. In order to execute an operation such as the one described above, the object has to be accessed, so that the class identifier can be extracted from it. In the case of invalid operations, type-check operations become costly and result in accessing disks unnecessarily. Other approaches to constructing OIDs and the performance of such approaches will be discussed in Chapter 8.

Another difference concerns the *visibility* of the OIDs outside the DBMS. Some systems allow the user directly to access an of object's OID, to print it out, for example. Obviously this has the main disadvantage whereby the system must ensure that the OID cannot be modified. Most other systems do not allow the user to access the OID directly. Certain systems, for example, GemStone and O_2, allow the user to assign *variable names* (*user names*) to objects. These names, in the case of GemStone, are stored in a dictionary of symbols. Different users can have different dictionaries. The names allow the user directly to access a given object from the database. Examples of how names are used is given in the section dealing with the GemStone and O_2 systems models.

2.1.2 Complex Objects

The values of an object's attributes can be other objects, both primitive and non-primitive ones. When the value of an attribute of an object O is a non-primitive object O', the system stores the identifier of O' in O. But if the system supports complex values, the whole complex value is stored in the object's attribute. In the first case, when an object O is loaded from disk into the main memory, all those attributes that are complex values are immediately visible. If, however, the attributes are complex objects, then the object O will contain only the OIDs of such objects and further disk access will be required to retrieve the values of the attributes of these objects. The main disadvantage of using complex values is that they mean that the data model is conceptually more complicated.

Complex objects are built by applying constructors to simpler objects. The simpler objects are integers, characters, variable length strings, boolean and real numbers. The minimal set of constructors which a system must provide includes sets, lists and tuples. Sets are crucial since they are a natural way of representing real world collections and they are used to define multi-valued attributes. Tuple constructors are important as they provide a natural means of representing properties of an entity. Lists or arrays are similar to sets but they impose an ordering on the elements and they are necessary in many scientific applications.

Object constructors must be orthogonal, that is, they must be applicable to any object. Relational model constructors are not orthogonal as set constructor can be applied only to tuples and the tuple constructor can be applied only to atomic values.

2.1.3 Encapsulation

Encapsulation was not firstly introduced in the framework of object-oriented languages. It is the end result of an evolution process which started with imperative languages. The reason behind it was:

- the need to make a clear distinction between the specification and the implementation of an operation;
- the need for modularity.

Modularity is an essential principle for developing software which exceeds a certain number of lines (100,000 lines) (Joseph *et al.*, 1991) and therefore for all the more significant applications designed and implemented by groups of programmers. It is also useful as a tool for supporting object authorization and protection.

Encapsulation in programming languages derives from the notion of abstract data types. In this context, an object consists of an interface and an implementation. The interface is the specification of the set of operations which can be invoked on the object and are its only visible part. The implementation contains the data, i.e. the representation or state of the object and the methods which provides, in whatever programming language, the implementation of each operation.

In databases, this principle is translated into the notion that an object comprises both operations and data but with one difference. In databases, it is not clear whether the structure is part of the interface or not, whereas in programming languages the data structure is clearly part of the implementation and is not visible. For example, it is clear that in a programming language the data type 'list' must be independent of the fact that lists are implemented as arrays or by using dynamic structures and this information is quite rightly hidden. In databases, it should not be considered a disadvantage that it is known of which attributes and references an object consists.

Representation of a set of employees provides a good example of encapsulation. In a relational system, a set of employees is represented by some relation in which each tuple represents one employee. This relation is queried using a relational language and application programs may possibly be developed. These programs are generally written in an imperative language incorporating DML instructions. They are stored in conventional file systems rather than in databases. This approach provides a clear distinction between programs and data and between query language and programming language. In an object-oriented system, however, the entity *employee* is defined as an object comprising a data component (probably very similar to the tuple defined in the relational system) and an operational component, for example, *increase in salary*, *dismissal*. This information is all stored in the database. Encapsulation provides a form of 'logical data independence' and means that the implementation of objects can be modified, while the applications that use them remain unchanged.

The Manifesto (Atkinson *et al.*, 1989), makes an interesting observation – real encapsulation is obtained only when operations are visible and the rest of the object is hidden. However, there are cases in which encapsulation is not necessary. Use of the system can be significantly simplified if strict encapsulation is not enforced. Query management (see Chapter 3) is one situation where violating encapsulation is almost obligatory. Queries are very often expressed in terms of predicates on the value of the attributes. Therefore, almost all OODBMS allow direct access to attributes supplying 'system-defined' operations which read and modify these attributes. These operations are provided as part of the system (and are not defined by the user) and they are implemented by the system in a highly efficient manner and at a low level. This avoids, among other things, the user having to implement a considerable amount of methods which have the sole purpose of reading and writing the various attributes of the objects.

Methods

Objects in OODBMS are manipulated with methods. In general, the definition of a method consists of two components: *signature* and *body*. The *signature* specifies the name of the method, the names and classes of the arguments, and the class of the result, if the method returns one.

Therefore the signature is the specification of the operation implemented by the method. Some systems, such as ORION, do not require the argument class to be specified. In fact, in this system, type checking is carried out at run-time and not at compile-time. Even in certain object-oriented programming languages, Smalltalk (Goldberg and Robson, 1983), for example, this specification is not required. An intermediate approach is used, however, in the CLOS language (Moon, 1989); in this language the specification of the argument class as well as the object attribute domain classes, are optional. An example, shown by Moon (1989) is given below:

```
DEFCLASS ANIMAL ()
        ((COLOR)
        (DIET)
        (NUMBER-OF-LEGS: TYPE INTEGER)))
DEFMETHOD FEED ((ANI ANIMAL) FOOD)
        (UNLESS (MEMBER FOOD (SLOOT-VALUE ANI 'DIET))
        (ERROR '''~As don't eat ~A'' ANI FOOD)))
```

In the example, a class named ANIMAL is defined. Its instances have three attributes. However, only for the attribute NUMBER-OF-LEGS the class of the values that are possible is specified. Similarly, the definition of named method FEED specifies that this method has two arguments. The first, named ANI, can assume as values only instances of the ANIMAL class, whereas no class is specified for the second argument. The semantics of this method is to check whether a certain type of food is present in an animal's diet. The following is an example of an answer returned by this method: Tigers don't eat grass.

The body represents the implementation of the method and consists of a set of instructions expressed in any given programming language. The various OODBMS use different languages; ORION uses LISP, while GemStone uses an extension of Smalltalk, O_2 uses C. Other OODBMS, such as Vbase/Ontos (Andrews and Harris, 1987), Versant (1990), and ObjectStore (Object Design, 1990) use C++ (Stroustrup, 1986).

Access and Manipulation of Attributes

As discussed, some OODBMS allow the values of the objects' attributes to be directly read and written, thus violating the encapsulation principle. The aim is to make less complex the development of applications which simply access or modify objects' attributes. Obviously these applications are very frequent in data management. There are two advantages, described below, of being able to access or modify directly the attributes of an object:

- it avoids the programmer having to develop a large number of generally conventional methods;

- it increases the efficiency of the applications, in that direct access to the attributes of objects is implemented as system-provided operations.

Obviously the violation of the encapsulation principle can cause problems, should the definition of the attributes of an object be modified. Since there are these two contrasting requirements, the various OODBMS provide different solutions. Some systems, such as Vbase/Ontos, for example, and the system presented in (Bertino *et al.*, 1990), provide 'system-defined' methods for reading and writing the attributes of an object. These methods are implemented efficiently and at low level by the system. However, these methods can be redefined by the user (*overriding*). This is very useful in certain situations, for example when data are imported from an external relational database. Other systems, such as O_2, allow the user to state which attributes and methods are visible in the object's interface and which can be invoked from outside. These attributes and methods are said to be *public*. Conversely, attributes and methods which are not visible outside are referred to as *private*. A similar approach is used in C++. Finally, in other systems, such as ORION, all attributes can be accessed directly, both while reading and writing and all methods can be invoked. In ORION authorization mechanisms can still be used to prevent access to certain attributes and the execution of certain methods.

2.1.4 Classes

Classes and types

Object-oriented systems can be classified into two main categories – systems supporting the notion of *class* and those supporting the notion of *type*. In research, there is much discussion on the distinction between classes and types and the lack of formal definitions merely compounds the problems. But, although there are no clear lines of demarcation between them, the two concepts are fundamentally different.

A *type* models the common features of a set of objects which have the same characteristics and which correspond to the notion of abstract data type (Guttag 1977). In programming languages, types are a tool for increasing the programmer's productivity, ensuring the correctness of programs. If the type checking system is carefully designed, types can be controlled during compilation; otherwise certain parts can be processed only at run-time. In general, in a type-based system, types are not objects in the true sense of the word and cannot be modified dynamically.

Often the concepts type and class are used interchangeably. However, when both are present in the same language, the type is used to indicate the specification of the interface of a set of objects, while class is an implementational notion. Therefore, as discussed in America (1990), a type is a set of objects which share the same behaviour – and this can be *observed* from outside. This means that the type to which an object belongs depends on which operations are invocable on the object, in which order, the type of arguments and the type of the result.

On the other hand, a class is a set of objects which have exactly the same internal structure and therefore the same attributes and the same methods. The class defines the implementation of a set of objects, while a type describes how such objects can be used. This distinction exists in the Pool language (America, 1990, 1991) which uses the concepts of type and class. A type can be implemented by several classes. Conversely, a class can implement several types; if a class implements a type, it automatically implements all the super-types of that type. An example taken from America (1990) is given below:

```
TYPE Int_Stack
      METHOD get () : Int
      METHOD put (Int) : Int_Stack
END  Int_Stack
CLASS AIS
      VAR a:= Array(Int).new(1,0)
METHOD get () : Int
BEGIN IF a@ub=0
          THEN RESULT NIL
          ELSE RESULT a@high
          FI
END get
METHOD put (n: Int) : AIS
BEGIN a@high :=n;
      RESULT SELF
END put
END AIS
```

In the above example a type is defined which has stacks of integers and a class which implements this type as instances. The class implements this type in that it provides methods which implement all the operations defined in the type. Note that the signatures of the methods in the class are compatible with the corresponding operations specifications in the type definition. The stack data type method signatures and the signatures of the corresponding class methods verify a number of conditions. These are, respectively, conditions of *contravariance* for arguments and of *covariance* for the result (America, 1990), which ensure that an object implemented by means of class AIS can always be used wherever a Stack type object is used. A definition of these conditions is provided in Appendix A.

A similar distinction exists in language systems like Emerald (Black, 1987). The distinguishing feature of this language is the concept of *abstract data types* which has the function of specifying the interface of a set of objects, and the concept of *implementation type* which has the function of implementing an abstract data type. In Emerald these two notions were introduced to support distributed applications. An abstract data type can have associated with it different implementation types, possibly one implementation type for each node in which there are instances of the abstract data type. The data model outlined by Bertino *et al.* (1990) provides a similar concept and is defined specifically for distributed applications. This model supports the concepts of *abstract class* and *implementation class* which can be seen as an analogue for data management applications of abstract data type and implementation type in Emerald.

Joseph *et al* (1991) make a similar distinction, given that the functionalities required of the system are the interface, implementation and management of the extent of each class. Interface functions are assigned to type definitions, whereas classes extend type definitions to include information on the names and types of attributes and on methods; in other words, classes represent their implementation. In a sense, class definition comprehends the corresponding type definition. Also, several classes can be compatible with a single type definition and the type-class relationship is not necessarily one to one. This means that, in principle, a type can be implemented by more than one class, and a class can implement more than one type. However, in the majority of OODBMS, there is no precise distinction between the two concepts and, therefore, between the two terms. For example, GemStone and O_2 use a concept of class which comprehends the functions of specification and of implementation, but the extent is managed separately, using constructs such as *set* or *bag*. The management of the extent through these constructs provides greater flexibility, in that, for example, several sets of objects of the same class can be defined, but the model is, however, more complex. In ORION, the class has associated all three functions, i.e. specification, implementation, and extent management.

Finally, in ENCORE (Zdonik and Mitchell, 1991), type is understood as interface specification and implementation, while class is understood as the extent of a type. A type can have several classes associated with it and classes can be defined by means of predicates. For example, given the data type 'Car', the class 'BlueCar' can be defined as a set of the instances of the data type 'Car', in which the 'color' attribute has the value blue.

Theoretically it would be correct to use the following three concepts of extent of type in an object oriented database model:

- type, meaning the specification of a set of objects;
- class, meaning the structure and implementation of a set of objects;
- collection of objects, supporting the concept of the extent of a type;

But the implications for other aspects of the model and for the implementation would be serious. For example, three different hierarchical mechanisms for inheritance would be required. Moreover, each object would need to have both its type and class associated with it.

Classes and Mechanisms of Instantiation

Instantiation means that the same definition can be used to generate objects with the same structure and behaviour – in other words it is a mechanism by which definitions can be reused. Object-oriented data models use the concept of class as a basis for instantiation. In this sense, a class is an object which acts as a template. In particular, it specifies:

- a structure, that is, the set of attributes of the instances;
- a set of operations;
- a set of methods, which implement the operations.

Objects that 'respond' to all the operations defined for a given class can be generated by using the equivalent of a *new* operation. Clearly, the values of the attributes of each object must be stored separately, but the definitions of the operations and of the methods do not have to be repeated. In fact, each class is associated with an object known as a *class-object* which contains the information common to the instances of the class and, in particular, the methods of the class; the class-object is therefore stored separately from the instances.

An alternative approach for generating objects is to use *prototype objects*. This involves generating a new object from another existing object, modifying its attributes and/or its behaviour. This is a useful approach when objects change quickly and are more different than similar.

In general, an approach based on instantiation is more appropriate where the application environments in use are more established, since it makes it difficult to experiment on alternative structures for objects, whereas an approach based on prototypes is more advantageous where experiments are being carried out at the application's initial design stages or in environments which change more quickly and where there are fewer established objects.

So far we have implicitly assumed that an object is an instance of a single class. The instances of a class C are also *members* of the super-classes of C. Therefore, as discussed in Moon (1989), a distinction is made between the concept of being an instance of a class and the concept of being a member of a class. An object is an instance of a class C, if C is the most specialized class associated with that object in a given hierarchy of inheritance. In systems in which the migration of objects between classes is not allowed, an object is an instance of a class C, if it was generated by

C (using the operation *new* invoked on C). An object is, however, a member of a class C, if it is an instance of C or an instance of a sub-class of C.

Most object-oriented data models restrict an object to being an instance of a single class. However, an object can be a member of several classes by means of inheritance hierarchy. Some models, for example the model defined in Zdonik and Mitchell (1991), do not impose this restriction. An object can be the instance of several classes. Consider, for example, the class Person, with subclasses Student and Pilot, in which Student and Pilot are not subclasses of each other; and suppose that a person P exists, who is both student and pilot. A model for such a situation can be easily worked out by making P an instance of both Student and Pilot. So P, as well as being an instance of both Student and Pilot, is also a member of Person. These models often provide mechanisms for the classification of names in order to resolve ambiguities arising from the fact that attributes and methods with the same name are used in the various classes of which an object is an instance. However, if the data model restricts an object to being an instance of a single class, multiple inheritance can be used to model situations such as the one in the example above. For example, a class Student-Pilot could be defined, with both Student and Pilot as superclasses, and P could be made an instance of this class. Obviously the main disadvantage of the latter solution is that it involves a more complicated database schema.

Exceptional Instances

As mentioned earlier on, all instances of the same class have the same structure and a similar behaviour. O_2, however, allows exceptional instances to be defined in terms of the class of which they are instances. In such a model an instance can be created which has additional attributes and/or methods to those specified in the class itself and which redefines attributes and/or methods inherited from the class itself. In the latter case, however, the new definition must be compatible with the definition given by the class. In this sense the compatibility rules that apply to subclasses also apply here.

Aggregation Hierarchy

In almost all object-oriented data models, an attribute has associated with it a *domain* which specifies the classes of the possible objects that can be assigned as values to that attribute. This is an important difference compared with certain object-oriented programming languages, in which instance variables have no type. For data management applications which require efficient management of large amounts of data and which therefore need to allocate the appropriate auxiliary structures, the system must know the type of the possible values of an attribute. Even GemStone, which is derived from Smalltalk, requires, in certain circumstances (for allocating an index, for example), the domain of the attributes to be specified.

The fact that an attribute of a class C has a class C' as a domain, implies that each instance of C assumes as the value of the attribute an instance of C', or of a subclass of it. An *aggregation relationship* is established between the two classes. An aggregation relationship from class C to class C' specifies that C is defined in terms of C'. Since C' is in turn defined in terms of other classes, the set of classes in the schema is then organized in an *aggregation hierarchy*. However, this is not a hierarchy in the strict sense of the word, since the classes can be defined recursively.

Migration of Instances Between Classes

The migration of instances between classes is important. The fact that an object can become an instance of a class that is different from the class from which it was generated is very important for the evolution of objects. More specifically, it means that an object can modify its own characteristics – attributes and operations – while maintaining the same identity. Certain systems, such as Iris and Encore (Zdonik, 1990), are able to do this, while most others are not. If objects can migrate between classes, problems concerning semantic integrity are likely to arise. In fact, as discussed earlier, the value of an attribute A of an object O is another object O', an instance (or member) of the class domain of A. If O' changes class and its new class is no longer compatible with the class domain of A, object O will contain an incorrect value in A. Zdonik (1990) proposes one solution. It consists of inserting in O' a flag (*tombstone*) to indicate that O has changed class. The main disadvantage of this is that the application must contain some code to manage an exception where the object referred to is an instance of a class which is different to the one expected.

Classes and Persistence

Another important issue is the *persistence* of instances of classes, i.e. the modalities under which objects are rendered persistent (inserted in the database) and are eventually deleted (removed from the database). There are two basic approaches.

(1)   Persistence is an implicit characteristic of all instances of classes.
       The creation of an instance (typically, by means of the operation *new*) has the effect of inserting the instance in the database. Therefore the creation of an instance automatically implies its persistence. This approach, used, for example, in ORION, is the simplest in that, in order to make an object persistent, it is not necessary to do anything other than create the object. Typically, it is used in systems where classes also have an extensional function.

(2)   Persistence is an orthogonal characteristic.

The creation of an instance does not have the effect of inserting the instance in the database. An instance created during the execution of a program is deleted at the end of the program, unless it is made persistent. One mechanism for making an instance persistent is to associate a name-user to the instance, or to insert the instance in a persistent collection of objects. O_2 is one system using this type of approach. In general, this approach is used by systems where the classes do not have an extendible function. It has the main advantage of being very flexible (we will give some examples in the section on O_2), but it is more complex than the first approach. A further possibility (Maier and Zdonik, 1989) is to provide a special operation which, if invoked on an object, will make it persistent.

An intermediate approach between these two extremes can be adopted. Classes are categorized into persistent classes and temporary classes. All instances of persistent classes are automatically created as persistent instances, whereas this does not happen with instances of temporary classes. This approach is used in the E language (Carey *et al.*, 1988).

There are two ways of deleting objects. The first involves providing an explicit delete operation. Obviously, being able to perform a delete operation raises the problem of the integrity of references. In fact, if an object is deleted and there are other objects which 'point' to that object, these references are no longer valid. A very costly solution is to keep information, for example a *reference count*, which is used to determine whether an object is referenced by other objects. Typically, an object can be deleted only if its reference count has the value zero.

Another solution, used by ORION, is not to keep any additional information and freely to allow delete operations. References to deleted objects cause exceptions. This solution makes the delete operation efficient. However, it requires additional code in applications and methods in order to handle the exceptions arising from references to deleted objects. Also, the OIDs of the deleted objects cannot be reused. The second approach is based on not providing an explicit delete operation. A persistent object is cancelled only if all external names and references associated with it are removed. This ensures integrity of references.

Metaclasses

As mentioned earlier it is useful to consider each class in turn as an object in itself, that is as a class-object, in which the attributes and methods common to the instances of that class are gathered together and in which those features of that class are stored that cannot be considered as features of the instances, for example the number of instances of the class present at any given time in the database or the mean value of an attribute evaluated on all instances of the class.

If one wishes to uphold the principle whereby each object is the instance of a class, and classes are objects, then, for the sake of uniformity, the system must support the concept of *metaclass* in the sense of the class of a class. In turn, a metaclass is an object and must therefore be the instance of a metaclass on a higher level, and so on. Most object-oriented systems do not provide metaclasses and only some of them provide metaclass functionalities – albeit only in part. In ORION, for example, a system's class, CLASS, represents both the class of all classes and the root of the class hierarchy, that is, it is the superclass of all classes present in the system. Generally, metaclasses, if present, cannot be directly accessed and manipulated by the user. Their purpose is to simplify the management of classes by the system, and to ensure the uniform application of the object-oriented paradigm to the classes themselves. For example, if the operation *new* is invoked on a class, this invocation triggers a search for the appropriate method of executing the *new* operation. This search operation, called *method look-up*, is the same one that was used when searching a method for an operation invoked on an instance of the class. Therefore, *method look-up* is essentially the same for operations invoked on instances and operations invoked on classes.

Finally, some models allow the definition of attributes and operations which characterize classes, understood as objects. These attributes and operations are therefore not inherited by the instances of classes. An attribute which contains the mean of the value of an attribute calculated taking into account all the instances of the class provides an example of this. Another example is the operation *new* which is used to create new instances. This operation is invoked on the classes and not on the instances.

2.1.5 Inheritance

The concept of inheritance is the second mechanism of reusability and Bancilhon (1988) points out that it is the most powerful concept of object-oriented programming. With inheritance, a class called a *subclass* can be defined on the basis of the definition of another class called a *superclass*. The subclass inherits the attributes, methods and messages of its superclass. In addition, a subclass can have its own specific attributes, methods and messages which are not inherited.

As an example of reusability, let us imagine that we must create two classes which contain information concerning a set of buses and trucks. The features of the two classes are shown in Figure 2.1 by means of a graphic representation similar to the graphic representation used in Rumbaugh *et al.* (1991) and Cattell (1991). This represents each class by means of a rectangle subdivided into three levels. The first level from the top down contains the name of the class, the second, the attributes, and the third, the methods. The third level can be empty if the class has no user-defined methods. This graphic representation will be further refined at a later stage.

In the relational model, two relations would have to be defined, one for Buses and one for Trucks, and the procedures implementing the various operations – three in all – would have to be encoded.

Using the new approach, it is recognized that buses and trucks are vehicles and that they therefore have certain features in common, and others which differentiate them. Thus the type `Vehicle` is introduced. This has the attributes `number-plate`, `model`, `date_of_last_overhaul`, and the method implementing the `next_overhaul` operation. Then it is stated that `Truck` and `Bus` are specific vehicles and therefore only the features that differentiate them have to be defined. Therefore the following inheritance hierarchy support is obtained, as shown in Figure 2.2. The figure shows an arc directed from class C to a Class C'; it shows that C is a subclass of C'.

Truck	Bus
number-plate:STRING model:STRING licence: NUMBER date_last_overhaul:DATE estimated_value():NUMBER	number-plate:STRING model:STRING seats: NUMBER date_last_overhaul:DATE
next_overhaul():DATE	next_overhaul():DATE

Figure 2.1   An extract from a database of vehicles.

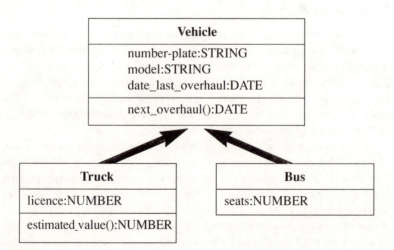

Figure 2.2   An example of inheritance hierarchy.

With this approach, less code has to be written. There is the added advantage which should not be under-estimated that inheritance hierarchies support a more precise and concise description of the reality of which one wants to make a model.

In certain systems, a class can have several superclasses, in which case one talks of *multiple inheritance*, whereas others impose the restriction of a single superclass, *single inheritance*. The possibility of defining a class from other classes simplifies the task of defining the classes. However, conflicts may arise, especially in multiple inheritance. Generally, if the name of an attribute or method defined explicitly in a class is the same as that defined in a superclass, the attribute of the superclass is not inherited, but is 'covered' by the new definition. In this case, one speaks of *overriding*, a concept which is discussed later in greater detail.

If the model provides multiple inheritance, other types of conflict may arise, for example, two or more superclasses may have an attribute with the same name, but with different domains. Generally, appropriate rules must be devised in order to solve these conflicts – if the domains are linked by an inclusion relation then the most specific domain will be chosen such as the domain for the subclass. If, however, this relation does not exist, the solution commonly adopted is to choose the domain on the basis of an order of precedence between the superclasses.

However, the essential aspect of inheritance is the relationship which is established between the classes, as the superclass, in turn, can be a subclass of other classes. The classes in a database schema can be organized, in the same way as for the aggregation hierarchy, in a inheritance hierarchy, which is an orthogonal organization with respect to that of the aggregation hierarchy. This graph is reduced to a tree when the model does not provide for multiple inheritance. The most consistent difference compared with the aggregation hierarchy is that the inheritance graph cannot have cycles for obvious semantic reasons.

In fact, in the literature and in the various object-oriented languages somewhat different concepts of inheritance exist. The differences between the various concepts depend upon the significance of the class and/or of the type. In Maier and Zdonik (1989), three different hierarchies are identified:

- the specification hierarchy;
- the implementation hierarchy;
- the classification hierarchy.

Each hierarchy relates to certain properties of the type system and the class system. However, these properties are often combined in a single inheritance mechanism.

The **specification hierarchy** (often called *subtype hierarchy*) expresses the consistency between the specifications of types in that it establishes subtyping relationships which mean that an instance of the subtype can be used in every context in which an instance of the supertype can correctly appear (*substitutability*). Therefore the specification hierarchy concerns the behaviour of objects as seen from outside. In order to obtain the correct substitutability, the system must only allow, in the definition of a subtype, the addition of new attributes or methods and very restricted modifications of the inherited attributes and methods. Indeed, the attributes and methods which are inherited can be modified, but in such a way as to remain compatible with the corresponding attributes and methods of the supertype. This applies only to attributes which are directly, visible from outside and to methods invocable from outside, given that the specification hierarchy concerns only the behaviour of the objects as perceived from outside.

The **implementation hierarchy** supports code sharing between types (or classes). Using this hierarchy, a type can be implemented in terms of its *difference* to another type. Both the attributes and the methods inherited from a type can be modified. Generally, no restrictions are imposed on the type of modifications that can be made to the inherited methods and attributes. The implementation hierarchy does not necessarily coincide with the specification hierarchy.

Finally, the **classification hierarchy** describes collections of objects and their inclusion relationships. Collections can be defined by *enumeration* or by means of a set of *predicates* which their members must satisfy (they are, therefore, prerequisites for membership).

A similar distinction is discussed in Atkinson *et al.* (1989) where the concepts of *substitution* and *inclusion* inheritance are introduced. The first concentrates more on behaviour. A class C inherits from C' only if more operations can be carried out on C than on C'. Inclusion inheritance is equivalent to the notion of classification. A class C is a subclass of C' if each instance of C is also an instance of C'.

Queries are another important issue in the context of databases as they are the tool with which information is extracted from a database. A query is generally formulated on a set of instances and/or members of a class and consists of a Boolean combination of predicates which express conditions on the attributes of the objects. Query languages, as defined in current OODBMS, in fact represent a break with the principle of encapsulation (the question is still very much under debate). Queries can invoke methods also, as will be discussed in the next chapter. When a query is applied to a set of class members (and, therefore, to instances of their subclasses) a different structure of the instances of a subclass can create certain problems. The fact that the structure – and thus the attributes – can be modified with respect to the structure inherited from the superclass can give rise to subclasses whose instances have structures which are radically different to those of the superclass. The result may be that some queries are poorly defined. It is precisely because of the queries in

OODBMS that restrictions are applied to modifications of the structure of objects that can be carried out within the context of the implementation hierarchy. A common example of this is that while attributes can be modified, they must still comply with compatibility conditions. These requirements apply even in cases where attributes are not directly accessible from outside.

Inheritance and Encapsulation

A problem of considerable importance concerns whether the structure of the instances of a class must also be encapsulated, with respect to the subclasses. In fact, the methods of a class can access directly all the attributes of its instances. However, where inheritance applies, the set of attributes of the instances of a class consists of the union of the inherited attributes and of the specific attributes of the class. The implementation of a method is therefore dependent, in part, upon attributes being defined not in the class in which the method is defined but in any superclass. A modification to the structure of the instances of any superclass can invalidate a method defined in any subclass. This limits the benefit of encapsulation insofar as the effects of modifications to a class are not limited to the class itself. Solutions have been proposed, for example, in Hailpern and Ossher (1990), for limiting the visibility of attributes with respect to the subclasses. Current OODBMS do not yet supply any mechanism for avoiding this type of problem.

2.1.6 Overriding, Overloading and Late Binding

The concept of polymorphism is orthogonal with respect to the concept of inheritance. There are many cases in which it is useful to be able to use the same name for different operations and in cases of objects this has precise characteristics. Consider a *display* operation that receives an object as input and performs the display of the object on the screen. Depending on the type of object, one wishes to be able to use different types of display. If it is an image, it must appear on the screen. If the object is a person, one wants the data concerning it, like name, salary, and so on, to be displayed. If, on the other hand, it is a graph, one wants a graphic representation. A further problem arises with the display of a set, the type of members of which is not known at compile-time.

In an application using a conventional system, there would be three operations – `display-graph`, `display-person` and `display-figure`. This forces the programmer to be aware of all the possible types of objects, of all the associated display operations, and, consequently, to use them properly. For example:

```
for x in X do
    begin
        case of type(x)
            person: display-person(x);
            figure: display-figure(x);
            graph: display-graph(x);
        end;
    end;
```

In an object-oriented system, the `display` operation can be defined in a more general class. The operation has a single name and can be invoked indiscriminately for various objects. However the implementation of the operation is *redefined* for each of the subclasses. This redefinition is called *overriding*. The result is a single operation name which denotes different methods. The system decides which one to use for execution. Therefore, the code above is compacted into:

```
for x in X do display(x)
```

There are numerous advantages to this. The programmers implementing the classes must write the same number of methods, but the designer of the applications does not have to concern himself or herself with it. The code is simpler and applications are more easily maintained, in that the introduction of a new type does not require any modifications to be made to them.

However, in order to be able to provide this new functionality, the system cannot bind the names of the operations to the corresponding methods at compile-time, but must do so during run-time. This delayed translation is called *late binding*.

2.1.7 An Example

Here is an example of an object-oriented database schema, which is graphically represented in Figure 2.3 (Bertino and Martino, 1991). The example describes a small database for the management of a number of projects. A project can be organized in the form of several sub-projects and the class `Project` is defined recursively in terms of itself. A work plan, consisting of several tasks, is associated with each project. Each task is assigned to a research group which consists of several researchers and has a leader. The leader of the task is also specified. It is noted that the task leader is not necessarily the research group leader assigned to the task, in that one research group can be assigned several tasks. For each project several documents produced during the project are also listed. The documents can be articles published in journals or conferences, or internal technical project reports.

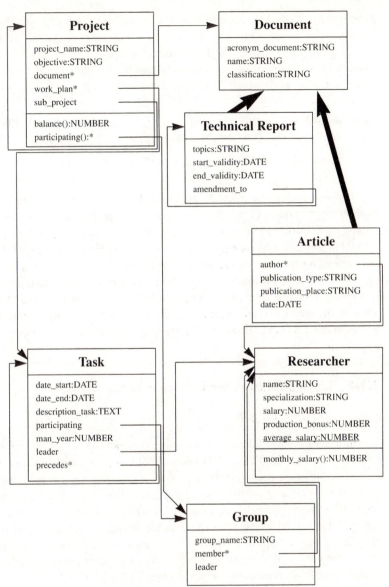

Figure 2.3   Example of a database schema.

In the figure each node represents a class. A node is sub-divided into three levels, the first of which contains the name of the class, the second the attributes and the third the methods. The attributes labelled with the symbol '*' are multi-valued attributes. The specific methods and attributes of the class can be distinguished from the attributes and methods of the instances by the fact that they are underlined. For example, in Figure 2.3, the

Researcher class has an attribute called average_salary which is underlined. This attribute has the value of the average of the salary calculated in all instances of the Researcher class. The nodes can be connected by two types of arc. The node which represents class C can be connected to the node which represents C' by means of:

- normal arc (i.e. thin), indicating that C' is the domain of an attribute A of C, or that C' is the class of the result of a method M of C;

- a bold arc, often indicating that C is the superclass of C'.

For example, the class Project, in Figure 2.3, is associated the method participant() which determines for a project all the research groups participating in the project. This method is associated the character '*' and is connected by means of an arc to the class Group to indicate that this method returns a set of instances of that class.

For the sake of simplicity, if, in the graph, the domain of an attribute is a basic class (for example, STRING, or NUMBER) the name of the class follows the name of the attribute after the symbol ':' for example, group_name : STRING. Basic classes are not explicitly shown as nodes in the schema.

2.1.8 Comparisons with Other Data Models

Semantic Data Models

Semantic data models, like the entity-relation model (Chen, 1976) and the functional model DAPLEX (Shipman, 1981), represent an attempt to capture explicitly as many sets of semantic relationships between entities of the real world as possible. The aggregation and 'instance-of' relationships are efficiently modelled. In terms of expressive power the object-oriented data model is less powerful than the semantic data model but the latter lacks the concept of methods. For reasons of performance and ease of use, the core of the object-oriented model must be extended to include functions such as versions or composite objects (Kim, 1990).

Generally speaking, the fundamental difference between these two types of data model is that the semantic models provide mechanisms for *structural abstraction* and in this sense are similar to knowledge representation models. By contrast, the major aim of object-oriented data models is to provide mechanisms for *behavioural abstraction*, therefore they are more similar to programming languages. However, this distinction is not sharp, and advanced object-oriented models provide powerful mechanisms for adequately supporting both types of abstraction (Bertino and Martino, 1991).

Network and Hierarchical Data Models

There are at least two types of similarities between network models and object-oriented models. Both support some form of data nesting, in that they accept objects which refer to other objects such as values of their attributes. But there is a fundamental difference. The aggregation hierarchy in a database schema can contain cycles. By contrast, the modelling of cyclic objects in the network data model requires artificial structures to be introduced in the schema.

A second similarity can be perceived between object identifiers and the use of pointers in the network model. An object identifier is however a logical pointer and, in addition, there are many systems where an identifier is never reused, even if the object is cancelled, whereas a pointer to a record is a physical pointer and cannot, therefore, be used for checking referential integrity.

In summary, the differences between the two models are clear, above all, from the viewpoint of their expressive power and of the simplicity of data manipulation (Kim, 1990).

Extensible Databases

Running in parallel with research on OODBMS, many projects on developing extensible DBMS are currently being carried out. The purpose of this research is to develop techniques for building a DBMS which can easily be extended to support new functions (Schwarz *et al.*, 1986) or for building a DBMS by assembling the appropriate components from a library of basic modules (Batory *et al.*, 1988).

If a DBMS is implemented using an object-oriented language, it is obviously easier to add new functions compared with those cases where it was implemented in a conventional language. Furthermore the extensibility of a DBMS is a characteristic of architecture. The difference between extensible DBMS and OODBMS can be better described by saying that the former provide 'physical (or architectural) extensibility' whereas the latter provide 'logical extensibility' (the ability to define new types of data and operations on them).

Relational Data Model

The differences between the object-oriented data model and the relational data model ought to be clear from the paragraphs above. However, we will give a brief summary of them. The relational model differs from the object model in that complex objects cannot be modelled directly, given that values of attributes can only be primitives, and in that it doe not provide the notion of inheritance. There are no mechanisms for associating operations defined by the users with the definition of data objects in the database schema, and the behavioural semantics of the objects are dispersed in application programs. Finally, the relational data model does not support the concept of the identity of objects as a concept that is separate from that of the state of the objects.

An extension of the relational model is the *nested-relational* model which has the sole advantage of obviating the first limitation and of defining relations in non-first normal form (¬1NF).

2.1.9 Criticisms of the Object-Oriented Data Model

Object-oriented databases, compared with the relational databases, have been the subject of certain criticisms, some of them valid, some not.

The navigational model of computation has been criticised for appearing to be a step backwards to the time of the network and hierarchical databases. However, there are CAD and artificial intelligence applications for which it is absolutely essential to navigate through the data, and the nested structure of objects is only one aspect of the object model.

Another common criticism is that the object data model is not yet based upon a coherent mathematical theory. However, it must be stressed that relational algebra or calculus do not in any way manage the many other aspects of database technology such as authorization, concurrency control, or recovery (Kim, 1990). Therefore, mathematical foundations appear to be useful in the development of a very limited number of components in a DBMS.

Generally speaking, the many drawbacks of existing OODBMS are essentially due to a lack of established technology and the difficulties surrounding the use of these systems is attributable to the model's effective complexity (Bancilhon, 1988).

2.2 Semantic Extensions

This section looks at certain semantic extensions to the basic model described in the above section. Most of these semantic extensions are proposals which are still at research stage and which, therefore, are not available in the data models of the various OODBMS. The sole exception is the concept of the composite object which has been incorporated in the data model of ORION.

2.2.1 Composite Objects

Objects can be defined in terms of other objects in the object-oriented data model. However, an aggregation relationship in an object-oriented data model establishes no additional semantics between two objects. For certain applications, hypertexts for example, it is also important to be able to describe the fact that an object is part of another object. Superimposing such semantics onto aggregation relationships between objects has considerable repercussions on operations performed on the objects, as we will see a little later. The concept of composite object has been introduced both into some OODBMS, for example, ORION (Kim *et al.*, 1987a) and into some programming languages (Steele, 1984), to enable applications to model the fact that several objects (known as component objects) constitute a logical entity. The fact that a set of objects constitutes a logical entity means that the system can handle that set of objects as a unit of locking, authorization and physical clustering.

An initial composite object model was proposed and implemented in the ORION project (Kim *et al.*, 1987). Tests carried out on a number of ORION applications showed that the concept of composite objects is extremely useful. However, a number of flaws in this model were brought to light. The first problem is that a component object can belong to a single composite object (the property of exclusivity). This restriction is somewhat limiting for some applications, for example, in an hypertext management system the same chapter could quite reasonably belong to two different books. The second problem is that the model requires that the composite objects should be built in top-down mode. Component object *O* cannot therefore be created if the father object was not created first (the father object of *O* is the object of which *O* is a direct component). This restriction means that composite objects cannot be created in bottom-up mode, that is by assembling objects which already exist. Finally, the model requires the existential dependence of the component objects from the composite objects to which they belong. If a composite object is deleted, all the component objects are automatically deleted by the system. This is useful as it means the application does not have to search for and explicitly delete all the component objects. However, in certain situations it means that it is not possible to reuse the components of a deleted composite object for creating a new composite object.

A second model which removes this disadvantage was also defined and implemented in the ORION project (Kim *et al.*, 1989a). In this model two types of references – weak and composite – are defined between objects. A weak reference is a normal reference between objects on which no additional semantics are superimposed. An object *O* has a reference to an object *O'* if this reference is the value of an attribute of *O*. A composite reference is a reference on which the part-of relationship is superimposed. A composite reference can, in turn, be *exclusive* or *shared*. In the former case, the object referred to must belong to a single composite object, whereas in the latter case it can belong to several composite objects. The semantics of a composite reference is then refined by introducing the distinction between dependent and independent composite reference. In the former case, the existence of the object referred to is dependent upon the existence of the object to which it belongs, whereas in the latter case, it is independent. The deletion of a composite object results in the deletion only of the component objects which are dependent for their existence. The objects whose existence is independent are not deleted. Obviously since the characteristic of dependence/independence is orthogonal with respect to the characteristic of exclusivity/ shared status, the following four possible types of composite references are obtained:

(1)   exclusive dependent composite reference

(2)   exclusive independent composite reference

(3)   shared dependent composite reference

(4)   shared independent composite reference

The reference type defined in the first composite object model above (Kim *et al.*, 1989a), coincides with the first reference type in the above list, whereas the other types were not supplied by the model. In (3), an object can be dependent upon several objects; this means that the deletion of a composite object results in the deletion of a shared component object only if all the other references to the object have been removed. In Kim *et al.* (1989a), rules are defined for the deletion of an object and the conditions establishing when an object can be made the component of a composite object are set.

By way of example, let us consider a class which creates a model for electronic documents and let us assume (obviously simplifying the example for the sake of brevity) that a document consists of a title, one or more authors, and one or more sections. One section, in turn, consists of several paragraphs. A section or a paragraph of a section can be shared by various documents. Let us also assume that annotations can be added to a document. The annotations are private for each document. Finally, let us assume that a document can contain images which are taken from predefined files. Therefore, a model document can be on the basis of a composite object whose components are: sections – shared dependent components; annotations – exclusive dependent components and images – shared independent components. A model of a section, in turn, can be modelled as a composite object consisting of paragraphs (shared dependent components).

When defining the revised model for composite objects, specific operations and predicates were also defined, whose format and semantics are presented in Kim *et al.* (1989a). These operations determine, for example, for a given object O, the composite objects to which O belongs, or the component objects of O. To support this extended model the list of parent objects must be associated with each object. For example, given a paragraph P contained in a section S, which is in turn, contained in a document D, that paragraph belongs to the composite object S, which is its parent object and is also indirectly part of the composite object D, by means of S. The concept of composite object, as well as being supported by ORION, is also supported in certain programming languages such as Loops (Stefik and Bobrow, 1984). A similar concept is also supported by some extended relational systems (Haskin, 1982).

2.2.2 Associations

An important concept which exists in many semantic models and in models for the conceptual design of databases (Batini *et al.*, 1990; Chen 1976), is the *association*. An association is a link between entities in applications. An association between a person and his employer (1) is one example; another (classic) example is the association between a product, a supplier and a customer (2) which indicates that a particular product is supplied to a particular customer by a particular supplier.

Associations are characterized by a *degree*, which indicates the number of entities participating in the association, and by *cardinality constraints* which indicate the minimum and maximum number of associations in which an entity can participate. For example, association (1) has degree 2 (it is therefore binary), whereas association (2) has degree 3 (it is therefore ternary). With regard to cardinality constraints, for association (1) if it is assumed that a person can have at the most one employer, the cardinality Person will be (0,1); conversely, if it is assumed that an employer can have more than one employee, the cardinality Employer will be (1,n). Finally, associations can have their own attributes; for example, one can imagine that association (2) has 'quantity' and 'unit price' attributes which indicate, respectively, the quantity of the product supplied to the customer by the supplier and the unit price quoted to the customer by the supplier. Refer to Tsichritzis and Lochovsky (1982) for an in-depth discussion on the various aspects of associations.

However, in most object-oriented data models there is no explicit concept of association. Associations are *represented* by means of references between objects. One way of representing association (1) using the concepts in the basic model introduced above is shown in Figure 2.4.

Figure 2.4. shows how the association adds to the class representing the Person entity a further attribute whose domain is the class which represents the Employer entity. An instance of the `Person` class will have as the value of the `employer` attribute a reference to an instance of the `Employer` class.

As discussed in Albano *et al.* (1991) and Rumbaugh (1987), there are a number of disadvantages to representing associations by means of references between objects. These include the difficulty of representing

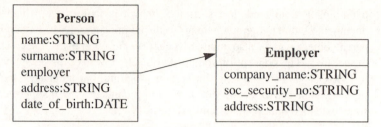

Figure 2.4 Representation of a binary association.

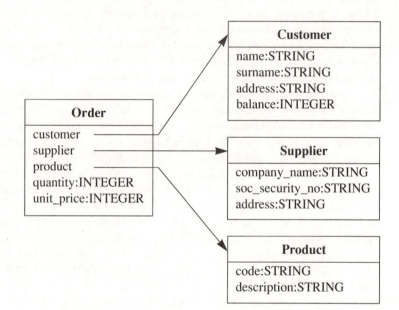

Figure 2.5 Representation of a ternary association.

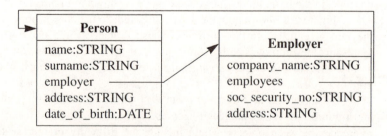

Figure 2.6 Classes with reverse references.

associations of the ternary grade and associations which have their own attributes. The associations are inherently two-way, and given a participating entity and an association, it must be possible to determine easily and efficiently the entity (or the set of entities) connected by a given association. If associations are implemented by means of references between objects, traversal is easy only in one direction. Figure 2.4 shows how, in order to determine the employer of a person – and therefore to traverse the association from person to employer – just the value of the `employer` attribute of the person in question has to be taken. Conversely, in order to determine the employees of an employer – and therefore to traverse the association from employer to person – it is necessary to access all the instances of the `Person` class and to determine which ones have as the value of the `employer` attribute, the OID of the employer in question. The second traversal is much more costly.

In order to obviate these problems certain proposals for extensions to the basic model have been proposed, for example in Albano *et al.* (1991) and Rumbaugh (1987). However, such extensions are not yet found in the data models supported by OODBMS which are currently available as products or prototypes. The reasons why this semantic extension has not been introduced are explained below.

- Increasing the semantic complexity of the data model has a number of repercussions on architecture (Bancilhon, 1988); therefore the introduction of a large number of semantic modelling constructs significantly increases the complexity of implementation and reduces the system's performance.

- If a large number of modelling constructs are available it is difficult for the user to design the database. In fact, it is not always easy for the user to decide which is the most appropriate representation for a given entity within the context of applications.

- Associations can be anyhow represented by means of constructs of the basic model. Figure 2.5 shows one way of representing association (2). The example shows how the association is represented by means of a class which has one attribute for each participating class and one attribute for each attribute belonging to the association. Representation strategies are discussed in depth in Rumbaugh *et al.* (1991).

Finally, the asymmetry of associations when implemented as references can be obviated by introducing so-called reverse references. Given an object O which has as the value of the attribute A, the OID of an object O', there is a reverse reference between O and O', if O' contains a reference to O. In some cases, reverse references are used to control specific integrity constraints, for example, ORIONs' composite object model provides for reverse references to exist between an object and its components. Given a component object in ORION, the objects of which it is a component can be efficiently determined. Finally, in other cases, reverse references can be introduced by the user by means of additional attributes. Figure 2.6 provides an example of this, in which the `employer` attributes of the `Person` and `Employee` class of the `Employer` class are the reverse of each other. In this case, the user is responsible for maintaining the consistency of the attributes. An exception is seen in the Vbase model (Andrews and Harris, 1987), in which, if the user declares an attribute to be the reverse of another one, the consistency of such attributes is automatically maintained by the system.

2.2.3   Integrity Constraints

In order to ensure the correctness and consistency of data, a DBMS has mechanisms for defining, managing and controlling integrity constraints. These constraints are assertions which must be satisfied by objects in a database. The integrity constraints are often classified as *static* constraints – conditions which relate to the state of the objects – and *dynamic* ones – conditions which relate to state transitions of the objects. An example of a static constraint is the assertion that an executive's salary must never fall below a given value, whereas a dynamic constraint is the assertion that an employee's salary may never decrease at all. The following are common types of constraints:

- *Domain constraints* – These specify a set of acceptable values for an attribute.

- *Keys* – These specify that the values of one or more attribute(s) identify an object univocally in a given collection of objects.

- *Referential integrity constraints* – If an object has a reference to another object, the latter must exist.

The above types of constraints were introduced in the relational model. Their application to OODBMS presents no particular problems. However, in OODBMS, referential integrity is automatically maintained by GemStone, O_2 and other such systems which do not allow the explicit deletion of objects and which use a *garbage collection* mechanism for determining which objects can be removed if they are no longer referenced by other objects.

In addition to the above types of constraints, there are others which, unlike the first ones, are peculiar to OODBMS. However, most OODBMS currently available as products or prototypes do not provide mechanisms for the definition, management and control of integrity constraints. In fact, in these systems it is however possible to encode integrity constraints as part of the update methods associated with the objects. The introduction of a language for defining the constraints would however enable such constraints to be defined in a declarative, rather than a procedural way. Moreover, the issues related to integrity constraints for object-oriented data models have not yet been dealt with adequately at research level, and in fact being able to define a constraints language depends considerably upon the specific characteristics of the model being used as a reference. The following are examples of the constraints peculiar to the OODBMS:

- *Constraints on the migration of objects between classes* – These constraints are significant only in the case of systems which allow an object to modify its own class. For example, suppose that a student then becomes a graduate student and then a teacher; on the other hand a graduate student can never become a non-graduate student. Therefore an instance of the 'Graduate' class can only migrate to certain specific classes and not to any class of the schema. This type of constraint is discussed in detail in Zdonik (1990).

- *Exclusivity constraints between classes* – These constraints are only significant where systems allow an object to be the instance of several classes. These constraints specify for example that the extents of two classes must be disjoint. This type of constraint is discussed in Zdonik (1990) and Lenzerini (1990).

- *Constraints on the definitions of subclasses* – With this type of constraint it is possible to specify that, in defining a subclass, certain methods or attributes inherited from a superclass cannot be redefined. This type of constraint can be seen as meta-level integrity constraints in that they deal with the definition of classes rather than with instances.

2.3   The GemStone Data Model

GemStone (Breitl *et al.*, 1989) is an OODBMS which combines the concepts of the Smalltalk object-oriented programming language (Goldberg and Robson, 1983) with the functions of a data management system. The data definition and manipulation language is called OPAL and it is derived from Smalltalk. Adopting the philosophy of Smalltalk, each entity in the system, including the programs written in OPAL, is considered to be an object. The discussion throughout the rest of this section is based on Version 2.0 of GemStone (Servio, 1990).

In GemStone, the methods and the structures common to all instances of a class are contained in an object referred to as CDO (*Class-Defining*

Object). Therefore, even class definition is an object. All instances of a class contain a reference to their CDO as part of the object identifier. In addition, each object is the instance of precisely one class. The internal structure of most of the objects consists of several attributes (in GemStone, the term instance variables is used) which can contain values and references to other objects. The domains of the attributes do not have to be specified. The specification of the domain class of an attribute takes, in GemStone, the form of an integrity constraint.

Objects are internally organized by means of structures, possibly complex, which are obtained by combining four different basic storage formats:

(1)   *Atomic* – These are objects such as integers and strings which have no internal structure.

(2)   *Named instance variables* – These are storage units which can be referred to by name.

(3)   *Indexable instance variables* – These represent storage units referred to by a number. An example of these is the instances of the *Array* class.

(4)   *Anonymous instance variables* – These differ from the two preceding formats in that they are accessed by name rather than by value. The instances of the *Set* class belong to this category.

Class Definition

A peculiar feature of GemStone is that it provides a number of predefined classes, referred to as *kernel classes*, which are organized in a class hierarchy. Each of these classes provides the structure and the methods for managing general purpose data types. The hierarchy of kernel classes establishes inheritance relationships on the basis of which each class inherits both the attributes and the methods of its superclass. The `Object` class is the root of the inheritance hierarchy and therefore each class is its subclass. When one wants to define a new class, this has to be defined as a sub-class of a class which is already present in the database. If the new class is a specialization of a previously defined class, the choice of superclass is natural, otherwise the user must determine, from among the kernel classes, the class whose characteristics are most suited to the new class. If no class is suitable, then the new class must be defined as a subclass of `Object`. Figure 2.7 shows, by way of example, part of the hierarchy of the kernel classes (the indent establishes the inheritance relationship).

The following is the syntax of the command for defining a class in OPAL:

```
Name_class_receiving subclass 'Name-subclass'
    instVarNames: ListofInstanceVariables
    classVars: ListofClassVariables
    poolDictionaries: LiistofCommonVariables
    inDictionary: DictionaryName
    constraints: ListofDomainConstraints
    instancesInvariant: False/True
    isModifiable: False/True
```

A subclass is defined by sending to the appropriate superclass (denoted in the preceding syntax by `Receiving_class_name`) the `subclass` message for which there is a method in all the classes. Therefore the creation of subclasses is one of the essential features of classes. The reception of this message by the receiving class triggers execution of the method for creating a subclass with the name, `Name_subclass`, whose characteristics are defined by the other creation command clauses. In particular:

- `instVarNames` has as arguments a list of strings with the following format: `#('string 1', 'string2', etc.);` each string specifies the name of an instance attribute.

- `classVars` has as arguments a list of class attributes which differ from the instance attributes in that their values can be read and changed by all the instances of the class; in other words, the class attributes are specific attributes of the class object, whereas the instance attributes are attributes of the instances of the class and therefore there is a pair of these for each instance.

- `poolDictionary` has as arguments a list of shared variables (*pool variables*); a shared variable is a particular storage structure which enables a certain number of classes and their instances to share information.

- `inDictionary` has as its argument the name of a predefined dictionary, in which the name of the class, assigned by the user, is inserted upon creation. The class can then be simply referred by that name.

- `constraints` specifies the values which each attribute may assume. The name of this keyword indicates that the attributes are 'constrained' to assume values from specified classes of objects.

- `instancesInvariant` specifies whether the instances of the class can be modified or must remain unchanged over time. The argument is False in the former case and True in the latter.

- `IsModifiable` specifies whether or not the class is modifiable; modifications to classes include the addition or deletion of instance attributes.

```
Object
  Association
    SymbolAssociation
  Behavior
    Class
    Metaclass
  Boolean
  Collection
    SequenceableCollction
      Array
        InvariantArray
        Repository
      String
        InvariantString
          Symbol
    Bag
      Set
        Dictionary
          SymbolDictionary
          LanguageDictionary
        SymbolSet
        UserSet
        UserProfileSet
  CompileMethod
  . . . . . . . . . . . . . . . . . . . . . .
```

Figure 2.7 An example of kernel classes.

Classes for which the clause `isModifiable` has the value True cannot have instances. These classes allow various types of modifications. Classes for which the clause `isModifiable` has the value False (and therefore normal classes) do not permit modifications such as the addition or the deletion of instance attributes. In fact, such modifications would result in modifications to all the instances of the class[1]. However, in normal classes, modifications such as addition and deletion of class attributes can be carried out, insofar as they do not have an impact on instances.

An Example

To illustrate the concepts described above, let us consider the definition, in OPAL, of a small database. The example relates to part of the database. Its schema is shown in Figure 2.3. The syntax of the definition of the classes is shown below, and some comments and observations are made:

```
Object subclass 'Researcher'
     instVarNames: #('name', specialization',
                                'salary', 'production_bonus')
     classVars: #('average_salary')
     poolDictionaries: #()
     inDictionary: UserGlobals
     constraints: #[ #[ # name, String ],
                        #] # specialization, String ],
                        # [ # salary, Integer ],
                        # [ # production_bonus, Integer ]]
     instancesInvariant: false
     isModifiable: false.

Set subclass 'Researchers'
     instVarNames: #()
     classVars: #()
     poolDictionaries: #()
     inDictionary: UserGlobals
     constraints: Researcher
     instancesInvariant: false
     isModifiable: false.

Object subclass 'Document'
     instVarNames: #('acronym_document', 'name',
                                'classification')
     classVars: #()
     poolDictionaries: #()
     inDictionary: UserGlobals
     constraints: #[ #[ # acronym_document, String ],
                        #] # name, String ],
                        #] # classification, String ]]
     instancesInvariant: false
     isModifiable: false.

Set subclass 'Documents'
     instVarNames: #()
     classVars: #()
     poolDictionaries: #()
     inDictionary: UserGlobals
     constraints: Document
     instancesInvariant: false
     isModifiable: false.
```

[1] In some recent articles the designers of GemStone have outlined the possibility of schema modifications whose execution results in modifications to instances. These functions are not yet available on the system, although certain extensions in this direction can be envisaged.

```
Document subclass 'Article'
        instVarNames: #('author', 'publication_type',
                            'publication_place', 'date')
        classVars: #()
        poolDictionaries: #()
        inDictionary: UserGlobals
        constraints: #[ #[ # author, Researchers ],
                        #[ # publication_type, String],
                        #[ # publication_place, String],
                        #[ # date, Date ]]
        instancesInvariant: false
        isModifiable: false.


Documents subclass 'Articles'
        instVarNames: #()
        classVars: #()
        poolDictionaries: #()
        inDictionary: userGlobals
        constraints: Article
        instancesInvariant: false
        isModifiable: false.


Document subclass 'Technical_report'
        instVarNames: #('topics', start-validity'',
                            'end_validity'', 'amendment_to')
        classVars: #()
        poolDictionaries: #()
        inDictionary: UserGlobals
        constraints: #[ #[ # topics, String ],
                        #[ # start_validity', Date ],
                        #[ # end_validity', Date ]]
        isVariant: false
        isModifiable: true.


Documents subclass 'Technical_reports'
        instVarNames: #()
        classVars: #()
        poolDictionaries: #()
        inDictionary: UserGlobals
        constraints: Technical_report
        isVariant: false
        isModifiable: false.
```

There are two types of array in the OPAL language syntax. The first type, called the *literal array*, can contain only literals, that is, characters, strings, symbols and obviously other literal arrays. A literal array is delimited by brackets where it is preceded by the symbol '#'. An example of a literal array is the set of the instance attributes of a class. For example, for the Article class:

#('author', 'publication_type', 'publication_place', 'date').

The second type of array, called *array constructor*, can also contain expressions and names of classes. In particular, expressions can contain messages. An array constructor is delimited by square brackets and it is preceded by the symbol '#'. An example of an array constructor is the set of domain constraints for the instance attributes of a class. In fact, such a set of constraints is a sequence of pairs of the form (name_attribute, class_domain). For example, for the class Article:

#[#[# author, Researchers], #[# publication_type, String], #[# publication_place, String], #[# date, Date]].

In the example above, each class definition is followed by the definition of a subclass of the Set kernel class whose constraints clause has the first class as its argument. For example, the class Researcher is followed by the definition of the class Researchers whose instances are sets of objects belonging to the class Researcher. Thus the class' extents, that is, the sets of its instances, can be defined at the same time, given that in GemStone the class has only the intensional concept. Any collection of objects in OPAL is defined as the instance of a subclass (direct or indirect) of the Set kernel class (also non-directly, as in the case of the Articles and Technical_reports classes). Therefore, a collection can be used as the value of an attribute of another class. The usual operations on the sets are inherited from the Set superclass. Subclasses of classes defined as subclasses of the Set class cannot have instance attributes. The constraints clause in such classes can have, at most, one element.

Another important characteristic of OPAL is that a domain for the instance attributes does not have to be specified and the constraints clause, in the definition of a class, need not necessarily contain a pair for each instance attribute defined in the class. However, the domain must be specified if associative queries on the class are foreseen.

The definition of the Technical_report class is a particularly interesting case in that it shows how recursive classes are defined in OPAL. We can see from the example that a domain has not been defined for the amendment_to attribute. In fact, in OPAL classes used as the domain in the constraints clause must have already been defined. Classes which have yet to be defined cannot be modified. However, where classes can be modified, domain constraints can be added after the class has been created using an operation provided by the system. Domain constraints can only be added if the class can be modified and so it has no instance. In fact, if a domain constraint were added to a class which already has instances, certain instances could have values which are not valid in terms of the domain. From the example we can see how the `Technical_report` class has been defined as modifiable (that is, the `isModifiable` clause: has a true value). Once defined, the `Technical_report` class can be sent the following message (the various message formats in OPAL are described later):

```
Technical_report instVar: 'amendment_to'
constrainTo: Technical_report.
```

This message has two arguments – the first is preceded by the keyword, `instVar:` and denotes an instance attribute; the second is preceded by the keyword, `constrainTo:` and denotes a class. The effect of this message is to add a domain constraint to the class receiving the message.

The class can then be made non-modifiable by means of the operation `immediateInvariant`, which is supplied by the system. For example:

```
Technical_report immediateInvariant.
```

Once the `Technical_report` class has been made non-modifiable, instances can be created from it. However, a non-modifiable class cannot then be made modifiable. In the initial definition of a schema it is probably better to define the classes as modifiable, insofar as the schema is not stable at that stage and it must be able to be modified. The evolution of objects and classes in GemStone is described in greater depth in Chapter 5.

Methods

In OPAL, the specification of a method consists of two components – a *message pattern*, which represents the signature of the method and the body of the method. A message expression in OPAL indicates that a message is sent to a receiving object just as it does in Smalltalk. A message expression can be seen as the invocation of an operation on an object. A message expression (or more simply, a message) consists of:

- an OID or an expression representing the object to which the message is sent;
- one or more identifiers, called *selectors*, which specify the method which must be invoked;

● possibly one or more arguments – the arguments can, in turn, be denoted by message expressions.

For example, in the message 2 + 8, 2 represents the receiving object, + represents the method to be executed and 8 represents the argument. The messages are classified into three categories:

(1) **Unary messages**. The simplest type of message consists of a receiving object and a single selector. For example, the expression, 7 negated which returns −7.

(2) **Binary messages**. A binary message consists of a receiving object, a selector and a single argument. For example, the sum expression seen above. Another example is the expression:

myObject = yourObject

which returns the Boolean value True if the objects myObject and yourObject have the same value, whereas myObject == yourObject returns True if the objects are identical, that is, if they have the same OID.

(3) **Keyed messages**. Keyed messages consist of one receiver and several pairs of the key-argument form (up to a maximum of 15). Each key is a simple identifier which terminates with the character ':'. For example, the message expression:

arrayOfStrings at: (2+1) put: 'Curly'
inserts the string 'Curly' in the third element of the array receiving the message. In this message expression, there are two pairs of key-arguments. The first pair has at: as its key and as its argument, a position in the array, the second has put: as its key and shows which string is to be inserted.

Several messages can thus be combined and messages can be sent in a cascade to the same object. The expression above, which inserts a string in the third element of the array, contains another message inside it. In fact, the argument of the key at: is denoted by the binary message 2+1.

A cascade message consists of a sequence of messages which are separated by the character ';' and which are sent to the same object. The receiver need not be repeated for each message. The following is an example of a cascade message:

arrayOfPainters add: 'Raffaello'; add: 'Giotto'

The above cascade message is equivalent to:

```
arrayOfPainters add: 'Raffaello'
arrayOfPainters add: 'Giotto'
```

The body of a method consists of:

- declarations of temporary variables;

- one or more OPAL expressions. This language includes the typical expressions of programming languages such as conditional expressions or assignment expressions;

- a *return* command which returns a value for the message expression which invoked the method.

As examples of methods, let us consider the `Document` class and two methods for reading and updating the `title` attribute. In GemStone, the attributes of an object can be directly accessed only by the methods of the object. For an attribute to be read and modified, the appropriate methods have to be defined. This encapsulation principle also applies to the attributes of instances with respect to the methods of the class to which the instances belong. In other words, a class method cannot directly access the attributes of the instances of the class. The following methods are defined for the attribute `title`:

```
method:    Document
title                          'message pattern'
           ^title              'return statement'
%
method:    Document
title:     aTitle              'message pattern'
           title := aTitle
%
```

In the above examples, the first and last lines of each method (i.e. `method: Document` and the symbol, `%`), relate to TOPAZ, the OPAL version for VAX/VMS. In particular, the `method: Document` clause denotes that what follows is a method to be compiled and installed in the `Document` class. The character `%` is a statement terminator. The character `^` denotes a value which is returned by the method. If there is no return statement the method returns the object on which the method was invoked (for example, in the second of the methods above). Finally, the strings between double apices denote comments. Although the two methods have the same name, i.e. 'title', they have different message schema. In fact, the first method's schema is a unary type message, whereas the second method's schema is a keyed message. The system determines on the basis of the type of message expression which code to use in order to respond to the invocation of the message. The following invocations:

```
aDocument title
aDocument title: 'Databases'
```

will have the effect of returning the title of the document and assigning a new value to the title of the document.

Class methods can also be defined. For example, let us consider a method which creates and initializes the `Document` class (example (a)).

```
classmethod:     Document
 newAcronym:  anAcronym     newTitle: aTitle
 newClassif:   aClassif
 | tempDocument |
tempDocument := self new.
tempDocument acronym: anAcronym;    title: aTitle;
                  classification:aClassif;
^tempDocument
 %
```

The above method has the effect of creating a new instance of the `Document` class and of assigning the arguments of the method to the attributes of the instance. The method has a keyed message pattern consisting of three key-argument pairs. In addition, the method contains the temporary variable | `tempDocument` |. The first statement executed by the method creates a new instance by means of the `new` message (which is in all classes) and assigns this instance to the `tempDocument` variable. Then three messages in cascade are sent to the new document. These messages assign the acronym, the title and the classification, respectively, which were received as input by the method. The initialization method calls the methods for modifying the instance attributes. As well as the method for modifying the `title` attribute, similar methods for modifying the other attributes need to be defined. The following is an example of the invocation of the initialization method:

```
newDoc := Document newAcronym: 'C1/27/03/92'
              newTitle: 'Databases' newClassif:  'Draft'
```

Inheritance

The GemStone data model only provides single inheritance mechanisms. In defining subclasses, two principal types of modification to the definition inherited by the superclass can be performed: adding attributes and adding and redefining methods. New attributes can always be added. The sole exception is superclasses whose storage format is the anonymous instance variable type (that is, classes whose instances have the set or collection type of structure – for example, the `Document` class defined above). Class attributes and global variables can also be added. If the instance attributes of a class have domain constraints, the constraints are inherited by the subclasses. An inherited domain constraint can be modified but it can only be made more restrictive. In other words, the domain specified in the subclass must be a subclass of the domain specified in the superclass. For example, the `Technical_report` class is a subclass of the `Document` class and it redefines the domain constraint inherited from `Document` by changing the domain from `Document` to `Technical_report`. This redefinition is correct insofar as `Technical_report` is a subclass of `Document`.

An inherited method can be completely redefined by defining a method with the same message schema and with a different body in the subclass. For example, let us consider the `Technical_report` class and let us assume that we want to redefine the creation and initialization method inherited from the `Document` class (see example (a)) insofar as we want to initialize one of the attributes with a default value. The following is one way of defining the method (example (b)):

```
classmethod: Technical_report
 newAcronym: anAcronym    newTitle: aTitle
 newClassif:  aClassif
| tempTechnical_report |
tempTechnical_report := self new.
tempTechnical_report acronym: anAcronym;  title: aTitle
                           classification:aClassif;
                           topics: 'Database';
^tempTechnical_report
 %
```

Those attributes which are not initialized assume a special 'nil' value (null reference). A method can be refined. Refinement is understood as the ability to add code to the body of an inherited method. For example, let us consider the definition of a method for the `Technical_report` class which creates a new instance and initializes all its attributes, including both the inherited attributes and the specific attributes. The following is one way of defining of this method (example (c)):

```
classmethod: Technical_report
 newAcronym: anAcronym    newTitle: aTitle
newClassif: aClassif
 newTopic: aTopic  startValidity': startDate
 endValidity': endDate  amendment: aTechnical_report
| tempTechnical_report |
```

```
tempTechnical_report := super newAcronym: anAcronym
                                 newTitle: aTitle
                                 newClassif:   aClassif
tempTechnical_report topics: aTopic;
                          start_validity': startDate;
                          end_validity': endDate;
                          amendment: aTechnical_report;

^tempTechnical_report
  %
```

In the above method, the **super** *pseudovariable* is used. By using the pseudovariable one can alter the usual search strategy of the method to be performed upon receiving a message. In the method in example (c), the creation and initialization method defined in the **Document** superclass is used. This method (example (a)) creates a new instance and initializes the attributes belonging to the **Document** class. Therefore, the method in example (c) only needs to add the code which is necessary to initialize the specific attributes of the **Technical_report** subclass.

Persistence

GemStone falls into the category of systems in which persistence is an orthogonal property of the objects. Not all the objects created are automatically persistent. The simplest way of making an object persistent is to associate an external name with the object. Let us assume that we want to create an instance of the **Document** class and to make it persistent, assigning to it the name, **MyDocument**. The following are the GemStone statements (example (d)):

```
| newDoc |
newDoc := Document  newAcronym: 'C1/27/03/92'
newTitle: 'Databases'
        newClassif:  'Draft'.
UserGlobals at: #MyDocument put: newDoc.
```

The above statements add to the **UserGlobals** dictionary an association which has **#MyDocument** as its key and the **newDoc** object identifier as a value. The **UserGlobals** dictionary is a default dictionary which each user has. Obviously other dictionaries can be created by defining the appropriate instances of the **SymbolDictionary** system's class.

In GemStone, each object which can be 'reached' by a persistent object is, in turn, persistent. Therefore the approach adopted in the above example is not the only one that can make an object persistent. Another widely used approach is to define a set of instances, and to make that set persistent (by assigning it a name, for example). All the objects which are elements of the set are made persistent, even if they have no external name explicitly assigned to them. Let us consider, for example, the Document class, and assume we want to define a set of documents, and to store certain documents in it. The GemStone statements to do this are:

```
| MyDocuments newDoc |
MyDocuments := new Documents
newDoc := Document newAcronym: 'C2/28/04/92'
           newTitle: 'Objects'
           newClassif:  'Revised'
MyDocuments add: newDoc.
newDoc := Document newAcronym: 'C3/18/01/91'
           newTitle: 'Objects'
           newClassif:  'Final'.
MyDocuments add: newDoc.
MyDocuments add: MyDocument.
UserGlobal at: #MyDocuments put: MyDocuments.
```

In the above example, an instance of Documents is initially created. This class has sets of documents as its instances. Then two new instances are created from the Document class and they are added to the set (a message with an add selector). In the example it is assumed that we are also adding the document created in example (d) to the set. This object is referred to by its external name. Finally, the set is made persistent by assigning to it the external name, MyDocuments.

To delete an object all its persistence 'roots' have simply to be removed. At that point, the system automatically deletes the object. GemStone does not provide an explicit delete operation but uses garbage collection. Suppose, for example, that the object created in example (d) needs to be deleted and then inserted in the set MyDocuments. To do this, the following steps must be executed: (1) remove the object from the set; (2) remove the association between the object and its external name. The GemStone instructions to do this are:

```
MyDocuments remove: MyDocument.
UserGlobal at: '#MyDocument put: nil.
```

2.4   The O_2 Data Model

O_2 (Deux *et al.*, 1990) is an OODBMS, the data model of which was defined from 'ex-novo', and which did not originate from an object-oriented programming language, like GemStone. In particular, the language for implementing methods, referred to as CO_2, is an extension of the C programming language. These extensions are, among other things, used for manipulating objects and for sending messages to objects. Therefore, CO_2 can be seen as an object-oriented extension of C. In the following, we refer to O_2, Version 1.0 (Altair, 1989).

Objects and Values

O_2 is obviously based on the concept of objects, in their conventional sense. Objects have an identity independent of the value and they encapsulate data and operations. The O_2 model allows, in addition, the definition of *complex values*. Complex values are defined by means of constructors, which can be nested arbitrarily. The main differences between complex values can be summarised as follows (Deux *et al.*, 1990); objects are pairs (identifier, value); they can only be manipulated with methods and they can be shared. Complex values have no identifiers, cannot be shared and can be manipulated directly by means of operators provided by the system. In order to illustrate the difference, let us consider two instances of the `Article` class. These instances have the date of publication as one of several attributes. Let us assume that the two articles have the same date of publication and this date is represented by a complex value rather than an object. Let us also assume that the state of the two instances is as follows:

```
I₁ tuple (acronym_document: 'R2/5/91',
          title : 'Databases for CAD applications – models',
          classification: 'Revised',
          author: set (R₁, R₂),
       publication_type: 'journal',
       publication_place: 'CAD Journal',
       date: tuple (day: 1,
                    month: 03,
                    year: 1992))


I₂ tuple (acronym_document: 'R3/5/91',
          title: 'Databases for CAD applications – architectures',
          classification: 'Revised',
          author: set(R₁, R₂, R₃),
          publication_type: 'journal'),
          publication_place: 'CAD Journal'),
          date: tuple (day: 1,
                       month: 03,
                       year: 1992))
```

In the above example R_1, R_2, R_3 represent instances of the Researcher class. In addition, note that each instance includes the attributes of the Article class plus the attributes inherited from the Document class.

Let us assume that the date of the instance I_1 is modified, changing the month from March to April. The resulting state of the object I_1 is:

```
I₁ tuple (acronym_document: 'R2/5/91',
          title : 'Databases for CAD applications - models',
          classification: 'Revised',
          author: set(A₁, A₂),
          publication_type: 'journal',
          publication_place: 'CAD Journal',
          date: tuple (day: 1,
                       month: 04,
                       year: 1992))
```

Since the date attribute is represented as a complex value, the dates contained in the two above instances are, to all intents and purposes, two 'distinct entities' and, as a result, modifications to the date of one document are not reflected in the date of the other document. The two documents have different dates once the modification has been made.

Let us assume that we want to create a model of the fact that the two articles must be published on the same date, and that the modification of the date of publication of one article entails modifying the date of publication of the other one. In other words, the date must effectively be shared between the two instances. It is appropriate to represent the dates with class. The two instances will have the following state:

```
I1 tuple (acronym_document: 'R2/5/91',
          title : 'Databases for CAD applications - models',
          classification: 'Revised',
          author: set(R1, R2),
          publication_type: 'journal',
          publication_place: 'CAD Journal',
          date: D1)
```

```
I2 tuple (acronym_document: 'R3/5/91',
          title : Databases for CAD applications - architectures',
          classification: 'Revised',
          author: set(R1, R2, R3),
          publication_type: ''journal'),
          publication_place: 'CAD Journal'),
          date: D1)
```

```
D1 tuple (day: 1,
          month: 03,
          year: 1992)
```

If the date is modified, by changing the month from March to April, the resulting state of the objects I_1 and I_1 is not modified in the sense that both have the identifier D_1 as the value of the date attribute. The state of D_1, after modification, is as follows:

```
D1 tuple (day: 1,
          month: 04,
          year: 1992)
```

Since the modification of an object does not change its identity, both documents have the same date.

Types and Classes

Type, in O_2, corresponds (albeit in a broader form which is dictated by the system's object-oriented basis) to the concept of type in normal, imperative languages and the concept of class has the peculiar characteristics of object-oriented models. In O_2 a type describes a data structure, i.e. it defines the structure of a set of objects. O_2 distinguishes between various type forms:

- *Atomic types* – These are provided by the system. They include the following types – integer, char, boolean, float, string, bitmap. Atomic types constitute the basis for constructing more complex types.

- *Structured types* – These are defined by means of constructors, tuples, sets and lists. They can be applied to any type (atomic and non-atomic) and thus define data structures of arbitrary complexity.

- *Classes* – A type can be a class; this means that aggregation between classes can be modelled. In fact, classes whose definition of type contains the names of other classes can be defined, with the result that the corresponding instances will have components which consist of other objects.

The following is an example of type definition in O_2:

```
date: tuple (day: integer,
             month: integer,
             year: integer)
```

The above definition defines a structured type which is defined with the **tuple** constructor. The constructors can be nested, for example:

```
data-person:
        tuple (name: tuple (first-name: string, surname: string),
            date-of-birth: tuple (day: integer,
                                   month: integer,
                                   year: integer),
        addresses: set(tuple (number: string,
                               street: string,
                               city: string)))
```

In the above example, a type is defined that describes the data concerning a person. In particular, the type, which is defined by the *tuple* constructor contains components which are, in turn, defined by constructors. For example, the **name** component is defined by the tuple constructor, whereas the **addresses** component is defined by the *set* constructor. The elements of this set are, in turn, defined by the tuple constructor.

The concept of class in O_2 corresponds to the description of a group of objects which are similar in structure and behaviour. The definition of a class consists of three principal components:

- the name of the class which must be unique in the system;
- the specification of the class type which defines the structure of all the instance objects of the class and which can be any type in accordance with the above definition. In particular, a class may appear in a class type. This enables recursive classes to be defined;
- a set of methods which define the behaviour of the class instances.

Class Definitions

The syntax of the command for class definition in O_2 is:

```
add class Class_name
      inherits ListofClassNames
      type TypeStructure
      public AccessAttributeSpecification
      method ListofMethodSignatures
```

In particular:

- **inherits** has a list of names of classes whose new class is a direct subclass as its arguments.

- **type** specifies the object's structure, and instances of the class. In defining the object structure, we can use all the constructors provided by O_2 (tuples, lists and sets); the constructors can be arbitrarily nested and a class name can be used in the type definition. For example, a class can be used as a domain of a tuple's attribute.

- **public.** This clause is followed by the specification of the attributes which can be accessed from outside the object and under which modalities. The modalities are in *read* and *write*. The default is that all attributes are private. Also, if an attribute is public in write then it is also public in read, whereas the opposite does not apply.

- **method.** This clause is followed by the class method signature specification. However, the methods' bodies are defined separately from the class definition. The signature specification of a method can be associated with the **public** or **private** clause to indicate whether or not the method can be invoked from the outside.

Both the **inherits** clause and the **method** clause are optional. In particular, if the creator of the class does not specify a superclass, the system makes the new class an **Object** subclass which represents the root of the entire database.

An Example

The following example illustrates how some of the classes defined above in OPAL are defined in O_2 :

```
addclass Researcher
        type tuple(name: string, specialization: string,
                salary: integer, production_bonus: integer)
        public write name, write specialization;
addclass Document
        type tuple(acronym_document: string, title: string,
                classification: string)
        public write acronym_document, write title;
addclass Article
    inherits Document
    type tuple (author: set(Researcher),
            publication_type: string,
            publication_place: string, date: Date);
addclass Technical_Report
        inherits Document
```

```
type tuple (argument: string, start_validity': Date,
            end_validity': Date,
            amendment_to: Technical_Report);
```

In the example, we used the public write clause for some attributes. These are accessible directly both in write and in read, without requiring the proper methods to be encoded. Note that O2 does not provide the notions of class attributes and class methods. Defining values with a name is one way of making up for this shortfall. Values with a name are similar to global variables. For example, the average_salary class attribute (of the Researcher class) can be defined as a value with a name using the following command:

```
add name: average_salary integer
```

With regard to the concept of extents of classes, O_2 has the same approach as GemStone insofar as the classes have the intensional meaning. Class extents in O_2 can be managed in the same way as GemStone. This involves defining a class whose instances are sets. The elements of these sets are the instances of the class of which one wishes to maintain the extent. For example:

```
addclass Researchers
        type set(Researcher);
```

The declaration above defines a class, the instances of which have a set structure. Each set contains instances of the **Researcher** class (and any subclasses it may have). Now let us consider a slightly more complex version of the class above:

```
addclass Researchers
        type tuple (average_salary: integer,
                    ins_researchers: set(Researcher));
```

The above example shows an alternative way of supporting class attributes. In fact, the class has as its structure a tuple, in which the first attribute contains the mean of the salaries of the researchers contained in the set which constitutes the second of the tuple's attributes.

Methods

The definition of a method in O_2 consists of a signature and a body. The signature specifies the method's name, type of arguments and result. The signatures for class' methods can be specified at the same time as the class definition or they can be added later. Let us consider, for example, an initialization method for the instances of the `Document` class. The signature of this method is defined as follows:

```
add method  init(string, string, string) : Document
in class Document is public
```

In the above example, the signature of the method is defined after the class is defined. If one wants to specify the signature at the same time as the class is defined, then the definition of the class will contain this signature in the method clause. Thus the definition of the class is:

```
addclass Document
        type tuple(acronym_document: string, title: string,
                    classification: string)
        public write acronym_document, write title
        method init(string, string, string) : Document is public;
```

Class methods cannot be defined in O_2. There are some specific system procedures for classes, for example, the `new` procedure for creating new instances. These procedures are provided by the system and the user cannot add new ones to them. A method cannot be defined for creating and initializing instances as in GemStone. The `new` procedure must be invoked and this creates the instance. The `init` method is, in turn, invoked on this instance. This performs the initialization. In GemStone, the initialization method is a class method, whereas the `init` method defined here is an instance method.

The body of a method consists of a set of commands expressed in CO_2, a language defined by means of extensions to C. O_2 provides other languages, including extensions to BASIC and to LISP. In the rest of the section we will refer to CO_2. A method's body is always defined separately from the class definition and must contain the specification of the signature, whose method constitutes the implementation. The signature associated with the body must contain the name, as well as the type of arguments. Let us consider the `Document` class with the associated specification of the `init` method. A possible body for this method is defined below:

```
body init(acronym_doc: string,  tit: string,
        classif: string) : Document
      in class Document co2 {
      self -> acronym_document = acronym_doc;
      self -> title = tit;
      self -> classification = classif;
      return(self);
   ]$;
```

In the above example, body represents a keyword in O_2 which indicates the start of the definition of the body of a method. In addition to the specification of the signature, the body contains the `in class` clause which specifies to which class the body belongs (note that the same signature can have different implementations in different classes). Finally, the code itself is enclosed between the strings `co2 {'` and `'}$`. In the above example, the pseudovariable `self`, which indicates the object on which the method is invoked, is used. The return statement in the example returns a reference to the object itself on which the method is invoked.

Given the `init` method, the body of which was defined in the above example, an instance of the `Document` class is created and initialized as follows:

```
execute co2 {
  o2 Document tmp;
  tmp = new(Document);
  [tmp init('C1/27/03/92', 'Databases', 'Draft')]
}$;
```

The `execute co2` statement denotes a sequence of CO_2 instructions to be executed. It can be executed interactively; in other words, class definitions can be introduced in the interactive interface and then the execution of CO_2 statements can be requested. O_2 also supports application programming in CO_2 (therefore, the above code will presumably be part of an application program). The above example illustrates the constructs used to invoke methods on objects. The invocation of a method generally has one of the following two formats:

```
[ receiver method_name ]
[ receiver method_name (arguments)]
```

The first format represents the invocation of a method which has no arguments, whereas the second represents that of a method with arguments.

Inheritance

O_2 has multiple inheritance. However, to enable a class C to inherit from a class C', the two classes must have some compatibility conditions. In other words, if C is declared to be a subclass of C' then the structure and methods of C must verify compatibility conditions with respect to the structure and methods of C'. In particular, structure compatibility means that the type of C is a subtype of the type of C'. A set of rules is defined for determining when a type T is a subtype of a type T'. Given two types, T and T':

(1) If *T* and *T'* are types with a tuple structure and if, for each *T'* attribute, there is an attribute with the same name in *T*, and if the type of such attribute in *T* is the same as, or a sub-type of the corresponding attribute in *T'*, then *T* is a subtype of *T'*. For example:

```
T = tuple (name: string,
              address: tuple (number: integer,
                                street: string,
                                city: string))
```

is a subtype of

```
T' = tuple (name: string,
              address: tuple (number: integer,
                                street: string)
```

(2) If T and T' are types with set structures defined, respectively, as *set(E)* and *set(E')*, and *E = E'* or *E* is a subtype of *E'*, then *T* is a subtype of *T'*. For example:

```
T = set(tuple (name: string, age: integer))
```

is a subtype of

```
T' = set(tuple (name: string))
```

(3) If *T* and *T'* are types with list structures defined, respectively, as *list(E)* and *list(E')*, and *E = E'* or *E* is a subtype of *E'*, then *T* is a subtype of *T'*. For example

```
T = list(tuple (name:string, age: integer))
```

is a subtype of

```
T' = list(name: string)
```

A subclass can redefine the structure specified in the superclass as long as the compatibility rules outlined above are verified. For example, let us consider the **Person** class defined below:

```
addclass Person
  type tuple(surname: string,
              name: string,
              age: integer,
```

```
                    telephone: tuple (prefix: integer,
                                      number: integer,
                    children: set(Person));
```

Let us assume that we want to define a subclass with the name Employee, which adds the position of each employee to the attributes above the salary. In addition, we want to redefine the telephone attribute adding the office's telephone number. The Employee class is defined:

```
addclass Employee inherits Person
   type tuple (redefines telephone: tuple (prefix: integer,
                                           number: integer,
                                           office-number: integer),
                salary: integer,
                position: string);
```

The keyword, redefines, in the Employee class, is used for overriding the definition of an inherited attribute. In the example, the definition of the telephone attribute inherited from the Person class is modified in the Employee class by adding a further attribute. However, the modified attribute is compatible with the inherited definition, on the basis of the first of the compatibility rules listed above.

Also, the Person class has an attribute which has the Person class itself as its domain. The definition of recursive classes in O_2 is much simpler compared with GemStone. In fact, classes in O_2 can be defined which have as a domain one or more attributes of classes which have yet to be defined. A class defined in terms of classes which have not yet been defined is called a *shadow class* and has a series of restrictions, the main one of which is that it cannot be instantiated.

Both the signature and the body of a method inherited from the superclass in a subclass can be redefined. Compatibility conditions can be defined on signatures. Therefore the signature of an inherited method can be redefined in a subclass as long as these compatibility conditions are complied with. The body of a method can be defined as the refining of the body of a method inherited from the superclass. Let us consider, for example, the init method as defined above for the Document class:

```
body init(acronym_doc: string, tit: string,
          classif: string) : Document
       in class Document co2 {
       self -> acronym_document = acronym_doc;
       self -> title = tit;
```

```
        self -> classification = classif;
        return(self);
}$;
```

Let us assume that we want to redefine this method in the Technical_Report class, a subclass of Document. Below is one way in which the init method can be redefined:

```
body init(acronym_doc: string, tit: string,
          classif: string) : Technical_Report
   in class Technical_Report co2 {
   [self Document @ init(acronym_doc, tit, classif];
    self -> start_validity = current_month;
    self -> end_validity = next_month;
    return(self);
}$;
```

In the above example, the inherited method is refined using the qualifier @. This is preceded by the name of a class. The effect is that the search for the method starts, rather than from the class associated with the qualifier @, from the class of the object on which the method is invoked. In the above example, the body of the init method defined for the Technical_Report class contains the invocation of an init method. The search for the body starts from the Document class. In the definition of the method it is assumed that the dates of start and end of validity are initialized with default values, which are, respectively, the first day of the current month and the last day of the month following the current month.

We can also see from the example that the signature of the init method for the Technical_Report class has precisely the same number of parameters as the signature of the init method for the Document class. And this leads us to the first compatibility rule for the method signatures in O_2. This states that there must be the same number of arguments in both signatures. Given the signature of a method defined in a class C and given a redefinition of such signature in a class C' which is a subclass of C, the two signatures must verify the following conditions:

(1)   there must be the same number of arguments in both signatures,

(2)   each argument type in the definition of the signature in class C' must be a subtype of the corresponding argument type in the signature definition in class C,

(3)   if, in the signature definition in class C, a type T is specified for the result, then the signature definition in class C' must also specify the type of result and this type must be a subtype of T.

Conditions defined for the O_2 model do not control conditions of contravariance on the arguments (see Appendix A) and, therefore, if a subclass instance in O_2 is used instead of a superclass instance, additional type controls are required at run-time. A theoretical formulation of the O_2 type and class system, including compatibility conditions for types and methods, is to be found in (Lecluse *et al.* (1990).

O_2 supports multiple inheritance. A class can be a subclass of several classes. In order to solve conflicts arising from the fact that superclasses may have different bodies for the same method, the O_2 model allows the user to specify from which superclass the method's body should be inherited. Let us consider, for example, the classes `Person` and `Employee`, and let us assume that we will add the classes: `Customer`, a subclass of `Person` and `Customer-Employee`, a subclass both of `Employee` and of `Customer`. The following are definitions of the classes (in which certain clauses are omitted for the sake of brevity):

```
add class Person .....
    method init (string, string, string) : Person;

add class Employee inherits Person
    .....
    method init (string, string, string): Employee;

add class Customer inherits Person
    .....
    method init (string, string, string): Customer;

add class Customer–Employee inherits Customer, Employee
    .....
    method init (string, string, string) : Customer–Employee
        from Employee;
```

In the above example, the body of the method `init` for the `Customer-Employee` class is inherited from the `Employee` superclass. The `from` qualifier can also be used in other circumstances. More specifically, it can be used for inheriting the method's body from a non-direct superclass. For example, add a `Regular-Customer` class to the preceding classes. This class is a subclass of `Customer`.

```
add class Person
    .....
    method init (string, string, string) : Person;
add class Customer inherits Person
    .....
    method init (string, string, string) : Customer;
```

```
add class Regular-Customer inherits Customer
    .....
    method init (string, string, string) : Regular-Customer
        from Person;
```

In the above example, the body of the `init` method for the `Regular-Customer` class was inherited directly from the `Person` class. Using the `from` qualifier, inheritance can therefore be changed for one or more methods, by inheriting the body from non-direct superclasses. The inheritance can be modified temporarily from a program, when the method is invoked by using the qualifier @ introduced earlier on.

Persistence

O_2's approach to persistence is similar to GemStone's. Objects are made persistent by inserting them in a persistent set, or by making them part of objects which, in turn, are persistent, or by assigning them an external name. Classes in O_2 have no extensional function. Extents of classes must be managed by the programmer with sets of objects. The simplest way of managing the extent of a class is therefore to define a set and add instances to it. Let us consider the `Document` class and assume that we want to define a set containing instances of `Document`. The instruction for doing this is:

```
add name Documents : set(Document);
```

It should be noted that the above instruction defines neither a class not an object. Rather it defines a complex value whose structure is a set of objects of the `Document` class. Both simple and complex values in O_2 can be made persistent by assigning a name. For example, the instruction:

```
add name pi : float;
```

assigns a name to a floating type of value and this means that symbolic constants can be defined. The following example initializes the set of documents created earlier on and then adds a new instance of the `Document` class:

```
execute co2 { o2 Document tmp;
            Documents = set();
            tmp = new (Document);
            Documents += set(tmp);
        }$;
```

The instructions in the above example are not schema instruction, as are, for example, the instructions for creating classes, rather they are instructions expressed in CO_2. The last instruction has the effect of adding a set consisting of a single element, denoted by the tmp variable, to the set of Document names.

However, the above approach is not very convenient, since each time a new instance of the Document class is created, the user must encode the appropriate instructions in CO_2 to add the instance to the set which represents the class extension. It is more convenient to define a suitable method or to insert such instructions in another method, in an initialization method, for example. The following example shows the init method for the Document class appropriately extended with the instructions for inserting the instance in the set called Documents. The external names are global and can be used inside the bodies of the methods.

```
body init(acronym_doc: string, tit: string,
        classif: string) : Document
    in class Document co2 {
    self -> acronym_document = acronym_doc;
    self -> title = tit;
    self -> classification = classif;
    Documents += set (self);
    return(self);
}$;
```

External names can also be assigned to specific class instances. For example, the instruction:

```
add name MyDocument : Document;
```

creates a new document and assigns to it the name MyDocument. This object can then be initialized by invoking, for example, the init method with the appropriate arguments. For example:

```
execute co2 {
    [ MyDocument init('C1/29/04/93', 'CAD/CAM', 'Draft')];
}$;
```

The names can be removed by means of the delete name instruction. For example:

```
delete name MyDocument;
```

removes the name, MyDocument. If the instance which has this name is not referenced by other persistent sets or objects, it is automatically cancelled by the system.

Exceptional Attributes and Methods

A peculiarity of O_2 is that instances with a name, for example the instance with the name `MyDocument`, can have attributes and methods in addition to those inherited from the actual class. Also, the body of the inherited methods can be redefined. Let us assume, for example, that we want to add a method which counts the number of words in the title of the object with the name `MyDocument`. The schema instruction to do this is:

```
add method count_word () : integer in name MyDocument;
```

2.5   The Iris Data Model

The Iris data model is based on three principal concepts: objects, types and functions. This model has its origins in semantic models, more than in object-oriented programming languages. However, its characteristics make it similar, in many ways, to the systems described above.

Objects, which are the entities present in the database, are instances of one or more types and are involved as arguments or as results in the definition of the functions. Thus we have the schema shown in Figure 2.8 which shows the relationships between the three basic concepts of the Iris data model.

Each object has its own unique identifier in accordance with the object-oriented model and, of course, the identity of the object is separate from the value of its attributes. The concept of type in Iris is more closely related to the concept of class in O_2, than to the concept of type in O_2. Types in Iris are treated as collections of objects to which a name is assigned. And functions of a type are defined in which the type's instance objects can participate.

Types, like classes in O_2 and GemStone, support specialization. A type can be defined as a subtype of another (called a supertype) in which case objects belonging to a type also belong to its supertype. A type in Iris can have several direct supertypes (multiple inheritance).

Type Definition

When a type is defined in Iris the name of the type and, as an option, its properties (that is, its attributes) and a list of its supertypes must be specified. Information can be provided on the implementation of the type and of its functions. The following is the syntax for the definition of a type in Iris:

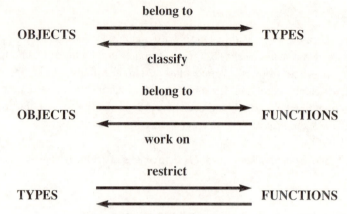

Figure 2.8 Basic concepts of the Iris data model.

```
CREATE TYPE type-name [SUBTYPE OF type-name-commalist ]
[ PROPERTIES ( function-commalist )]
[ AS FORWARD | STORED | CLUSTERED ];
```

The syntax for defining a function, in the list of functions which follows the PROPERTIES clause, is:

```
[ KEY | NONKEY ] function-name res-type-name
[ KEY | NONKEY ] [AS FORWARD | STORED | CLUSTERED ];
```

In the definition of the properties of a type the cardinality constraints between the keywords KEY and NONKEY can be defined. KEY denotes that the argument and/or the result is a key for the function, in that a given object can be used as a function argument and/or result no more than once. A function which has a KEY argument is also called a single-valued function (for each argument value there is a single result value); a function with a KEY result is called a unique function (for each result value there is a single argument value). NONKEY denotes that an object can appear several times as a function argument and/or result. A function which has a NONKEY argument is also called a multiple-table function (for each argument value there can be several result values). A function with a NONKEY result is called a non-unique function (for each result value there can be several argument values). If these specifications are not provided in the definition of a function, the defaults are KEY for the argument and NONKEY or the result. For example, if, in Iris, we want to represent a situation in which a person has a single name which may be common to several people, a single vehicle which cannot belong to others, and is involved in several activities which are common to other people, a `Person` type must be created, as defined below:

```
CREATE TYPE Person PROPERTIES
        ( KEY   name        Charstring NONKEY,
          KEY   car         Vehicle KEY,
          NONKEY activity Work NONKEY);
```

In addition to the definition of the functions which specify the properties of the type, certain specifications can be provided on the implementation both of the type and of the properties. More specifically, the keyword `FORWARD` denotes that the specification of the implementation of the type or of the function is deferred and will be defined later by means of a `CLUSTER` or `IMPLEMENT` instruction. The keyword `STORED` indicates that the type or the function are implemented by means of a table. Finally the keyword `CLUSTER` indicates that the type and associated properties must be stored next to each other.

An Example

The following example shows how the classes defined above in OPAL and in O_2 are defined in Iris.

```
CREATE TYPE Researcher PROPERTIES
        ( KEY   name              Charstring NONKEY,
          KEY   specialization    Charstring NONKEY,
          KEY   salary            Integer NONKEY,
          KEY   production_bonus Integer NONKEY);

CREATE TYPE Document PROPERTIES
        ( KEY   acronym_document Charstring KEY,
          KEY   title             Charstring NONKEY,
          KEY   classification    Charstring NONKEY);

CREATE TYPE Article SUBTYPE OF     Document PROPERTIES
        ( NONKEY author                Researcher NONKEY,
          KEY     publication_type  Charstring NONKEY,
          KEY     publication_place Charstring NONKEY,
          KEY     date                  Dates NONKEY);

CREATE TYPE Technical_Report SUBTYPE OF Document PROPERTIES
        ( KEY   topics            Charstring NONKEY,
          KEY   start_validity    Date NONKEY,
          KEY   end_validity      Date NONKEY,
          KEY   amendment_to      Technical_Report NONKEY);
```

In Iris, as well in O_2, the equivalent of the class attributes cannot be defined directly.

Functions

Functions defined according to types represent, uniformly, attributes, associations and operations. In Iris, functions:

(1)   Define **properties** (attributes) of the objects belonging to the type on which the function is defined (for example, the name attribute of a Person type object is seen as a function from the Person type to the string type); this type of function is defined at the same time as the type is created with the PROPERTIES clause.

(2)   Specify **associations** between objects of the same type or of different types (for example, the parent association between Person type objects, or the belongs to association between Person type objects and Vehicle type objects).

(3)   Specify **operations** on objects to change their internal state, i.e. the set of values which the properties of the object have at any point in time (for example, the promotion function which modifies the qualification property of an Employee type object).

Functions (1) and (2) are supported in O_2 and GemStone using attributes (simple and/or complex ones), while the functions referred to in point (3) would be translated into defining appropriate methods.

Not all the functions in Iris can be defined by using the PROPERTIES clause of the type definition. In particular, the only functions which can be defined in this clause are those which have just one type as their argument, the type to which the property functions are associated. Functions which have several types as their argument and/or result must be defined with the CREATE FUNCTION instruction. The only constraint on the definition of these functions is that the types used in the function signature should be existing types. The keywords KEY and NONKEY can also be used for these functions with the same meaning as for the properties.

The CREATE FUNCTION instruction specifies the function signature whereas its implementation can be specified in OSQL (Beech, 1988) – the Iris query language (defined as an extension to the SQL language) – or linked by means of the LINK clause to a file containing the code obtained from the compilation of the function body written in a programming language. Functions of this type are referred to as *external functions*. The implementation of a function can be specified while the function is being defined – i.e. in the CREATE FUNCTION instruction – or after by means of the IMPLEMENT FUNCTION instruction. In the latter case, the IMPLEMENT FUNCTION instruction must repeat the function signature which has been implemented.

The following is the syntax of the CREATE FUNCTION instruction:

```
CREATE FUNCTION func-interface [ implementation ];
```

The above instruction has two principal components. The first component specifies the function signature and is defined as follows:

```
func-interface ::= function-name arg-spec -> res-spec
arg-spec ::= ( [ argument-commalist } _
res-spec ::= result | < result-commalist >
argument ::= type-name [ argres-name ] [ KEY | NONKEY] |
             BAG OF type-name [ argres-name ]
result   ::= type-name [ argres-name] [ KEY | NONKEY]
```

A function signature in Iris contains the name of the function, a list of arguments and a list of return parameters. A name can also be specified for the arguments, as well as for the result of a function, in addition to the type. A function can also have a BAG of objects as its argument. A BAG is a collection of objects, possibly with duplicates. However, a function cannot have a BAG as its result.

The second component in a function definition specifies its implementation and is defined as follows:

```
implementation ::= AS [function-body | FORWARD | STORED ]
function-body ::= OSQL-body | foreign-body
OSQL-body ::= select-expression | procedure-body
foreign-body ::= LINK file-name
```

Iris is particularly flexible in defining the implementation of functions. In fact, such bodies can be implemented declaratively using the OSQL language – an extension of SQL – by using an imperative programming language (even though, in the current version of the system, this is somewhat restricted). It can be requested that the function be stored as a table (STORED option) and that its implementation be defined later (FORWARD option).

If a function is implemented as STORED, then an empty table will initially be created for the function. This table can then be modified by means of insertions, deletions and modifications. The OSQL language defines both access and update operations. If a function is expressed in SQL it is called a *derived function*. A function in Iris which has side-effects is called a *procedure*. If no implementation is specified in the function definition, the default is the FORWARD option. Below are some examples of function definitions.

- A `Parenthood` function is defined, connecting three instances of the `Person` class, respectively a mother, a father and their child:

```
CREATE FUNCTION
  Parenthood (Person mother NONKEY, Person father NONKEY)
                -> Person child KEY AS STORED);
```

It should be noted that the function arguments in the above definition are both associated with the keyword `NONKEY` whereas the result has the keyword `KEY`. This means that two people can have several children, whereas a child can have only one father and one mother. This function is implemented as a table insofar as the implementation specified is `STORED`.

- A function is defined which determines a given child's father. This function is implemented in terms of the `Parenthood` function defined above:

```
CREATE FUNCTION Father (Person child) -> Person father AS
      select f
      for each Person f, Person m
      where Parenthood(m,f) = child;
```

- A function is defined with several return parameters. This function determines the name and grade of the school of a given student:

```
CREATE FUNCTION
InfoSchool (Student s) -> <NameSchool n, Grade g>
```

Only those functions which are implemented in the form of tables can be modified. This, in fact, means that function components can be added, removed and updated (respectively, by means of the `ADD`, `REMOVE`, and `SET` commands). Generally speaking derived functions, defined in OSQL, cannot be modified. They can only be modified in particular cases. The following are some examples of modifications. The `Parenthood` function defined in the above example is used in the examples.

- `:P1`, `:P2`, and `:P2` are three variables which, respectively, point to three `Person` type objects, the `ADD Parenthood` instruction (`:P1`, `:P2`) = `:P3` extends the `Parenthood` function. Since the function is implemented from a table, the effect of this modification is to add a new tuple to the table.

- `:P1`, `:P2`, and `:P2` are three variables which, respectively, point to three `Person` type objects, the `REMOVE Parenthood` instruction

(`:P1`, `:P2`) = `:P3` removes the object pointed at by `:P3` as the result of the `Parenthood` function for the arguments `:P1` and `:P2`.

Predicates can be used in the modification instructions to determine the tuples of the function which are to be modified. The modification instructions can be used in a wholly similar way to the `INSERT`, `DELETE` and `UPDATE` instructions of the SQL language.

Procedures

Procedures are user-defined functions by which objects can be modified. The `ADD`, `REMOVE` and `SET` instructions are used to modify functions and they are defined by the system. By using procedures, one can define more complex modification operations which are obtained by combining the modification commands provided by the system. Procedures restrict the type of values which can be returned, in that the only type allowed is the 'Boolean' type. The following is the syntax for defining procedures:

```
CREATE FUNCTION function-name arg-spec res-type-name
                AS procedure-body;
res-type-name ::= single boolean type
procedure-body ::= procedure-body-stmt | block
procedure-body-stmt ::= add-stmt | remove-stmt
                        set-stmt | call-stmt
block ::= BEGIN [ procedure-body-stmt-list ] END
```

The body of a procedure can contain several modification instructions. The following is an example of a procedure which initializes the attributes of the `Document` type defined above:

```
CREATE FUNCTION init(document d, string acronym_doc,
string tit, string classif) -> Boolean
     AS begin
         set acronym_document(d) = acronym_doc;
         set title(d) = tit;
         set classification (d) = classif;
     end;
```

Unlike GemStone and O_2, the object on which the modifications must be carried out is passed explicitly as argument of the procedure. In the preceding example, it is the first argument.

Inheritance

Iris supports multiple inheritance insofar as a type can have several direct supertypes. Automatic conflict solving mechanisms are not as yet supplied. So, if two supertypes of a single type have a function with the same name, the system does not accept the definition of that type. Overriding can be carried out for one or more functions inherited from supertypes.

One difference of Iris compared with other systems is that it uses an *early binding* mechanism. The choice of implementation to be used for a given function depends upon the declaration of the type of variable and not the type of the object which the variable is effectively referencing when the procedure is carried out.

Persistence

The approach to persistence used by Iris is the simplest and the most similar to the approach used in relational systems. Each object is automatically persistent until it is explicitly deleted by the user by means of the `DELETE OBJECT` instruction. For example `:P1` is a variable which references a `Person` type object; the instruction `DELETE OBJECT :P1` deletes this object. Functions involving this object are modified automatically by the system.

A characteristic of the Iris model is that an object can belong to several types which may not even be connected by inheritance. Types can be added to and removed from an object dynamically, by means of the `ADD TYPE` and `REMOVE TYPE` instructions which have, among other arguments, the object to which the type is added or from which it is removed.

Any object is thus an instance of the `UserTypeObject` system type. Therefore, if we remove from an object all the types to which it belongs, the object is not deleted, rather it remains as an instance of the `UserTypeObject` type. The `DELETE OBJECT` instruction has to be used to delete the object from the database.

2.6   Summary

In this chapter, we discussed various aspects of object-oriented data models. We have looked at the data models of three systems and portrayed the various differences between the different models.

The discussion clearly shows that no agreement has yet been reached on a definition of the characteristics which an object-oriented data model ought to have. There are also differences in the semantics of the various concepts, for example, class/type concepts and concepts of inheritance hierarchy. Certain aspects, for example, integrity constraints, have not yet been studied in sufficient depth. The differences are greater if we compare object-oriented database models and object-oriented programming languages. Whereas, in the latter, only the interface and the implementation of the objects need to be defined, in the former, the problem of the management of the object extents must also be tackled. This is reflected, for example, in a greater complexity and in the numerous variations on the concept of type/class in database models, compared with programming languages. Among the operations associated with a database model there are queries, whereas this type of function is not present in programming languages.

In conclusion to this chapter, Table 2.1 shows the principal characteristics of the models discussed and include the ORION model, although this was not discussed in detail in the chapter.

The following points are taken into account in the table:

(1)   With regard to persistence, the term 'root' in Table 2.1 means that an instance is persistent if it can be reached by a persistent object or if it has an external name. Automatic persistence means that each object created automatically becomes persistent, until it is deleted.

(2)   In the entry on access to the attributes of an instance, the term, 'on demand', indicates that the attributes are made public or private as specified in the definition of the classes.

(3)   In Iris, there is no explicit construct for modelling associations. However, the 'multiple-type' functions which do not belong to the definition of a specific class can directly model associations.

	Gemstone	Iris	O_2	Orion
Class extent	NO	YES	NO	YES
Persistence	root	auto	root	auto
Deletion of instances	NO	YES	NO	YES
Direct access to attributes	NO	YES	on request	YES
Obligation to specify attributes' domain	only in some cases	YES	YES	YES
Composite objects	NO	NO	NO	YES
Class attributes and methods	YES	NO	NO	YES
Exceptional instances	NO	NO	YES	NO
Integrity constraints	NO	NO	NO	NO
Associations	NO	YES	NO	NO
Multiple inheritance	NO	YES	YES	YES
Object migration	NO	YES	NO	NO

Table 2.1   Main features of GemStone, Iris, O2 and Orion models.

2.7 **Bibliographical Notes**

Object-oriented data models are described in various articles already referred to in the bibliographical notes in the previous chapter, including articles by Bertino and Martino (1991), Joseph *et al.* (1991), Maier and Zdonik (1989). The book by Cattell (1991) contains a chapter in which the fundamental concepts of these models are outlined. Finally, Atkinson *et al.* (1989) came up with a so-called 'manifesto' – a very succinct description of the foundations of these models. The various semantic extensions for the objects are described in the following articles: Kim *et al.* (1987) and Kim *et al.* (1989a) for composite objects. Albano *et al.* (1991) and Rumbaugh (1987) discuss associations. Urban and Delcambre (1990) and Zdonik (1990) describe integrity constraints.

The GemStone database model is described in Breitl *et al.* (1991). The O_2 database model is described in the article which comes under the name of the whole group of system designers (Deux *et al.*, 1990) – this article provides a good overall description – and the article by Lecluse *et al.* (1990), which gives a formal definition of this model. Finally, the Iris database model is introduced in the article by Fishman *et al.* (1989), and a summary description can also be found in Wilkinson *et al.* (1990).

3 Query Languages

Query languages are an important functionality of DBMS. The user can retrieve data simply by specifying the conditions the data must meet. Generally speaking, a language should be:

- high-level, so that complex operations can be easily formulated;

- declarative – that is, attention should be focused on 'what' is sought and not on 'how' it is to be obtained;

- efficient – constructs must provide space for optimizations;

- application independent, so that it can be used on any database schema.

The advantage of these characteristics, which we have already seen in relational databases is that they simplify the task of application development.

Computational Completeness

This property is self-evident for programming languages, but is not so obvious for databases. SQL, for example, does not have the necessary constructs for expressing all possible computable functions. However, we are not saying that the OODBMS designers should also design new programming languages. Computational completeness can be achieved with a reasonable interface using an existing programming language. For example, ORION uses LISP, O_2 uses its own extended C language, GemStone is based principally on Smalltalk, but can also import code from other languages.

However, computational completeness is different from 'resource completeness', that is, the possibility of accessing all of a system's resources, such as video and remote access, for example, from within the language. The language, even if computationally complete, may not be sufficiently powerful to express a complete application.

Impedance Mismatch

One of the main problems highlighted by the object-oriented approach as applied to DBMS is impedance mismatch (Bancilhon, 1988), that is, the difference between the type system of the programming language and the type system of the DBMS DDL and DMl.

As well as requiring the programmer to learn two different languages, impedance mismatch involves writing extra code for 'translating' data structures from the programming language into the structures of the DDL and DML of the DBMS. Relational models satisfactorily support *ad hoc queries*. However, they are not suitable for developing applications requiring close communication between query language and programming language. Generally speaking, in solutions used in existing relational systems, the two languages are not adequately 'mixed'. They have different type systems and different computational models. In particular, query languages use sets as the logical computation units, whereas programming languages are more suited to reasoning on the basis of one 'entity' (record) each time.

The solution to the problem of impedance mismatch requires the integration of programming language technology with database technology. The solutions proposed so far involve adapting the main programming models – logical, functional and object-oriented models – so that they become valid DMLs. In particular, the object-oriented model has become the most promising model as it provides a structure for uniformly representing and manipulating both data and application programs.

A good query language model has yet to be proposed. There are various reasons for this problem.

In the first place, the more complex structure of the data model and the lack of a formal foundation are clearly obstacles to defining a language which is simple yet powerful. Languages deriving from semantic and functional models have been suggested. Until now, none has emerged, but studies have shown that to design a simple query language for such a complex data model is far from easy.

A second problem is that query languages and encapsulation are in some way contradictory, as was hinted at in Chapter 2. The principle of encapsulation stipulates that the structure of data (implementation) must be hidden from users, whereas for queries it is essential to be able to see the attributes of objects.

Despite these difficulties, it is crucial that the problem of impedance mismatch is overcome – not only to achieve integration of form between the languages involved, but also to increase the programmer's productivity. Applications developers, who for their tasks require a data model able to model complex objects directly, cannot easily represent these objects with simpler data structures. However, even if the data model available is complex and if it does not strictly correspond to that of the host programming language, the programmer is forced to use the models of the two environments. In many applications, 30% or more additional code is needed for translating between the data structures of the application language and the structure of the database (Joseph *et al.*, 1991). In this article, the authors use the term *seamlessness* to mean a smooth transition between the two environments.

In the rest of this chapter, we discuss briefly some characteristics of query languages for object-oriented databases, highlighting some of the differences between them and query languages for relational databases. Then we will illustrate the concepts involved with a query language defined as an extension of the SQL language.

3.1   Characteristics of Object–Oriented Query Languages

In this section, we focus on the salient features of object-oriented query languages. Many of the concepts are, in fact, merely an extension of the principles already referred to in relational languages. Technology for these is established and many features are applicable to the object-oriented model. We will attempt to point out the similarities, but, primarily, we shall discuss the problems raised by the new data model. In the following section, we also take an informal look at a model for queries encompassed by a query language.

Access to Objects

In the relational DBMS, query languages are the only way of accessing data, whereas OODBMS, in general, have two ways. The first is *navigational* and exploits object identifiers and aggregation hierarchies. Given an OID, the system accesses the object directly and it navigates through the objects referred to by its attributes. The second is based upon SQL-like query languages.

These two types of access can be used in a complementary fashion. A conventional query is considered useful for selecting a set of objects which are then accessed and processed by applications using navigation capabilities. Therefore, one can assume that the queries result in sets of object identifiers, rather than in the objects themselves, without any loss of generality.

Equality, understood in the sense we have used elsewhere, is reflected in the semantics of queries. It is important to establish which type of equality is used, since it determines the semantics and strategies involved in the execution of operations, for example, union, difference, intersection and removal of duplicates.

Aggregation Hierarchies

The concept of aggregation hierarchy implies certain extensions to the language. The conditions appearing in a query in the form of combinations of predicates are imposed on attributes which are nested in the hierarchy of the object in question – and it is an advantage to be able to navigate through this structure with ease.

For example, let us consider the query referred to in Figure 2.3 of Chapter 2:

> Find all projects which have at least one task which has a researcher specialized in databases as its leader.

In a relational calculus-like language, this could be translated as follows:

$$\{v \ \mid \ (\exists w)\,(\exists g)\,(\exists i)\ \textsf{Project}\ (w) \land \textsf{Task}\ (g) \land \textsf{Researcher}(i)$$
$$\land\ (w = v) \land g \in w.\ \textsf{Workplan} \land g.\ \textsf{Leader} = i$$
$$\land\ i.\ \textsf{Specialization} = \text{"DB"})\}$$

By analyzing this expression from the viewpoint of the new model, we can see that this requires the explicit introduction of two variables g and i, and the two join predicates. A reasonable simplification would be to have *path* expressions included in the language so that the joins which are intended for obtaining one of the components from an object can be easily formulated.

Join

In object-oriented languages, there is a distinction to be made between an *implicit join* derived from the hierarchical structure of the objects, and an *explicit join*, that is, one which, as in the relational model, explicitly compares two objects using identity or value-equality. The above query then becomes more succinct:

$$\{v \quad | \quad (\exists w) (\exists g) (\exists i) \; \texttt{Project} \; (w) \land (w = v)$$
$$\land \; (\text{"DB"} \in w. \texttt{Workplan.Leader.Specialization})\}$$

A predicate on a nested attribute is called a *nested* or *complex* predicate. A nested attribute in a query is denoted by a *path expression*. It is worth noting that using *path expressions* does not add expressive power to the language, since, as we have seen, this can be obtained by other means, although it does increase their conceptual conciseness. A language is said to be conceptually concise if artificial elements need not be used to specify a query. *Path expressions* or equivalent constructs are available in many object-oriented query languages. However, not all of them provide the constructs for expressing explicit joins, since, generally speaking, implicit joins are sufficient for most applications.

A different way of looking at implicit and explicit joins – and one which leads to a better classification of queries – is by distinguishing between *single operand* and *multiple operand* queries. The single operand queries retrieve object instances of a single class (target class) or of subclasses of the target class, whereas multiple operand queries represent operations which can be compared with relational joins and therefore with explicit joins, using the terminology of the object-oriented data model, and with operations on sets. The significance of this distinction will be clarified later.

Inheritance Hierarchy

There are other important aspects which concern the inheritance hierarchy. Firstly, a class or a class and all its subclasses can be queried. In most languages of existing systems, for example, ORION, both of these are available.

Given that each subclass can have its own attributes as well as those which are inherited, it is useful to be able to express queries by means of *alternative predicates* with the following form:

```
if class(x) = C₁ then pred₁
if class(x) = C₂ then pred₂
...
if class(x) = Cₙ then predₙ
```

where x is a variable which denotes an object and `class(x)` is a special message which, applied to an object, returns its class. Alternative predicates are useful where the query also contains other predicates on common attributes of the inheritance hierarchy, for example:

```
Find all documents with the classification C2. If
they are technical reports, they have databases as
```

their topic, and if they are articles, they have been
published in the journal called 'databases'.

Recursive Queries

Object-oriented query languages very often have constructs for expressing
recursive queries even if recursions are not a peculiar characteristic of this
model and is already used in relational models. Therefore, it is important to
be able to introduce a form of recursion since objects which are relevant to
many advanced applications are naturally modelled by recursion.

Cycles in the Class Hierarchy

This area deserves further consideration since it was not covered in our
discussion of the relational model and some definitions need to be
introduced at this stage. As we have seen, the aggregation relationship
does not define a hierarchy in the strict sense of the word in that it admits
cycles. In several systems, including Iris, ORION and O_2, a class can be
defined directly in terms of itself.

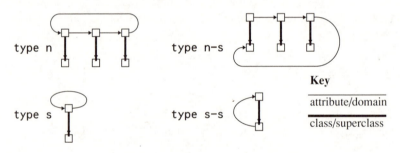

Figure 3.1   Possible cyclic branches.

A branch in a hierarchy of classes is *cyclic* if it contains two classes,
C_i and C_j, that meet one of the following conditions (Kim, 1990):

- C_j is the (indirect) domain of an attribute of C_i and C_i is the domain
  of an attribute of C_j;

- C_j is the (indirect) domain of an attribute of C_i; and a superclass or
  subclass of C_i is the domain of an attribute of C_j.

This definition implies four different types of cycle as shown in
Figure 3.1, two of which, types n-s and s-s, can be considered as quasi-
cycles since they are not cycles in the usual sense of the word.

Assuming that the branch has n nodes, and that each node can be
the root of an inheritance hierarchy, the following are definitions of the
four types of cycle:

(1)   A type n cycle is a cycle consisting of n>1 nodes on the branch.

(2)   A type ns cycle is a quasi cycle corresponding to an n type cycle. It consists of n>0 nodes on the branch and of a superclass or a subclass of one of the n nodes.

(3)   An s type cycle is a cycle consisting of a single node.

(4)   An ss type cycle is a quasi-cycle corresponding to an s type cycle. It consists of a class and of its superclass or a subclass.

These structures are needed in order to provide a consistent form of manipulation of the queries in which they appear and as an extension of the normal structures. In the following section, we will give some examples of queries in which cycles arise.

Methods

Methods can be used in queries either as *derived attributes* or as *predicate methods*.

A method used as a derived attribute has a function comparable with that of an attribute, but, whereas an attribute contains a value, a method is a procedure which calculates a value on the basis of the values of the attributes of an object or of other objects in the database. In the latter case, executing a method results in methods being invoked on other objects. The following is an example of a query which invokes a derived attribute type method:

```
Determine all projects in which there is a
participating group with a leader specializing in
databases.
```

The method used in the above query returns the groups participating in a given project. If a method, for example, a derived attribute, returns objects (primitive values or identifiers), a predicate method has a similar function, but returns Boolean True or False values. A predicate method therefore makes comparisons between the objects in question and can, therefore, form part of the Boolean expressions determining which objects satisfy the query.

Query Results

Let us now look at query results. One of the most important properties of the relational model is the fact that the result of a query is a relation, owing to the flexibility of the relational construct. Queries can thus be nested, so the result of one query can be provided as operand to another query.

Generally speaking, it can be expensive to apply the same principle to queries on objects. In particular, the result must be an object, or a set of objects, of a class which often does not yet exist in the database schema, and which must be defined by the query. But this approach is expensive and certain languages impose restrictions on operations on classes. A restriction common to many query languages is to restrict projections by imposing that all the attributes must be retrieved from each object selected, that is, the object itself, or a single attribute. Thus, the result of a query is a set of objects of an existing class. Another solution is to consider results as a set of object instances of a general class which accepts all objects and whose only methods are those for printing out objects or displaying them on screen. However, this prevents the objects from being used again for other manipulations and limits the idea of nested queries. The most restrictive solution, i.e. allowing only limited forms of projection, is the solution adopted by ORION.

3.2   An SQL-like Language

In this section, we look at a proposal for an SQL-like query language which was defined for ORION (Kim, 1989), but has yet to be implemented. This language is presented to put into concrete form the query model described in the previous section.

3.2.1 Overview of the Language

A query, in its simplest form, can be specified as follows:

```
SimpleQuery ::=
   select TargetClause | select TargetClause from
RangeClause |
   select TargetClause where QualificationClause |
   select TargetClause from RangeClause where
QualificationClause
```

The syntax follows SQL syntax, i.e. it is an example of syntax (**select**, **from**, **where**). TargetClause (**select**) specifies the attributes to be retrieved. RangeClause (**from**) denotes sets of class instances. QualificationClause (**where**) specifies a Boolean combination of predicates that must be satisfied by the retrieved objects.

As in the case of SQL, the RangeClause can contain a declaration of variables, called *object variables*, which reference the instances of classes specified in the RangeClause. In addition, the concept of *path expressions*, discussed earlier, is introduced.

For example, the query:

```
Find all the tasks which have two man-years, which
have as their leader a researcher specialized in 'DB'
and in which there is, as the participant, a group
whose leader specializes in 'Information Systems'
```

can be formulated as follows:

```
Q1:select :T
   from Task :T
where : T man_years = 2
   and : T leader specialization = 'DB'
   and : T participant leader specialization ==
          'Information Systems'.
```

Q1 can be formulated more concisely if, omitting the object variable, no ambiguities arise:

```
Q1' :select from Task
            where man_years = 2
            and head specialization = 'DB'
            and participant head specialization ==
                'Information Systems'.
```

3.2.2 Single Operand Queries

These are queries for which no explicit joins are required since they find objects belonging to a single class target, on the basis of the terminology which has already been introduced.

Acyclic Queries

Aggregation hierarchy

Because of the nested definition of objects, the language must support the simple specification of predicates on nested sequences of attributes, and the concept of *path* needs to be introduced. This denotes a nested sequence of attributes of an object.

A path can be denoted by means of a *path variable* which is specified as follows:

```
ScalarVariable ::=
        ObjectVariable ScalarPath |
        ScalarPath
```

in which, as mentioned earlier, the ObjectVariable can be omitted if there are no ambiguities. A ScalarPath is a sequence of names of attributes preceded by a qualifier if they denote multiple-valued attributes. If there is no quantifier, the existential quantifier is assumed by default:

```
ScalarPath ::=
        ScalarPathElement |
        ScalarPathElement ScalarPath
ScalarPathElement ::=
        ScalarAttributeName |
        Quantifier ScalarAttributeName

Quantifier ::=  each | exists
```

The following is an example of the use of the universal quantifier, **each**:

Q2: select Project
   where each work_plan leader ==
   work_plan participant leader

The above query determines the projects in which each task has as its leader the same researcher who is responsible for the group participating in the task. Query Q2 has an explicit join represented by the predicate in which it is determined whether the researcher who is the leader of the task is the same researcher heading the work group participating in the task.

Q3: select Project
   where exists work_plan leader ==
   work_plan participant leader

The above query is similar to query Q2, with the difference that query Q3 is satisfied by the projects for which there is at least one task in which the task leader is the same researcher who is the leader of the participating group (therefore, all the project's tasks will not necessarily have to be like this).

The presence of multiple-valued attributes requires relation operators to be used for the sets, *has-subset*, *is-subset*, =, *is-in*, *etc*. The following example shows relation operators being used for sets and illustrates that the same query can be expressed in two different ways. The query selects projects in which all the tasks start on '1-3-90', or on '1-4-91'.

Q4: select Project
   where work_plan start_date **is_subset** {'1-3-90', '1-4-91'}.

Q5: **select** Project
     where each work_plan start_date **is-in** {'1-3-90' , '1-4-91'}.

It should be noted that in both the above queries, the work_plan start_date path indicates a set of values and not an individual value. In fact, the work_plan attribute of the Project class is multiple-valued. Given an instance of this class, the work_plan start_date plan denotes the set of the starting dates for all the tasks of that instance.

Inheritance hierarchy

As discussed in the section on the model for queries, the user must be able to specify whether or not the scope of a query also includes the inheritance hierarchy rooted in that class. In the query language, this is specified by the operator '*', which appears immediately after the name of the class indicating that the hierarchy must be included in the evaluation of the query.

Class expression is used to express these queries with the following syntax:

```
ClassExpression ::=
        (ClassExpression) |
        (ClassExpression Union ClassExpression) |
        (ClassExpression Difference ClassExpression) |
        Class |
        ClassHierarchy.

Class ::= ClassName.

ClassHierarchy ::= ClassName*.
```

For example, let us consider the Document class as the root of a class hierarchy and the following queries:

```
Find all the documents which have the classification 'C2'
```

```
Find all the documents, except the technical reports, which
have the classification 'C2'.
```

These queries are expressed as follows:

Q6: **select** Document*
     where classification = 'C2'.

Q7: **select** Document* difference TechnicalReport
     where classification = 'C2'.

Cyclic Queries

As mentioned in the section above which describes the query model, cyclic queries can also be expressed. There are four possible types, depending on whether the cyclicity is due to the aggregation hierarchy, the inheritance hierarchy or a combination of the two.

To illustrate these types of queries and the constructs for expressing them, let us consider a query obtained by taking into consideration the `amendment_to` attribute of the `Technical_Report` class where the domain of the `amendment_to` attribute is the `Technical_Report` class itself. The query

> Find all the amendments of the technical report with
> the acronym ZZ122

is formulated as follows:

> Q9: select Technical_Report (recurses amendment_to)
>   where acronym_document = 'ZZ122'

The expression **recurses amendment_to** specifies that, as soon as an instance of the `Technical_report` is found which qualifies the predicate (`acronym_document = 'ZZ122'`), the values of the attribute, `amendment_to` must be returned recursively. This means that we can then express recursive queries.

Expressions concerning other types of cyclic queries are derived in a similar way.

Use of methods

As explained earlier, methods can be used in queries as *derived attributes* or as *predicate methods*.

The following query shows how a method is used as a derived attribute. Let us consider the `Project` class and the `balance` method which calculates the balance of a project on the basis of the man-years of the various tasks comprising it. Let us suppose that we want to determine all the projects with a balance greater than 20,000. This query is expressed as follows:

> Q10: **select** Project
>   **where** balance > 20,000.

Methods can return objects other than values. Let us consider the `participant` method defined in the `Project` class which returns all the groups participating in a project. The query:

> Determine all projects in which there is a participating
> group with a leader specialized in databases

is expressed as follows:

> Q11: **select** Project
>   **where** exists participating leader specialization = 'DB'

The query above is an example in which a path expression is applied in cascade to the objects returned from a method. Whether the task leader is specialized in databases is determined for each task returned.

Let us now assume that the Project class is extended to include a method with the name reserved_project, which returns True or False, depending on whether or not the project is reserved. The following is an example of a query in which a method is used as a predicate:

> Q12: **select** Project
>   **where** reserved_project.

Query Results

The projection operation of a class onto the attributes applies to nested and simple objects, but if the attributes are nested this can be specified by path expressions which do not contain quantifiers. The projected attributes can be multiple-valued. The following are both possible:

> Q13: **select** Task start_date, participating leader name
>   **where** man_years ≥ 5.

> Q14: **select** Project project_name, work_plan
>   **where** recurses subproject reserved_project.

Query Q13 returns the start date and the name of the leader for tasks with at least 5 man_years. Query Q14 returns the name and the set of the tasks for each project with at least one reserved subproject.

3.2.3 Multiple Operand Queries

Let us consider explicit joins between classes. Each class involved in the join can be the root of a hierarchy of subclasses and it must be possible to express whether or not one wants to include the whole hierarchy in the evaluation of the query. It must also be possible to make comparisons with multiple-valued attributes. The following is the syntax of join predicates:

```
JoinPredicate ::=
    ScalarVariable ScalarOperator ScalarVariable |
    SetVariable SetOperator SetVariable |
```

Let us consider, for example, the query

Find all the documents in which the title is the same
as the name of a project

which can be formulated as follows:

Q15: **select** :D **from** Document :D, Project :P
     where :D title = :P project_name.

3.2.4 Operations on Sets

Indeed, queries are specified completely when operations are introduced on sets.

```
Query ::=
    (Query) |
    Query Union Query |
    Query Intersection Query |
    Query Difference Query |
    SimpleQuery.
```

The operands of set operations are sets of class instances. It is interesting to see that union, difference and intersection operations are available that determine object memberships based on value-equality rather than identity; these operations are called **UnionOfValue**, **DifferenceOfValue**, **IntersectionOfValue**.

3.3 The Languages of GemStone, Iris and O_2

There are considerable differences between the languages of the systems examined in the previous chapter. The Iris and O_2 languages are very powerful. Both of these were defined with a syntax which recalls the syntax of SQL and they have an expressive power comparable to that of SQL. For example, they can formulate both explicit and implicit joins. O_2 can also restructure the result of a query in a highly sophisticated way.

However, they are not compatible with SQL. The syntax of GemStone's query language is different to that of SQL. GemStone's query language is rather limited in terms of its expressive power. However, as yet, no in-depth comparison of the respective expressive powers of the query languages of these systems has been made.

Another difference concerns the integration of the query language with the method definition language. Queries in O_2 cannot be issued from within methods, whereas in Iris, functions which contain queries (derived functions) can be issued. In fact, in GemStone, methods containing queries can be written.

Below we give a brief illustration of some examples of queries expressed in the languages of these systems.

GemStone

Querying in GemStone is only supported on collections of objects whose class has been defined. The `constraints` clause of the class whose instance is the collection queried must not be empty.

Queries are issued by means of a special `select` message. This message has as its argument a string which denotes the Boolean combination of predicates which defines the query. The result returned from a query is a set of objects whose class is the same as that of the objects of the set to which the query is sent. For example, the query which selects all tasks with a number of man-years greater than 20 is expressed as follows (in the examples, let us assume that `Tasks` is a variable referencing an object defined as a set of instances of the `Task` class):

```
Tasks select: {t | t.man_years > 20}
```

The result of this query is a set of tasks.

Queries can contain Boolean combinations of predicates and path expressions. For example, the query which selects all tasks with a number of `man_years` greater than 20 and whose leader specializes in databases is expressed as follows:

```
Tasks select: {:t | (t.man_years > 20 &
            (t.leader.specialization = 'DB')}.
```

In addition to the `select` message, the query language provides other query protocols. The `reject` message selects all objects which do not have a particular predicate, whereas the `detect` message returns an object which satisfies the query. For example, the query:

```
Tasks reject: {:t | t.man_years > 20}
```

returns all tasks with a number of man_years less than or equal to 20.

Iris

The Iris query language, known as OSQL, is the most similar to the SQL language, in terms of functionality. More specifically, OSQL also has cursor mechanisms for accessing the results of a query sequentially. With OSQL, user-defined functions can be invoked in queries. Obviously, the system checks that arguments of correct type are passed to functions to ensure that the query is correct.

In OSQL, the query which selects all tasks with a number of man_years greater than 20 is expressed as follows:

```
select t
for each Task t
where t.man_years > 20;
```

whereas the query which determines all tasks with a number of man_years greater than 20, and whose head specializes in databases, is expressed as follows:

```
select t
for each Task t
where t.man_years > 20 and t.leader.specialization = 'DB';
```

With the Iris query language, one can also specify projections and use the distinct clause which, as in SQL, removes duplicates.

O_2

The O_2 query language, as mentioned previously, can be used only as a *standalone* language and cannot be used either within methods or within the CO_2 application language. This somewhat limits the application scope of the query language. Since the query language can be used only as a *standalone* language – at least in the system's current version – no cursor mechanisms are provided. The query language is used principally from the interactive graphic interface, in which a small environment is specifically provided for queries. This environment is for formulating queries, for saving them, for assigning a name to them and for browsing the result.

The two examples queries seen above are expressed as follows in O_2:

```
select t
from t in Task
where t.man_years > 20
```

```
select t
from t in Task
where t.man_years > 20 and t.leader.specialization = 'DB'.
```

Both projections, joins and sub-queries can be executed in O_2.

3.4   Bibliographical Notes

The area of query languages has been studied in great depth within the context of extended relational models, including the nested relational model, models for complex objects, object-oriented models and semantic models. Developments in this area have not yet been treated systematically. Some discussion of, and comparison with, relational languages are included in articles by Abiteboul and Beeri (1988), Bertino *et al*. (1992b), Alasqhur *et al*. (1989), and Dayal (1989).

Articles by Abiteboul and Bidoit (1984) and Ozsoyoglu *et al*. (1987) on extended relational models present proposed languages for a relational model with multiple-valued attributes and aggregate functions. The article by Pistor and Traunmuller (1986) presents a language for a relational model with multiple-valued attributes which can be defined by means of lists or sets. Roth *et al*. (1988), Sudkamp and Linneman (1990) and Osborn and Heaven (1986), present languages for relational models extended with abstract data types. Campbell and Embley (1985), Shipman (1981), Velez (1985) and Zaniolo (1983) present languages for semantic models. Most of these languages are defined in the context of the Entity-Relationship and functional models.

Finally, the object-oriented query languages of greatest interest are those developed for the OODBMS. The models of some of these systems are discussed in the previous section. The Iris query language, OSQL, is discussed in an article by Beech (1988). The O_2 query language is discussed in several articles, including those by Bancilhon (1989), and Cluet *et al*. (1989). The ORION language is discussed in the article by Banerjee *et al*. (1988), in which mapping techniques from the object-oriented model to the relational model are discussed. Some extensions to the language proposed by Banerjee *et al*. (1988) are presented in a later article by Kim (1989). However, these extensions have not been implemented and the ORION query language is the language described in Banerjee *et al*. (1988). The GemStone language is discussed briefly in Maier and Stein (1986). The article by Shaw (1989) describes the algebraic object-oriented query language developed for the Encore system.

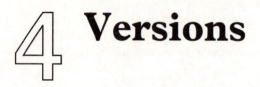

4 Versions

In management applications, once transactions have modified data, the previous values of the data that have been changed are lost – consider, as an example, a company's salaries database and transactions which modify the amount of basic pay. In more advanced applications, especially those in which a database has to support the design of a manufactured product, *versions* of objects have to be managed, given the experimental nature of the design process. This is the case in software design and CAD (*Computer Aided Design*) applications in general.

A version of an object can be thought of as a semantically significant snapshot of the object, taken at a given point in time. 'Semantically significant' means that not all the modifications to an object necessarily create a new version. Normally, a new version is created after the modifications made have been passed to the designers for them to look at, and deemed by them to be acceptable or to conform with the requirements specified.

Derivation and *history* are basic conceptual mechanisms of version management. A new version is *derived* from a preceding version and a *history* is used to keep track of how a given version was arrived at over a period of time.

A set of organizational concepts and a set of operational mechanisms are needed to manage DBMS versions. The former must be incorporated in some way in the data model, whereas the latter are the result of operations which can be applied to the entities of the data model. As will be seen in later sections, object-oriented database models are characterized by complex objects and inheritance. Defining basic concepts of version management is highly complex, as is the provision of operational support mechanisms.

As mentioned, applications such as CAD and Software Engineering have been the greatest boost, within the context of the so-called OODBMS engineering, to research and to the development of both OODBMS and of models and mechanisms for the management of versions. In this chapter, after a brief look at the requirements posed by design applications, we will first discuss the basic concepts, for example, *design objects*, *versions*, *history*, *workspaces* and other related concepts, such as *configurations* and *revisions*. Then, in order to put this into context and to look at this area in greater depth, we will give a detailed analysis of the model and mechanisms for the management of versions proposed and implemented in ORION, based on work by Chou and Kim (1988). Finally, as an overview of the various approaches, we shall briefly describe the proposed version models, based on the work of Katz (1990).

4.1   Basic Concepts

In this section, we shall introduce the basic concepts and problems of version management systems, with reference to databases for design applications. We should point out that the concepts introduced here are not necessarily used in all the models discussed in Section 4.3 and, in general, there is a lack of common terminology for the various models.

In databases for design applications, a *design object* is an aggregation of design data which designers treat as a coherent unit. A design object is usually a complex object (for example, the wing of an aircraft or an integrated circuit, or the release of a software package), obtained by bringing together a number of component objects which can be either primitive or complex objects. For example, in Software Engineering, a design object could be the release of a software package, consisting of original source code modules, libraries of executable modules and documentation manuals. In VLSI design, a design object could be an ALU (*Arithmetic and Logic Unit*), consisting of an aggregation of geometric masks, logic gates and a program written in a hardware description language. Design objects are stored in a *design database*.

A *version* is a semantically significant snapshot of a design object created at a given moment in time. Obviously, the concept of semantic significance cannot be defined unambiguously for all applications. For example, in OODBMS engineering, the concept of version has been used to model both different implementations of the same object and revisions of an object. Apart from the semantics attributed to the concept of version, a version of a given object is created from the modifications made over time to the previous versions of it, starting with the initial version. An outline of these *derivations* is provided by a version's *history*, the graphic representation of which finds its most natural form in a tree (see Figure 4.1). The tree's nodes identify the versions and the arcs represent the derivation relationships.

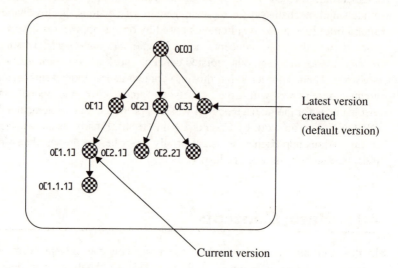

Figure 4.1   History of a version.

Several 'parallel' versions can be derived from a given version. These 'parallel' versions are defined as *alternatives*. In Figure 4.1, O[1], O[2] and O[3] are alternatives of version O[0].

In general, a version of a complex object can consist of specific versions of its component objects; to this end, the concept of *configuration* was introduced in several models. This establishes a link between a version of a composite object and a version of each of its component objects. For example, in software engineering, a configuration could consist of a version, RPS[w], of a release, RPS, of a software package aimed at a specific country and a specific machine, consisting of a version, RT[i], of the run-time, of a version, L[j], of a library and a version, D[k], of the documentation, as illustrated in Figure 4.2.

A configuration can be *static* or *dynamic*. In the former case, as shown in Figure 4.2, the user explicitly and permanently defines the link between the configuration and specific versions of component objects, whereas, in dynamic configuration, one or more specific versions making up the configuration are identified at run-time. In this case, as will be seen in greater detail in Section 4.2, the reference, called the *generic* reference, identifies a specific design object, but not a specific version of it.

A specific version, such as the *current* version, must be identifiable within the history of any given version. Generally speaking, the *current* version does not necessarily coincide with the latest version (see Figure 4.1). The version management system must provide the user with the primitives that enable him or her to select the current version and, if the user fails to select it, the system must also maintain a current default version (which is usually the most recent version).

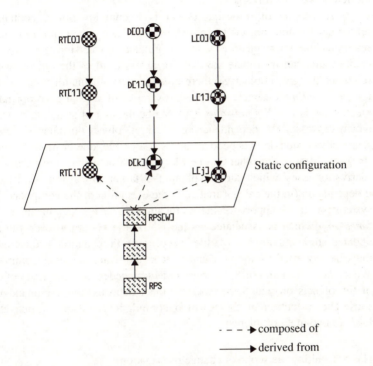

Figure 4.2   Example of a configuration.

In design applications, objects and their versions in a design database have to be organized into different *workspaces*, so that objects in a *private* workspace which are likely to be modified can be distinguished from those in a *public* workspace, or *public database*, which can be considered to be a final stage of processing. A workspace is a named repository which constitutes both a work area that is shared by users and an access control unit. Only a specific user can access and modify objects in a private workspace; other users are denied access, precisely in order to prevent objects that are still being worked on from being made generally available. But all users can access objects in a public database in read and *append* modes, as the system controls access with *check-in/check-out* protocols. However, splitting the organization of a design database into two separate levels fails to deal with situations where an 'incomplete' object combining the work of several designers has first to be 'assembled' before another, that is to be placed in the public database, can be obtained. And so a third type of workspace, known as a *semi-public* workspace, has been created. Users can access it in read and append modes, controlled by a check-in/check-out protocol. As will be seen later in Section 4.2 on the ORION model, different types of versions can be defined on the basis of operating rules that determine which type of version can be stored in a particular type of workspace.

A version of a design object is a complex object containing references to other objects (primitive or complex), which can, in turn, be referenced by other objects or versions. When a new version of an object is created, this can invalidate some of, or at most, all of the objects which reference the given object. So there must be mechanisms for *notifying* and for *propagating* changes. A simple example of a change propagation mechanism is UNIX's *makefile*. This can be thought of as a data structure which expresses the dependence of a 'target' object on other objects (a given object module is dependent on its source file, one or more libraries, 'include' files and/or other source files). The structure also expresses the 'derivation rules' which allow to obtain the 'target' object from the objects it depends on (in the case of makefile, the execution of the compiler). The system provides support for the notification of change (by means of the *timestamp* which is associated by the UNIX file system to each file and updated automatically when a file is accessed). Propagation of the change must be requested by the user and is executed using the *make* command. Where the timestamp of the 'target' object precedes the timestamp of any of the objects on which the 'target' object depends, this command will cause the execution of the required compilations. Change propagation leads to two main problems:

(1) Limiting the scope of change propagation.

(2) Defining the path along which the changes must be propagated.

The first problem arises because the history of the versions of a given object is in the form of a tree. If we replace version V[i] with version V'[i], this could require propagating the change right back to the root node. As can be seen from Figure 4.1, the replacement of the version $O[1.1.1]$, with a new version $O'[1.1.1]$, could require propagating the change back to the root version $O[0]$. And it is worth noting that the other versions previously generated from $O[0]$ may no longer be valid. The second problem arises in the case of configurations. For example, in Figure 4.3, the two configurations RPS[w] and RPS1[j] share the version RT[i] of run-time. It may happen that a new version of RT'[i] of run-time is needed and then it would have to be decided whether RPS[w] or RPS1[j], or both configurations, need to be changed.

There are various ways of managing ambiguities in situations such as this. The first involves preventing any change propagation if there are DAG structures. However, this may be too restrictive. The second possible solution is to propagate the change to all the branches concerned and to consider the resulting versions as alternatives of the root version. However, this would lead to a proliferation of versions, not all of which would be useful to the user. A third solution is to propagate the change, interrupting it as soon as ambiguity arises. Another solution is to define operational mechanisms, whereby users can make their intentions unambiguous by defining appropriate rules which modifications of versions must obey and by using check-in/check-out mechanisms.

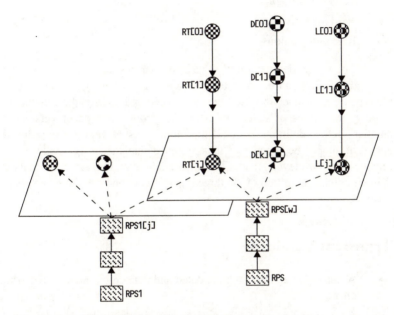

Figure 4.3 Ambiguous propagation of a change.

The final aspect of version modelling and management is the extension to include cases in which versions are applied not only to instances but also to classes and schema. In fact, due to the nature of design applications, a significant change of a design object could involve not only modifying its 'value', but also modifying its structure. It could be helpful to have a versions and history mechanism which applies to the schema.

With regard to the versions of objects (instances), the schema versions make it necessary to keep track of the objects created under each specific schema version and to define rules both for updating and for deleting versions of a class. This topic is related to the concept and the mechanisms of schema evolution discussed in Chapter 5, and will be discussed in greater depth in the section on ORION's version management system.

4.2 The ORION Model

In this section, we describe in greater detail the versions model developed in ORION (Chou and Kim, 1988) and its implementation.

This is based upon a model formulated by (Chou and Kim, 1986), which identifies three types of versions:

- Transient versions
- Working versions
- Released versions

These are defined on the basis of various factors, such as the operations which can be executed on them, the user who executes them, the type of workspace in which they are stored and, finally, the constraints on any 'transitions of state' that may arise from one type of version to another. Before defining in detail the three types of versions introduced above, it should be noted that it is assumed that the design database is organized on two levels, that is, a public database and private workspaces. A more precise definition of the three types of versions mentioned above is given below.

Transient Versions

- A transient version can be updated and deleted by the designer who created it.
- A transient version can be created from scratch or by checking-out a released version from a public database. It can be also derived from another transient version or from a working version in a private database.
- It is stored in the private workspace of the designer who created it.
- If a new transient version is derived from an existing transient version, the latter is 'promoted' to a working version.

Working Versions

- A working version is considered to be 'stable' and cannot be updated.
- It can be deleted by the designer who created it.

- A transient version can be derived from a working version.

- A working version can be derived from a transient version by 'promoting' the latter. The promotion can be explicit (requested by the user), or implicit (determined by the system).

- It is stored in the private workspace of the designer who created it.

There are restrictions on updating working versions mainly because, if a working version is updated *after* one or more transient versions are derived from it, appropriate algorithms for insertion, update and deletion would have to be defined in order to ensure that the derived versions do not 'see' the effects of updating the working version.

Released Versions

- A released version is stored in a public database.

- It cannot be updated or deleted.

- A transient version can be created from a released version.

- A released version can be derived from a working version by 'promoting' the latter.

- A released version is created from the check-in of a working version which is stored in a private workspace.

Figure 4.4 shows some of the above concepts.

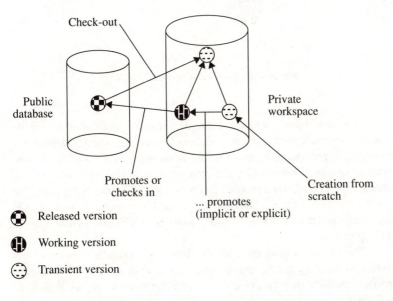

Figure 4.4   Types of version in ORION.

The model distinguishes between *versionable* objects and *non-versionable* objects. A versionable object, also called a *generic object*, is an instance of a versionable class and consists of the derivation hierarchy of its versions. The model also distinguishes between generic objects and version instances, which identify a specific version of the generic object.

Both generic objects and specific version instances have OIDs. These concepts are illustrated in Figure 4.5, which shows a generic object, its version instances and associated OIDs.

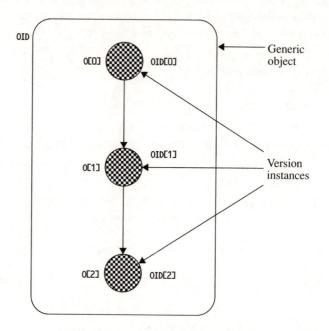

Figure 4.5 Generic object in ORION.

Version numbers, which are unique within the derivation hierarchy, are also associated with version instances. An object which references a versionable object can reference both a generic object and a specific version instance. In the former case, the reference is called *dynamic* and it identifies the *default version* of the generic object. In the latter case, the reference is called *static*. Dynamic references are useful where objects reference transient or working version instances, which can then be deleted (see Figure 4.6).

The system allows the user to identify a particular version of the derivation hierarchy as the default version. If none is identified by the user, the system selects the version instance with the most recent timestamp as the default version.

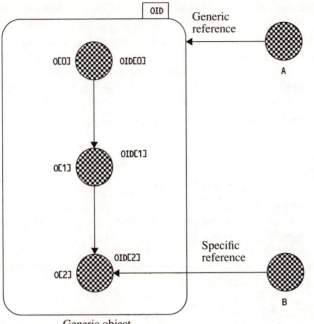

Figure 4.6   Generic and specific references in ORION.

A versionable object is an instance of a *versionable class*. When an application creates an instance object of a versionable class, ORION creates a generic object and, at the same time, the first version instance. From the implementation point of view, a generic object is essentially a data structure which describes the version derivation hierarchy of the versionable object. As mentioned earlier, the system assigns an OID both to generic objects and to version instances. A generic object and the version instances described by this are instances of the same class. In order to distinguish between them, the system associates a special flag to the generic object.

A generic object consists of the following attributes defined by the system:

(1)   Version-counter.
(2)   Next-version-number.
(3)   Default-version-number.
(4)   Default-switch.
(5)   Derivation-tree.

The version-counter contains the total number of version instances of the versionable object. The next-version number is the number to be assigned to the next version instance of a versionable object when this is created. The next-version number is increased after it is assigned to the new version instance. The default-version-number is the number of the version instance to be used when a dynamic reference to a generic object needs to be resolved. The default-switch indicates whether the default version instance was specified by the user. The derivation-tree descriptor contains a tree of version descriptors.

A version descriptor is associated with each version instance. This descriptor includes:

(1)   The version-number of the version instance in question.

(2)   The OID of the version instance.

(3)   A list of the children of the version, consisting of references to version descriptors for all version instances which derive directly from the version instance.

Each version instance also contains the following attributes which are defined by the system.

(1)   Version-number.

(2)   Type-of-version.

(3)   OID of its generic object.

Version numbers are used to distinguish between version instances of the same versionable object. The type-of-version denotes whether version instances are transient versions or working versions and allow the system to refuse requests for updating working versions. The OID of a generic object allows the system efficiently to find other version instances of the versionable object, starting with a given version instance.

It should be noted that the generic object is examined and updated each time a new version instance is created, so that the most recent version instance can be kept track of and, of course, so that the derivation hierarchy can be updated. The processing overhead due to version management is limited to versionable classes, and it is fairly low. Storage overhead depends on the level of 'granularity' of the versionable objects. To limit storage overhead, the designers of ORION advise that versions should only be generated for rather large objects.

In order to integrate the versions model into ORION's data model, the latter has been extended to include an additional set of messages and limited extensions to some of the basic messages.

The message **define-class** was extended to include an additional argument, **versionable**, as shown below in order to define a versionable class:

(define-class Classname **:versionable** TrueOrNil**)**

When the argument :versionable has the value True, versions can be generated for object instances of the class; when it has the value Nil, versions cannot be generated. When the user sends a create message to a versionable class, ORION simultaneously creates a generic object and the first version instance of the versionable object. The new version instance is a transient version and becomes the root of the derivation hierarchy for the versionable object. Other optional arguments of the message define-class provide the names and values of the attributes for the version instance.

The following message has to be sent to a generic object or to a version (identified by VersionedObject), in order to create a new version from an existing one:

(derive-version VersionedObject)

If VersionedObject is a transient version, ORION 'promotes' it to a working version and makes a copy of it. The copy becomes a new transient version, to which a new version number and an OID are assigned. If VersionedObject is a generic object, the message is redirected to the default version.

An application can 'promote' a transient version to a working version by sending the message promote to a VersionedObject. If VersionedObject is a working version, the system takes no action. Conversely, a working version can be 'demoted' to a transient version by means of the message demote. If VersionedObject is already a transient version, or if VersionedObject is a working version and there are other versions which have been derived from it, the system takes no action. If VersionedObject is a generic object, the message, whether promote or demote, is redirected to the default version.

The default-version-number of a generic object can be changed by means of the message change-default-version.

(change-default-version VersionedObject [NewdefaultVersionNumber])

If the argument NewdefaultVersionNumber is specified, the default-version-number is fixed and is not changed even if new versions are created; in this case it can be changed only by another change-default-version message. If the argument NewdefaultVersionNumber is not specified, the version number of the most recent version is used by default.

To delete a version instance or a generic object, the message delete-object is used. If the message is sent to a generic object, the whole derivation hierarchy is deleted, that is, all the version instances of the versionable object and the generic object itself. If the message is sent to a version instance, the latter is deleted. If the version instance is a transient version, or a working version from which no other versions have been derived, the descriptor of the version is also removed. If the version instance is the only version instance of the generic object, the latter is also removed. Finally, if the message is sent to a working version from which other versions have been derived, the descriptor of the version is not removed.

The system also provides the message `parent-version` which is used to obtain the father version of a version instance, the message `child-version`, which is used to obtain the child versions of a given version instance, the message `generic-object` which is used to obtain a generic object starting from one of its version instances and the message `default-version` for requesting the default-version-number from a generic object.

It should be noted that the attribute version-number can be used in specifying QueryExpression (which, it should be recalled, is a Boolean expression of predicates), to find all (or some) of the version instances of a versionable class, or to find the user-defined default version or the most recent version instances, which satisfy a given QueryExpression.

Finding all the version instances of a specific versionable class presents no particular difficulties. In fact, these can be scanned sequentially to find those which satisfy the QueryExpression, or a subset of them can be scanned using a secondary index defined on some class attributes. Queries which involve the user-defined default version, or the most recent version instances, cause implementation and performance problems, in that information on the user-defined default version and the most recent version instance are stored in the generic object and not in the individual version instances. ORION does not support this second type of query.

4.2.1 Notification of Changes

In ORION, there are two main ways of notifying changes, namely, using *messages* and using *flags*. In the message-based approach, the system notifies changes in objects by sending users appropriate messages (whether these users are humans or applications). Notification can be *immediate* or *deferred*, depending on whether the users are notified of the change immediately after it happens or later (at a time also specified by the user).

In the flag-based approach, the system simply updates a system data structure and users are advised of the change only when they access the modified object. Obviously, the use of flags results in deferred notification. Changes resulting in notification can be updates, deletions and the creation of new versions.

ORION supports flag-based change notification. Each object which participates in change notification has two different timestamps. The first, called *change-notification-timestamp*, denotes the moment the object was created or the moment of the last update. The second, called the *change-approval-timestamp* denotes the last point at which the owner of the object approved all changes made to objects referenced by the given object; the attributes referencing the changed object are referred to as *notification-sensitive*.

ORION provides three system attributes for classes involved in change notification:

(1)   Change-notification-timestamp.

(2)   Change-approval-timestamp.

(3)   The set of events which generate a notification of change.

Events which generate change notification include updating and/or deletion. Deletion is the default value and updating subsumes deletion.

If a class D is the domain of an attribute a, which is sensitive to the notification of a class C, then each instance of D and each instance of the subclasses of D contains a change-notification-timestamp. Each time a new instance of D (or of a subclass of D) is created, its change-notification-timestamp stores the instant the event occurs. At a later instant, when an instance c of class C references an instance d of class D through a notification-sensitive attribute, the user (or the application) can compare the change-notification-timestamp of c with the change-notification-timestamp of d and decide whether the change to d has to be approved.

Here, two new concepts should be introduced; *reference-consistent* objects and *reference-inconsistent* objects. An object, V, with a change-approval-timestamp, $V.CA$ and a change-notification-timestamp, $V.CN$, is reference-consistent in respect of the set, R, of objects that the object references, if no object belonging to R has a change-notification-timestamp greater than the change-approval-timestamp of V. And V is said to be reference-inconsistent with respect to R, if one or more objects in R have been updated and the effects of these updates on V have not been determined. In order to make V reference-consistent, the effects of updates on the objects of R must be determined and if appropriate, V must be updated. If the updates on the objects of R have no impact on V, $V.CA$ is simply updated to the current time instant, otherwise $V.CN$ will need to be updated (and possibly $V.CA$, if the changes are approved) to the current time. A deletion of an object which results in a dangling reference is an indication of the inconsistency of references if the reference to the deleted object occurs through an attribute which is notification-sensitive. The system keeps the necessary information for determining whether an instance is reference-consistent, but responsibility for determining the consistency of references and also responsibility for taking appropriate steps for making the instance reference-consistent, falls to the application user.

ORION provides a utility program to assist the user (or the application) in determining inconsistent references in a complex object. The program recursively controls all notification-sensitive objects referenced directly or indirectly from a given object. At the end of the control, the program returns a list of *warnings*, each of which consists of a triple in the form $< from - object, to - object, event >$, indicating that the reference from the object *from - object* to the object *to - object* is potentially inconsistent with respect to the result of *event*.

4.2.2 Schema Versions

Problems relating to modelling and managing schema versions have been studied in the ORION project (Kim and Chou, 1988). The proposed model has not been implemented. It is an extension of the ORION version model, described in the section above.

Kim and Chou (1988) identify three possible approaches to modelling and managing schema versions. The first two approaches differ in terms of the 'granularity' of the versionable object. In fact, in the first approach, called the *schema versions*, the entire schema is dealt with as a versionable object, whereas in the second, called *class versions*, the versionable object is the individual class. Finally, the third approach involves providing *dynamic views* of the schema rather than versions in the real sense. Whereas in the first two approaches objects are 'linked' to the schema or class version which created them (or from which any of these are accessible), in the third approach all objects are associated with a single underlying schema, on which different views are dynamically superimposed.

Initially, the model identifies operations which can result in the creation of a schema version, namely the modifications to the class definition and the schema's DAG structure (and therefore of inheritance relationships between classes). Modifying class definition can involve adding or removing an attribute of the class involved, whereas modifying DAG stems from adding or deleting a class or adding another superclass S to a given class C.

The types of schema versions are slightly different from those of object versions (in fact, there are transient and working versions in the definition, but no released versions). Transitions of state from one schema version type to another, as well as the allowed primitives (promote and demote) are also essentially the same as those defined for object versions.

The most significant problem in schema version management concerns keeping track of those objects which have been created under a given schema version and controlling access of applications to them. In fact, an object O created under a schema version S_1 may have a different structure from that of an object instance of the same class in another version S_2 of the schema.

To this end, as shown in Figure 4.7, the concept of a *creator schema version* of an object is introduced into the model. It identifies the schema version in which a given object was created, the *access scope of a schema version* and the *direct access scope of a schema version* which identifies the set of objects created from a given schema version.

Using these concepts as a baseline, the model defines a set of rules for schema versions. These identify the possible transitions of state from one type of schema version to another – and the operations which activate them. According to the procedures laid down by the rules, objects belonging to a schema version's access scope are inherited from the access scope of a schema version derived from that to which it belongs. The rules also define the operations allowed on objects which are accessible in the access scope of a given schema version.

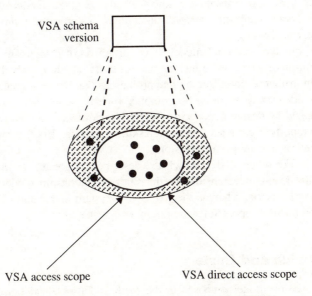

Figure 4.7   Access scope of a schema version in ORION.

4.3   Proposed Models

In this section, we describe some of the models proposed for managing versions and the corresponding management mechanisms. This survey is based on the work of Katz (1990). The models and systems presented, which we do not claim to be exhaustive, show that, beyond terminological differences, the issues are those already described in Section 4.1 and that there are relatively few basic mechanisms and concepts.

Generally speaking, the temporal dimension is of fundamental importance in modelling and managing versions. Time-oriented data models (Clifford and Ariav, 1986), provide many of the elements needed to represent the evolution of data over time. Representation of data in these models is extended to include additional properties, such as the creation time of a certain object and the point in time at which an object is replaced by a new instance. However, time-oriented databases do not take into consideration such operational aspects as inheritance, propagation of changes and workspaces. And versions cannot be considered simply as objects which change over time as they are updated. Creating a version is an explicit operation, which is semantically significant and related with changes to other design objects. Time-oriented data models provide support for operations such as temporal series analyses (for example, determining the rate of increase of sales for a given model of car as a function of time) which are not relevant to design applications. For the latter, it is more important to know whether a given version was derived from another specific version, rather than to know the point in time at which this happened.

In the relational model, it is certainly not difficult to extend the definition of a relation to include one (or more) attributes which describe a given instant of time. But the real problem is that the relational data model fails adequately to describe complex objects which are modelled and managed by design applications. Extensions of the relational model focus on supporting complex objects (Haskin and Lorie, 1982), rather than on modelling and supporting versions.

The other models which are described in greater detail further on are the result of extensions to the Entity-Relationship model or object-oriented models, whereas the SUN NSE system and Apollo DSSE were developed to support Software Engineering activities.

Dittrich and Lorie

The version model proposed in the work of Dittrich and Lorie (1988) is based on the concepts of design object, generic references and clusters of logic versions. In this model, a design object is a set of versions with a specific current version which is different from other versions. Design objects can reference other design objects, thereby forming hierarchical aggregations. References can be *direct*, when they identify a specific version of a design object, or *generic*, when they identify a specific design object but not a specific version of it. *Generic* references are resolved by means of an *environment* mechanism: an environment defines a link between design objects and their specific versions, or recursively, between design objects and another environment. A relationship of order can be established between environments, so that, in the resolution of a generic reference, the links between objects and versions defined in an environment can take precedence over the links defined in other environments. The model also introduces the concept of clusters of logic versions, whereby the user can further structure versions, grouping them according to criteria defined by that user. For example, all versions which are revisions of the same alternative can be grouped together in one cluster. The model enables arbitrary hierarchies of version clusters to be defined and a specific version can be inserted in several clusters.

Klahold, Schlageter and Wilkes

The model described in the work of Klahold *et al.* (1986) is based on the concept of a *version graph*, which is similar to the concept of history. Taking as its starting point the fact that the least recent versions are those which, presumably, have undergone the most verifications, the concept of *partitions* is also introduced in the model. These are superimposed on the version graph, where a partition groups together a set of versions which have a certain level of 'consistency'. The model also supports views of subsets of a version's graph. These consist of a subset of a given graph which satisfies a given criterion.

Landis

The model described in the work of Landis (1986) is an initial version of the Ontologic data model for CAD applications. It is based on four concepts: *non-linear history, version references, change propagation* and *limiting of change scope*. The model organizes the versions of an object into several derivation 'branches'. The history consists of several derivation branches. Each branch of the history represents an *alternative* and the system explicitly identifies the *current version* and the *default branch*. Versions references are a mechanism for supporting dynamic configurations. 'Historical' references always have a specific value. In other words, when a version is made obsolete by a new version, references which leave the old version cannot be changed. And the references which originate in the current version and which have no specific value always reference the current version of the target object. As far as change propagation is concerned, the user can instruct the system to activate it in the following circumstances:

(1)   Whenever a new version is created.

(2)   When changes are made to the schema (for example, when a new property is added to a version).

(3)   Whenever the value of a property is modified.

To keep changes under control, the model provides two additional mechanisms: *delta sets* and *pended version creation*. Delta sets are similar to the log of changes – sets of changes to related objects, which are considered as units for undo/redo operations – which is managed by transactional systems. The second mechanism is similar to *checking-in* in semi-public workspaces. The propagation of a change made to an object cannot result in the creation of more than one new version.

Batory and Kim

The model proposed in the work of Batory and Kim (1985) is based on the extension of the E-R model by means of inheritance of object-oriented models. The model has four new concepts: *molecular objects, type-version generalization, instantiation* and *parametrized versions.*

Essentially, molecular objects can be traced back to complex objects of object-oriented data models. They are used to define complex objects by aggregating several primitive objects and the relationships (as defined in the E-R model) that exist between them. In a molecular object, the model explicitly distinguishes between *interface* and *implementation.* The type-version generalization mechanism is used to model the history of the versions of a molecular object. In the model, all versions are considered to be instances of the type of a given molecular object and, consequently, they all have the same interface. The versions are seen as alternative implementations of a given type of molecular object or as revisions of previous versions. Parametrized versions allow to use any version of a component object as the component of a molecular object. They provide support for dynamic configurations, since a molecular object can reference both a specific version of its component and the type of that component. The model also proposes a support mechanism for change notification based on *timestamps* to limit the number of messages which the system must send.

Ketabachi and Berzins

The model proposed by Ketabachi and Berzins (1987) assimilates versions with *refinements*, that is, versions are a tool for modelling different descriptions of the same object. The following three types of refinement are identified:

(1) *Template* refinements, which are for describing the various aspects of an object.

(2) *Explosion refinements* which list the versions of the component objects constituting a version of a composite object.

(3) *Instance refinements* which describe the revisions and alternatives of a given object.

The model uses the concept of *incremental refinements* to describe the evolution of an object. These represent the differences between an object and an object derived from it. The history of a version is represented by means of two graphs. The first, called the *refinement graph*, describes the derivation relationships between various versions, whereas the second, called IRG (*Incremental Refinement Graph*), stores differences (or deltas) between a version and the father version.

A refinement graph can represent: *dependent* refinements, for which modifications to an ancestor of a given object are reflected in the object; *independent* refinements, in which the differences between parallel paths do not result in changes to the same object; and *alternative* refinements, in which changes to parallel paths are reflected in the same information.

Beech and Mahbod

A proposal for the management of versions was developed in the IRIS project (developed at Hewlett-Packard's research laboratories) and is described in an article by Beech and Mahbod (1988). In this model, a version is an object with its own OID. Version instances are organized into *version sets*, each associated to a single generic instance. *Generic* and *Version* are types which are predefined by the system and they can be used to the same extent as other types. Version graphs are obtained with functions associated with Generic and Version instances. These functions define *first*, *last*, *next version* and *preceding version* operations and so on. New versions can be generated automatically using the following two methods: *mutation* or *propagation*. In the first case, a change to a 'significant' previously specified property causes the system to make a copy of the object (*copy on write*) before it makes the change. The current version is 'frozen' and a new version is created before the change is made. The second method is used to propagate changes. When a new version of a subcomponent is created, this results in the creation of a new version of the object which contains the subcomponent. References can be either *specific* or *generic*. The former identify a specific version, whereas the latter identify a generic instance and the set of versions associated with it. A mechanism based on *contexts* is used to resolve generic references. This consists of a trigger, which can be activated before, or after, an operation is invoked; a user-defined rule is associated to it, which specifies how the references should be resolved.

Vines, Vines and King

The work of Vines *et al.* (1988) describes the change control and versions model of GAIA – an object-oriented development environment for the ADA language – being developed at Honeywell. In this model, versions are identified with timestamps instead of version numbers. This serves to put a version clearly in relation to the event which generated it. Specific relations are created between objects – *version sensitive* relations and *change sensitive* relations – to define the effect of changes. The former type of relation causes an object to be notified of a change to a related object, whereas the latter causes an object which is, itself, not sensitive to the change, to redirect the change notification to another object related to it.

The model provides specific objects for managing changes. The first, called the *change request object*, is created when the user or the system itself generates a request for a change. This object is associated with the object which has to be changed, keeps track of the changes to it and acts as an 'anchor' for an *audit trail*. The second, called the *change notification object*, is created when a request for a change is propagated along version-sensitive or change-sensitive relations. Finally, configuration objects are defined so that changes can be grouped together. These associate specific versions of objects with those objects. A new configuration object can be created as a result of a request originating from a change made to the objects making up the configuration.

SUN NSE

The SUN NSE system (SUN Microsystems, 1988) is a software development environment in which the various 'design objects' are manipulated with specific tools and generic commands. The system defines and manages the following types of object:

- FILE. A file can be of the source, derived, or generic type. Versions of the files can be made.

- TARGET. A target consists of a derived file, the objects on which it depends and a procedure for reconstructing it when it changes any one of the objects on which it depends.

- COMPONENT. These are the 'building blocks' of hierarchical structures where such a hierarchical structure can be composed of objects of different types. Components are similar to directories of a file system; the difference is that components are organized in revisions, which are time-sensitive 'snapshots'. The components are essentially a hierarchical space of names for objects.

- LINKDB. A linkdb represents arbitrary connections between related objects. Versions of linkdb can be made.

Versions are stored in the form of *interleaved deltas* inside an object. The access paradigm is based on *acquire, modify* and *reconcile* operations. The effect of an acquire operation is to copy (check-out) an object from one 'environment' (and hence a workspace) to another. The reconcile operation (check-in) copies the object back into the environment, as a new revision. The system provides tools for assisting in merging parallel revisions. Environments are organized hierarchically. The system also supports change notification. Users register notification requests in the system and, when there is a significant event in an environment of interest to the user, for example, the recompilation of a specific file, the system sends an E-mail to registered users.

Apollo DSEE

Apollo DSEE (*Distributed Software Engineering Environment*) (Leblang and Chase, 1984) is a software development environment. It consists of the following five components:

(1)   *History Manager*, which governs version control.

(2)   *Configuration Manager*, which enables a complex system to be built from more primitive components by using a system's model

(3)   *Task Manager*, which ensures correct sequentialization and activation of tools.

(4)   *Monitor Manager*, which supports change notification.

(5)   *Advice Manager*, which provides on-line help to users carrying out a task.

History Manager provides the operations, *Reserve* and *Replace*, which can be traced back to check-in and check-out operations, respectively. The versions of a program module are stored by using *interleaved deltas* inside the same file. Configuration Manager uses a system's model to describe the composition of a module, the sequence of tasks which are required to recompose the object if there is a change and to build the dependencies which can exist between module's components and other objects known to the system. Configuration Manager defines the composition of modules in terms of *configuration threads* which associate a list of versions of the components which have to be used with the names of the components. References can either be to specific versions or, by default, to the most recent version of a given component. A configuration thread which contains only references to specific versions for each of its components is called a *bound configuration thread*. The configuration thread of a module can also refer to the configuration threads of each of that module's components. Finally, a *release* comprises a software system, its bound configuration thread and a keyword which identifies it.

4.4   **Bibliographical Notes**

One of the first version models for semantic data models was proposed by McLeod *et al.* (1983). In this model, a version can represent different things, namely: alternative implementations, revisions, or different representations of an object. The model also makes an explicit distinction between instances and definitions, so that all the instance versions of a given definition share the attributes of the definition.

The work of Katz (1990), makes a survey of the various version models proposed in the relevant literature or implemented in certain systems, and proposes a reference model which aims to standardize the various previously developed models. The papers of Kim and Chou (1988) and Chou and Kim (1988), on version management in ORION, include an in-depth discussion of implementation problems (necessary data structures and algorithms) deriving from version management as well as providing a detailed description of the model.

Models and mechanisms for change notification and propagation have been investigated in works by Chou and Kim (1986) and Rumbaugh (1988), among others. The model proposed by Chou and Kim (1986), and used in ORION, is a revision of the model by Batory and Kim (1985). The model proposed in Rumbaugh (1988) associates with a relation a set of *propagation attributes*, which represent those operations which result in change propagation. A propagation attribute can have the value *none*; where the associated operation must not be propagated, the value *propagate*; where the operation must be applied both to the instance of a relation and to objects participating in it, the value *shallow*, if the operation must be applied only to the instance of a relation; and finally, the value *inhibit*, if the propagation must not occur until there is at least one instance of the relation.

By contrast Sciore (1991) proposes to model and manage versions by using annotations. An annotation is a piece of information which is used by the system 'behind the scenes'. In the model proposed by Sciore, the user only sees the current version of an object. Alternative versions, as well as the history of versions, are managed by the system with annotations and these are hidden from the user.

5 Evolution

As stated earlier on, application environments that OODBMS support are characterized by the fact that schema changes are the rule rather than the exception. In fact, it is natural that, for example, during a design application, there are changes in the way in which objects are classified and in which relations between them are established. This is also due to the length of time that these applications last.

There are many aspects to the problem of object evolution in object-oriented databases. Not all of them have been investigated in sufficient depth. Generally speaking, one can distinguish between evolution of schemas – for example, modifying a class definition – and of instances – for example, the migration of an instance from one class to another. In the latter type of evolution, an instance can modify its own structure while maintaining the same identity. In this chapter, we discuss both types of evolution and illustrate certain approaches to implement schema modifications. Finally, we discuss the types of schema and instance evolution that are possible in GemStone, O_2 and Iris.

5.1   Schema Evolution

The primitives supplied by relational DBMS are used to create and delete relations and to add attributes to a relation. Normally, it is fairly simple to manage this somewhat limited type of modification, since modifications to a relation have no effect on other relations. The situation is more complex in OODBMS, since the repertory of possible modifications is significantly larger, due to the increased complexity of the model, and to the fact that modifications to a class can involve several classes. If, for example, an attribute is deleted from a class, it must be removed from all subclasses. The concept of inheritance hierarchy requires other schema modification operations to be defined, in addition to those which are semantically significant in the relational model. Another important issue concerns mechanisms for on-line execution of such schema modifications. Efficiency of execution is crucial. These and other issues of schema modification are discussed in the rest of this section.

5.1.1 Taxonomy and Semantics of Schema Modifications

To place the problem more specifically within the context of the OODBMS, Figure 5.1 shows the taxonomy described by Banerjee *et al.* (1987), of possible schema changes. These obviously depend on the specific details of the data model involved. The taxonomy concerns ORION's database model. However, since this is the most complete model proposed thus far, it of course covers most of the schema modifications that are possible in almost all the object-oriented models proposed. In particular, the ORION database model supports the specification of default values for instance attributes. If an instance is created without specifying the value of one or more attributes, these attributes are assigned the default values, if these are specified in the class definition. Finally, the database model provides the concept of shared attributes. The value of such attributes is shared between all class instances. The concept of shared attributes is very similar to the concept of class attributes (described in Chapter 2).

A list of similar modifications is proposed for GemStone in Breitl *et al.* (1989). But there are some differences, as this system does not support multiple inheritance and it does not provide the concept of composite objects. Modifications which change the order of superclasses or which change a composite attribute into a non-composite attribute have no significance. However, the current version of GemStone does not yet have the functions for executing the schema modifications proposed in Breitl *et al.* (1989). Some of these modifications can be executed only for classes which have no instances. In Section 5.3, we discuss evolution in GemStone. By contrast, all the modifications in ORION's system definitions can even be executed for classes with instances.

Rules for Schema Consistency

When executing modifications to a schema, the changes proposed must maintain a consistent schema and both in ORION and GemStone, rules

(1) Modifying the class definition
    (1.1) Modifying attributes
        (1.1.1) Adding attributes
        (1.1.2) Deleting attributes
        (1.1.3) Renaming attributes
        (1.1.4) Modifying the domain's attributes
        (1.1.5) Modifying the inheritance of attributes
            (attributes inherited from another superclass
            bear the same name)
        (1.1.6) Modifying the default value attributes
        (1.1.7) Manipulating shared attributes
            (1.1.7.1) Transforming non-shared attributes
                into shared attributes
            (1.1.7.2) Modifying the value of shared
                attributes
            (1.1.7.3) Transforming shared attributes into
                non-shared attributes
        (1.1.8) Modifying composite attributes into
            non-composite attributes
    (1.2) Modifying methods
        (1.2.1) Adding methods
        (1.2.2) Deleting methods
        (1.2.3) Modifying the names of methods
        (1.2.4) Modifying the implementation of methods
        (1.2.5) Modifying inheritance of methods
            (a method inherited from another superclass
            bears the same name)
(2) Modifying the inheritance hierarchy
    (2.1) Making a class S the superclass of a class C
    (2.2) Removing a class S from the list of superclasses of
        a class C
    (2.3) Modifying the order of the superclasses of a class C
(3) Modifying the set of classes
    (3.1) Creating new classes
    (3.2) Deleting classes
    (3.3) Modifying class names

Figure 5.1   Taxonomy of schema modifications in an object-oriented database.

have been defined for schema consistency. These must be complied with as each schema is modified. Consistency rules are referred to as *schema invariants*.

However, almost all such invariants can be applied to other data models. Let us consider, by way of example, the schema illustrated in Figure 5.2. An extended graphic notation is used in the schema. This indicates not only the specific attributes and methods of each class, referred to from now on as *local* class attributes and methods, but also the methods and attributes inherited from superclasses. The latter are shown in a rectangle. For example, the age method is defined in the Person class and is inherited from all subclasses without being redefined. It appears in all subclasses within a rectangle. The monthly_salary method is defined in the class Researcher and is redefined in the class Part_Time_Researcher. Therefore, the latter class does not appear in a rectangle in the graphic definition.

The following is the set of schema invariants defined for the ORION database model:

- *Inheritance hierarchy invariant*
  The inheritance hierarchy must be a graph with a direct and acyclic root (that is, a DAG). The graph must have a single root, that is, an OBJECT system's class. The graph must be completely connected, that is, there must be no isolated nodes. Each node must be accessible from the root. A similar invariant is defined in Breitl *et al*. (1989) for the GemStone database model. Each node represents a class and must have a different name.

- *Unique names invariant*
  All attributes and methods of a class, whether of instances or of the class, must have different names.

- *Single origin invariant*
  All class attributes and methods must have a single distinct origin. In other words, a class *C* cannot have two different attributes and methods which have as their origin the same attribute or method of a superclass (direct or indirect) of *C*. For example, as the schema in Figure 5.2 shows, both direct superclasses of the class Researcher_Student have an age method. However, this method has a single origin class – the class Person – so that both the class Part_Time_Researcher and the class Student which are direct superclasses of the class Researcher_Student, inherit this method from the class Person.

- *Complete inheritance invariant*
  A class inherits all the attributes and methods of each superclass, except when complete inheritance results in violations of the unique name invariant and of the single origin invariant. Therefore:
  - if two attributes or methods have a different origin but the same name in two different superclasses, at least one of these attributes or methods must be inherited.
  - if two attributes or methods have the same origin in two different superclasses, only one of these attributes or methods must be inherited.

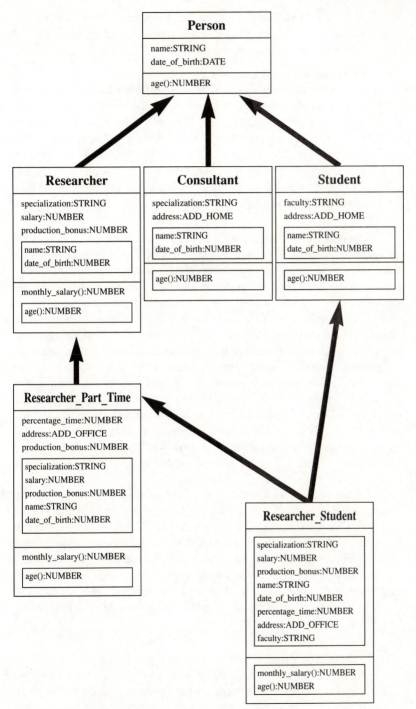

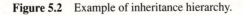

Figure 5.2   Example of inheritance hierarchy.

A similar invariant is defined for GemStone's database model. However, invariants in GemStone are simplified by the fact that only single inheritance is supported.

- *Domain compatibility invariant*
  If an attribute A_i of a class C is inherited from an attribute A_j of a superclass of C, then the domain of A_i must be the same as A_j or a subclass of the A_j domain class. However, this invariant is common to most models and has been discussed, for example, in relation to the GemStone and O_2 database models. This invariant in GemStone applies only to attributes for which the domain is specified (remember that a domain for class attributes has to be specified only in certain circumstances in GemStone).

There is another invariant for the GemStone database model, called the *preserving information invariant*, which ensures that there is no loss of information. This invariant depends specifically on the fact that there is no explicit delete operation in GemStone and the system guarantees that the values of both variables and objects referenced by other objects are maintained. For example, the effect of deleting an instance attribute from a class is that the attribute is lost for all the class instances, with the resultant loss of the value of that attribute for all instances. If one of these instances is 'pointing' towards other objects, there will be a problem if the 'customers' of the instances use the deleted attribute. The solution to this problem, put forward in Breitl *et al.* (1989), is to delete the attribute but to notify the 'clients' that the object has been modified, at the same time providing the value of the deleted attribute, so that the 'clients' can reconstruct the necessary information. However, this approach has so far only been proposed, has yet to be implemented and it is not yet clear how valid it is.

When defining a mechanism for a schema modification, the rules by which modifications are executed must be specified in such a way that schema invariants are respected. These rules are classified in four groups in Banerjee *et al.* (1987). The first group of rules concerns the resolution of conflicts caused by multiple inheritance and the redefinition of attributes and methods in a subclass. Any schema modification, such as the addition of a superclass or the deletion of an instance attribute from a class, can result in conflicts of inheritance. The following three rules belong to the first group:

[S1] Rule of precedence of subclasses over superclasses.
      If, in a class C, an attribute or method is defined with the same name as an attribute or method of a superclass, the definition given in the subclass takes precedence over the definition of the superclass.

[S2]   Rule of precedence between superclasses of a different origin.

If several superclasses have attributes or methods with the same name but with a different origin, the attribute or methods of the first superclass is inherited by the subclass. For example, let us consider the class `Researcher_Student` represented in the schema in Figure 5.2. This class has two superclasses (`Student` and `Part_Time_Researcher`) which have an attribute with the same `address` name but a different origin, since this attribute does not come from a superclass which is common to the two `Researcher_Student` superclasses. Therefore, since this attribute is defined differently in the two superclasses and their domains cannot be compared, the attribute is inherited from the first superclass, and the definition inherited is the one which assigns the class `Adr_Office` as the domain to the `address` attribute.

[S3]   Rule for precedence between superclasses of the same origin.

If several superclasses have attributes or methods with the same name and with the same origin, the attribute or method is inherited only once. If the domain of the attribute has been redefined in any superclass, the attribute with the most specialized domain is inherited by the subclass. Finally, if domains cannot be compared, the attribute is inherited from the first superclass.

The second group of rules concerns the propagation of modifications to subclasses. In fact, a modification which, for example, relates to an attribute, is only propagated to those subclasses in which the attribute has not been redefined. The following three rules apply to this group:

[P1]   Rule for propagation of modifications.

Modifications to an attribute or method in a class are always inherited from subclasses, except from those subclasses in which the attribute or method has been redefined.

[P2]   Rule for propagation of modifications in the event of conflicts.

Introducing a new attribute or method or the modification of the name of an attribute or method is propagated only to those subclasses for which there are no conflicts of name as a result of the modification of the schema.

[P3]   Rule for modification of domains.

The domain of an attribute can only be modified by means of generalization. And the domain of an inherited attribute cannot be made more general than the domain of the original attribute in the superclass.

The rule governing the propagation of modifications in the event of conflicts (Rule P2 of the second group) takes precedence over Rule S2 of the first group. A class which inherits modifications propagates them to its own subclasses, although with the constraints highlighted in the above rules. However, those modifications which are not inherited from a class are not propagated to the subclasses of that class.

The third group of rules concerns the aggregation and deletion of inheritance relationships between classes and the creation and removal of classes. The following rules belong to this group:

[E1]   Rule for inserting superclasses.
       If a class C is added to the list of superclasses of a class C', C becomes the last of the superclasses of C'. Therefore, any conflict of inheritance caused by inserting the class C is resolved by Rules S1, S2, and S3.

[E2]   Rule for removing superclasses.
       If a class C has a single superclass C', and C' is deleted from the list of superclasses of C, then C becomes a direct subclass of each of the direct superclasses of C'. The ordering of the new superclasses of C is the same as that of the superclasses for class C'.

[E3]   Rule for inserting a class into a schema.
       If no superclass is expressly shown in the definition of a class C, then C becomes the subclass of the OBJECT class (root of the whole schema).

[E4]   Rule for removing a class from a schema.
       The deletion of a class C from a schema involves the application of Rule E2, since C must be removed from the list of the superclasses of all its subclasses. The OBJECT class cannot be deleted.

The OBJECT class cannot be deleted from the list of the superclasses of a class C if the OBJECT class is the only superclass of C. This ensures that the schema is completely connected and that there are no disconnected nodes.

There is a fourth rule governing composite objects. Whereas the groups of rules above are generally applicable to several data models, this group of rules applies only to those models which support the concept of composite objects.

[C1]   Rule for the modification of the definition of composite attributes.
       An attribute defined as an exclusive composite can be transformed into a non-composite or shared composite attribute. An attribute defined as non-composite or shared composite cannot be transformed into an exclusive composite attribute. An attribute defined as

dependent composite (whether exclusive or shared) can be transformed into an independent composite attribute and vice versa.

The reason for this rule is that, if a class attribute is initially defined as non-composite or shared composite and is then changed into an exclusive composite attribute, it would be necessary to determine that all class instances are referred to, at most, by a single object. Executing this type of check is very costly and if objects are referred to by more than one object, the modification would not apply. A modification to the schema would not, in fact, be executed on all instances, making the schema inconsistent with the database's contents. The formulation of the rule referred to here differs from the original rule presented in Banerjee *et al.* (1987). The original formulation refers to a simplified model of composite objects in which the references are exclusive and dependent. The formulation presented here, on the other hand, refers to the extended model of the composite objects presented in Kim *et al.* (1989).

Semantics of Schema Modification Operations

The various modification operations have different effects on schemas. For example, if an instance attribute is removed from a class, this attribute must also be removed from the subclasses of that class. We provide below an analysis, by Banerjee *et al.* (1987), of the effect of each type of modification listed in Figure 5.1.

[1]   *Modifications to class definitions*

   [1.1]   *Modifications to attributes*

      [1.1.1]   *Adding an attribute*
      If there are no conflicts, i.e. there are no attributes with the same name, this modification results in a schema modification for all subclasses (whether direct or indirect). In fact, for the complete inheritance invariant, all subclasses must inherit each attribute of superclass C. If there are several specialization paths from C to any subclass (obviously not direct ones), the new attribute will be inherited only once by the subclass in question, in accordance with Rule S3 governing inheritance of attributes with the same origin. If conflicts arise, i.e. class C inherits from any superclass an attribute with the same name, the new attribute replaces the inherited attribute, in accordance with Rule S1 (governing precedence of classes over superclasses). If, finally, class C already has an attribute which has been defined locally to C and which has the same name, then the current definition of that attribute is replaced with the new definition. In all cases, the new attribute is propagated to all the subclasses (direct and indirect) of C. The only exceptions are the subclasses which have a local definition of an attribute with the same name (in accordance with Rule P1) or which inherit an attribute with the same name from any superclass other than C (in accordance with Rule P2).

[1.1.2] *Deleting an attribute*

To delete an attribute of C, the attribute must have been defined locally in C, since an inherited attribute cannot be deleted. Deleting an attribute from class C results in the attribute being deleted from all the subclasses (direct and indirect) of C (in accordance with Rule P1). If C has any superclasses which have an attribute with the same name as the deleted attribute, the attribute of the superclass is inherited. If several superclasses have an attribute with the same name, the attribute is inherited in accordance with Rules S2 and S3. Similarly, if any subclass C' of C, from which the attribute was removed as a result of the attribute being deleted in C, has a superclass SC, which is different to C, which has an attribute with the same name as the deleted attribute, then C' inherits the attribute from SC. Finally, if C' has several superclasses which have an attribute with the same name as the deleted attribute, then the superclass from which the attribute is inherited is chosen on the basis of Rules S2 and S3.

[1.1.3] *Modifying an attribute's name*

Modifications of this kind can only be executed if they do not create conflicts. They are accepted if there is no other attribute in C which is inherited or defined locally and which has the same name. If modifications are accepted, they are also propagated to subclasses of C. However, they are only propagated to those subclasses in which they do not cause conflicts (in accordance with Rule P2).

[1.1.4] *Modifying attributes' domains*

In accordance with Rule P3, the domains of attributes can only be generalized. Moreover, invariants concerning the compatibility of domains must not be violated. Such modifications are propagated to subclasses in accordance with Rule P1.

Modification of this kind are only propagated to those subclasses in which the domains of attributes have not been redefined locally.

[1.1.5] *Modifying the inheritance of attributes*

Modifications of this kind require that an attribute, A, currently inherited from a superclass, SC, should be inherited from another superclass, SC'. If attribute A of superclass SC – indicated by $SC.A$ – is the attribute A of superclass SC' – indicated by $SC'.A$ – have different origins, the modification is equivalent to the deletion of $SC.A$ from C, and to the addition of $SC'.A$ to C.

If $SC.A$ and $SC'.A$ have the same origin, they represent two different situations. If the domain of $SC'.A$ is the same as the domain of $SC.A$, or the domain of $SC'.A$ is a superclass of the domain of $SC.A$, the properties (for example, the domain and default values) of $SC'.A$ are inherited in C. If not, the two attributes are treated as if they had different origins and $SC.A$ is deleted from C and $SC'.A$ added to C.

[1.1.6] *Modifying the default values of attributes*

The default value of an attribute is expressly declared in the definition of C, or has a null value. Therefore, adding a default value d for an attribute will modify the value from null to the value d. The value d must be an instance of the domain of the attribute (on the basis of the domain compatibility invariant). Deleting the default value of an attribute is equivalent to assigning the null value to that value. Modifications to the default value of an attribute are propagated only to those subclasses which have not redefined the default value locally (Rule E4).

[1.1.7]   *Manipulating shared attributes*

[1.1.7.1]   *Transforming instance attributes into shared attributes*
Modifications of this kind are propagated to subclasses in accordance with Rule P1 and they are only propagated to those subclasses which have not redefined such attributes.

[1.1.7.2]   *Modifying the values of shared attributes*
Modifications of this kind assign new values to shared attributes. The new values must be instances of the attributes' domain class. Such modifications are propagated to subclasses in accordance with Rule P1 and are only propagated to those subclasses which have not redefined such attributes.

[1.1.7.3]   *Transforming shared attributes into non-shared attributes*
Modifications of this kind are propagated to subclasses in accordance with Rule P1 and are only propagated to those subclasses which have not redefined such attributes.

[1.1.8]   *Modifying composite attributes into non-composite attributes*
Modifications of this kind are propagated to subclasses in accordance with Rule P1.

[1.2]   *Modifying methods of a class* C
The rule governing execution and propagation of modifications of methods are similar to those discussed previously for modifications to attributes.

[2]   *Modifying inheritance hierarchies*

[2.1]   *Making a class S a superclass of a class* C
Modifications of this kind can only be carried out if they do not cause cycles in inheritance hierarchies. This means that S must not be a subclass, whether direct or indirect, of C. All the attributes of S are inherited from C and from its subclasses on the basis of Rule E1 (on the addition of arcs to inheritance hierarchies). If there are inheritance conflicts during the propagation of the attributes of S to C and to its subclasses, they will be resolved in accordance with Rule S3 (on inheritance of attributes with the same origin).

[2.2]   *Removing a class S from the list of superclasses of a class* C
When executing operations of this kind, class C should not become disconnected from its inheritance hierarchy. When defining the semantics of this operation, which superclasses class C is connected to following this modification has to be be determined. If S is the only superclass of C, then C becomes a direct subclass of all the direct superclasses of S. These superclasses assume, in relation to C, the same order that they had in relation to S. C loses all the attributes and methods defined specifically in S. However, it keeps all the attributes and methods which S inherited from its superclasses. If, however, S is not the only superclass, then C remains connected to the remaining

superclasses after removing S. C, in this case, does not become a direct subclass of the superclasses of S, as it does when S is the only superclass. C loses all the attributes and methods it had inherited from S. As a result, C can inherit certain of the attributes and methods which it had inherited earlier from S from any other of the remaining superclasses, as was discussed for the modification operations 1.1.2 and 1.2.2.

[2.3] *Modifying the order of the superclasses of a class* C.
Operations of this kind result in a complete revaluation of the inheritance of attributes and methods, since they may result in the class C inheriting an attribute A (or a method) from a superclass other than the one it inherited it from before the modification. Inheritance must, therefore, be re-evaluated in accordance with Rules S1, S2 and S3. Any modifications to the inheritance of attributes or methods are as described for operations 1.1.5 and 1.2.5.

[3] *Modifying a set of classes*

[3.1] *Creation of a new class* C
If no superclass is specified for C, C becomes a direct subclass of the OBJECT class (in accordance with Rule E3). If, however, one or more superclasses are specified, C becomes a direct subclass of these classes and inherits its attributes and methods. Any conflicts are resolved in accordance with the rules on the solution of conflicts (Rules S1, S2 and S3).

[3.2] *Deleting a class* C
Initially, this operation has the effect of removing C from the list of super-classes of all its subclasses. Therefore, operation 2.2 (to remove classes from the lists of superclasses of classes) is applied to all the subclasses of C in which C is the class removed. It should be noted that the subclasses of C are not deleted. The definition of C is deleted and C removed from the schema. If C is used as the domain in the definition of an attribute, A, of any class C', A is automatically assigned the first superclass of C as the new domain. Deleting C results in the deletion of all its instances. Therefore, all references to such objects become pending. This approach is consistent with the choice made by the designers of ORION to allow the explicit deletion of objects. However, in systems in which the objects with references cannot be deleted, operations relating to deletion of classes ought only to be possible if they have no instances, or if all the instances of those classes do not refer to other objects (the latter strategy, however, can be costly). Finally, another possibility is not to delete instances; instead they can be made instances of any other class, for example, a subclass or a superclass of C.

[3.3] *Modifying class names*
Operations of this kind can be carried out if other classes do not have the same name (in accordance with the unique name invariant).

Let us consider, by way of an example of schema modification, the deletion of the method **age** from the class **Person** (note that this method cannot be deleted from **Person** subclasses, because an inherited attribute or method cannot be deleted). This modification results in the method in question being deleted from **Person** and from all its subclasses. The schema resulting from this modification is shown in Figure 5.3. Let us now assume that we want to delete from the schema in Figure 5.3 the method `monthly_salary` of the class `Researcher`. The modification is not propagated to the subclass `Researcher`, since this redefines the method. Figure 5.4 shows the schema resulting from this modification. As a final example, let us assume that we want to delete the attribute `address` from the class `Part_Time_Researcher`.

This modification results in the removal of the attribute from that class and from its subclass `Researcher_Student`. However, since `Researcher_Student` has another superclass which has an attribute with the same name and a different domain, the effect of the deletion is that the `Researcher_Student` class inherits the attribute `address` from the superclass `Student`. And one of the effects of the modification of the class `Researcher_Part_Time` is to modify the domain of the attribute `address` of the class `Researcher_Student` from `Office_Address` to `Home_Address`. Figure 5.5 shows the schema that results from this modification.

5.1.2 Approaches to Implementation

It is important to understand how modifications of classes can be applied to class instances. Obviously, this concerns only certain types of modifications, for example, deleting attributes. Other types, for example, modifying methods, have no impact on instances. The first approach we shall look at, which we shall call the deferred approach, involves deferring (even indefinitely) the modifications of these instances. A proposal based on this approach is described in Zdonik (1990) and involves using a mechanism of class versions, generating a new version of a given class C each time C is modified. Each instance object of C is 'connected' to the version of the class in which it is created. Exception managers are defined for each new version of the class. When an application tries to read or write an attribute of an object which was created with a class version other than the one used in the application, this constitutes an exception. This activates the appropriate manager which, in most cases, executes the appropriate transformation of the attribute concerned into the correct class version.

A second mechanism, based on the deferred approach, was defined and implemented as part of the ORION system – see Banerjee *et al.* (1987). Instances are modified only when they are accessed by applications. If, for example, modifications involve deleting an attribute from a class, the attribute is not removed from the instances when the class definition is modified. Later, when an instance of that class is accessed, the system does not present the deleted attribute to the application; it 'screens' it. However, if the modification is an addition of an attribute, the attribute is not immediately added to the object. For each request to read the attribute, following modification, the attribute's default value is returned, if a default

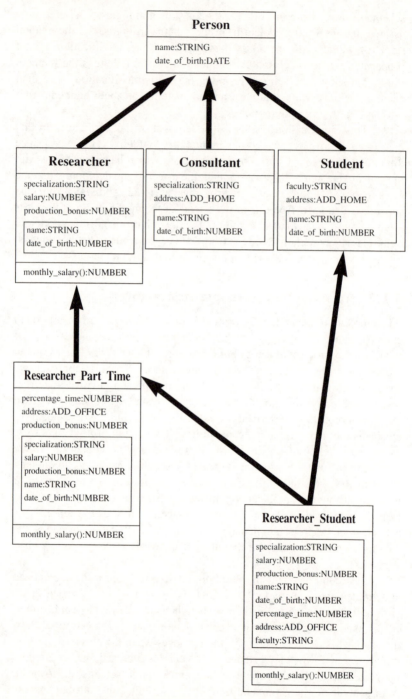

Figure 5.3 Inheritance hierarchy obtained from the hierarchy shown in Figure 5.2 following deletion of the method **age** from the class **Person**.

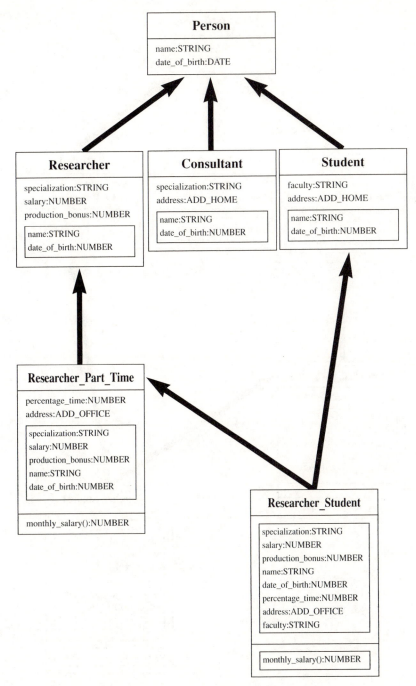

Figure 5.4 Inheritance hierarchy obtained from the hierarchy shown in Figure 5.3 following deletion of the method `monthly_salary` from the class `Researcher`.

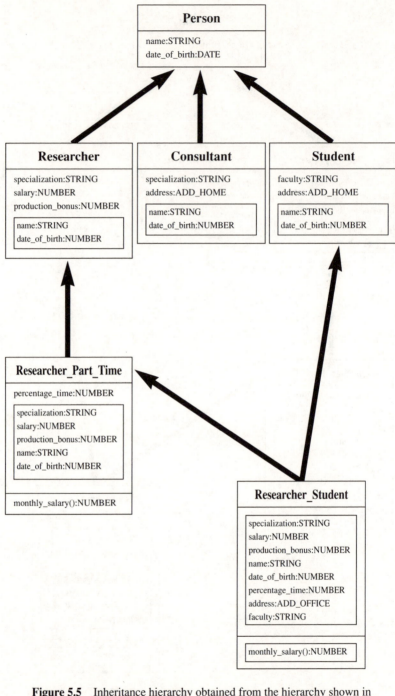

Figure 5.5 Inheritance hierarchy obtained from the hierarchy shown in Figure 5.4 following deletion of the method `address` from the class `Part_Time_Researcher`.

value was specified in the definition of the attribute. If not, a special 'nil' value is returned. The attribute is effectively added upon the first request of modification to the attribute value. Consequently, the cost involved is not much higher than that of a normal modification to an attribute's values.

Another approach, called the immediate approach, involves modifying all instances as soon as a class definition is modified. This approach has been proposed for GemStone, but has not yet been implemented.

Obviously, each of the two approaches has its advantages and disadvantages. The advantage of the deferred approach, especially the one used in ORION, is that the modification is inexpensive. However, access to instances can take longer because of 'screening'. The immediate approach makes modification operations very costly. Applications supported by OODBMS frequently modify schemas, and research continues into combining these two approaches into a flexible mechanism which would permit either approach to be used in any given situation.

5.1.3 Consistency of Methods

The consistency of modifications to methods is a significant problem in schema evolution. In fact, the treatment of this evolution described in the preceding subsections refers to a type of consistency known as *structural* consistency. The purpose of the set of invariants in subsection 5.1.1 is to ensure that the structure of a schema includes a certain set of properties, for example, the absence of isolated nodes and classes with the same name. However, the invariants described concern only the structural component of the schema, and, therefore, classes and their organization in terms of inheritance and aggregation hierarchies. Another type of consistency which ought to be looked at is known as *behavioural* consistency, which concerns the dynamic aspects of objects. For example, if an attribute is deleted or modified, a method referring to that attribute in its implementation would no longer be consistent in terms of the current schema.

One solution is to recompile the entire schema and its methods. This solution can be rather expensive if schemas are frequently modified and, moreover, it can only be applied in systems using compilation. For other interpretation-based systems, inconsistency of methods relating to schema modifications can result in type errors. And, even if there are no type errors, schema modifications can result in semantically incorrect methods being executed.

Broadly speaking, there are no solutions that can be applied generally. This is mainly due to the fact that methods are often implemented in imperative programming languages, and it is not easy to determine the effects of a schema modification to the set of methods of the classes involved in the modification. The problem has not been extensively studied. One possible solution, proposed in Coen-Porisini *et al.* (1992), is to use a set of interactive tools which, when a schema is modified, can show the effects of the modification to the user, and suggest alternative modifications if inconsistencies occur. The work focuses mainly on structural consistency, although behavioural consistency and avoiding type errors is also dealt with.

5.1.4   Other Approaches to Schema Evolution

Other approaches which enable OODBMS to support modifications to schemas include the use of *versions of schemas* (Kim and Chou, 1988) and *object-oriented views* (Bertino, 1992a). These approaches differ from the approach described earlier on in that the old schema is not replaced by the modified schema. Instead, there are two schemas; one is the original schema and the other reflects modifications executed on the original. Obviously, several modifications can produce a sequence of later versions of the schema or different views of the schema. An essential difference between using schema versions and views is that, by adopting the former approach, an object created in a specific schema version is only visible in that specific schema version, whereas by adopting the latter approach, an object is visible in all views, if the conditions for belonging to these are met.

View mechanisms developed for relational DBMS must be extended in order to support schema evolution. One such extension consists of views that add attributes and methods in addition to those received from the classes on which they are defined. In addition, it must be possible to access instances of the views with OID, as well as queries. In Bertino (1992a), it was shown that almost all the schema modifications presented in the taxonomy in Figure 5.1 could be simulated by using object-oriented views with such extensions. An advantage of using views instead of directly modifying the schema is that no information is lost. If a schema modification proves to be unsatisfactory, the original schema can always be returned to without loss of any information. For example, if an attribute is deleted from a class, all its instances will lose the attribute. But a view can be defined that screens out all attributes except the one that has to be removed. The original schema does not undergo any modifications and so the values of the attribute are not lost.

5.2   Instance Evolution

The object-oriented model introduces different types of evolution for objects. As well as modifications to an object's attributes (state evolution), other types of evolution are possible, in which individual objects can modify their own structure and behaviour, while keeping their own identity constant. Whereas state evolution finds its counterpart in the relational model in modifications of the values of the attributes of a tuple, other types of evolution are specific to object systems. In particular, an object's structure and/or behaviour can be modified with:

- migrations of the object to different classes;
- the dynamic addition of classes, even those not related by inheritance;
- specialization of instances.

It should be noted that migration of an object to a new class is different from adding a new class to that object. In fact, in the first case, the class to which the instance belonged previously is lost, in the second case, it is not. In the latter of these two options, an object must be able to be the instance of several classes at the same time. These types of evolution are not as yet supported by many systems, as they create problems of both implementation and consistency.

In particular, some research prototypes envisage object migration to a new class – see, for example, the extension proposed for the Galileo language (Albano *et al.*, 1991). Very often objects are restricted to being able only to migrate to any subclass of the class to which they belong. Here, objects, in one sense, also keep the previous class to which they belonged, since they remain a member of the class to which they used to belong despite becoming the instance of a new class.

Types in the Iris system can be added to and removed from an object[1]. The object can thus be migrated from a type T to a type T' – type T' just has to be added to the object and the type T deleted from the object to do this. And a type T' can be added without losing the previous type to which it belonged – to do this, the type T' has to be added to the object.

Finally, in O_2, instances can be specialized. This enables attributes and methods to be added and redefined for an individual object. In redefining an attribute or a method, the new definition must be compatible with the definition given by the class. In this sense, the rules governing subtype definition are used. For example, the domain of an attribute in an instance can be specialized with respect to the domain specified for the attribute in its class. However, the domain used in the instance must be a subclass of the domain specified in the class.

If an object is to be able to migrate to different classes or to acquire and to lose classes dynamically, appropriate constraints must be imposed on it to ensure that correct evolutions are defined. Taking the schema in

---

[1] Note the use of the term, type, instead of class. It is considered appropriate to use Iris' own terminology. For our purposes, here, the term type can be considered to be synonymous with class.

Figure 5.2 as an example, it is meaningful for a student to become a researcher later in life, but not for a student to become an instance of the Document class. Semantically significant migrations have to be defined within the applications domain. One option is to specify special integrity constraints (Zdonik, 1990). They include:

- Specifying classes as *essential*
  A class, C, is essential if an object which is a member of class C cannot at a subsequent point in time migrate to another class and stop belonging to the set of members of class C. This means that migrations of an object which is a member of C are confined to the inheritance hierarchy which has C as its root. For example, in the schema in Figure 5.2, the class Person is an essential class. As Zdonik (1990) points out, an object can have several essential classes, if the model has multiple inheritance.

- Specifying a class as *exclusive*
  A class is exclusive, if, belonging to a class as an instance, precludes its ability to belong to another class. The class Consultant in the schema in Figure 5.2 could serve as an example of an exclusive class, if we assume that a consultant can be neither a student nor a researcher employed on a permanent basis. This constraint can then be refined by introducing the property of exclusivity of one class in relation to another. For example, we can assume that a consultant cannot be a researcher employed on a permanent basis, but he could nevertheless be a student, albeit not a student who is a part-time researcher. Consultant is exclusive in relation to the classes Researcher_Student and Researcher.

The fact that a class is essential does not imply that it is exclusive. An essential class C can be added to an object O, even if the object already has essential classes. The only constraint is that O cannot later 'lose' C. Conversely, an object can 'lose' an exclusive class.

The migration of objects also poses problems in the consistency of a database. It is these very problems which mean that migration is not supported, or is limited to migrations to subclasses. Problems of consistency are caused by the fact that, if an object O, which is an instance of a class C, is used in an object O', as the value of an attribute A, whose domain is C, the migration of O to a superclass of C violates the integrity constraint established by specifying the domain for A. In other words, object O', after the migration of O, will have as the value of A, an object which is neither an instance nor a member of the domain of A. Let us consider, for example, the two objects in Figure 5.6a. The objects are, respectively, instances of the Researcher and Group classes. The schemas of Person, Researcher and Group are shown in Figure 5.6b. Let us assume that we want to migrate the object, Researcher[i] from the class

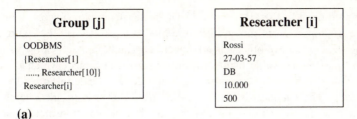

(a)

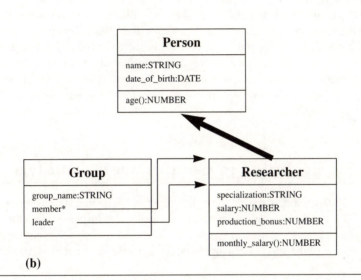

(b)

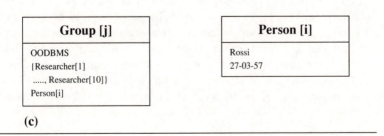

(c)

Figure 5.6   **(a)** State of objects before modification,   **(b)** Fragment of the
database schema,   **(c)** State of objects following modification.

Researcher to the class Person. The state of the two objects, following the modification, is shown in Figure 5.6c. As can be seen in Figure 5.6c, the state of the two objects is no longer consistent, in that the object, Group [j] has, as the value of the attribute leader, an object which is not an instance of the class Researcher as requested by the definition of the class Group. The database is inconsistent. One solution is to allow temporary inconsistencies of this type and to provide a notification mechanism for determining which objects are inconsistent. In the example shown, an access to the value of the attribute leader of the object Group [j] would cause an exception to be returned, to indicate that the object currently pointed to by Group [j] as the value of the attribute leader is not an instance object or a member of the class Researcher. Following this notification, the application can show that the object Group [j] is in a consistent state. It should be noted that, in the example in Figure 5.6, we have assumed, for the sake of simplicity, that the instances have the name of the class of which they are instances, as well as their OID. In fact, if object migration is to be possible, it ought not to cause the modification of objects' OIDs.

5.3   Evolution in GemStone, O_2 and Iris

The system models which were illustrated in Chapter 2 do not provide a full spectrum of evolution functions in schemas and instances – but they do provide a good subset of such functions. Of course they all support evolution of the state of instances and the dynamic creation of classes.

GemStone

In GemStone, all types of modification to a class definition can be executed, if the class is modifiable. Whether or not a class is modifiable can be determined from the class definition itself by means of an appropriate flag (isModifiable). However, a modifiable class cannot be instantiated. Therefore all those modifications which have an effect on instances cannot be executed on classes with instances. Such modifications include adding and deleting an attribute and adding a constraint on an attribute's domain[2]. However, those schema modifications which do not affect instances can be executed on classes with instances. Examples of these modifications

---

[2] It should be remembered that the domains for the attributes in GemStone do not have to be specified when the class is defined. However, the domains can be specified later, only if the class is modifiable and has no instances.

include all modifications of class attributes and methods. A class can be made non-modifiable with an appropriate message. A class which has been made non-modifiable can no longer be made modifiable.

No explicit deletion operation exists for deleting classes since the same rules apply to classes as apply to deleting an object. In practice, the system automatically deletes a class if it has no instances, no subclasses, is not used as the domain in the definition of another class and its name has been removed from every user dictionary in which it appeared.

The only type of instance evolution supported is the state evolution and migration between classes. GemStone allows state evolutions of objects to be controlled, since the state of objects can be 'frozen' by using the `immediateInvariant` message which, when sent to an object, does not allow any further modifications to be made to the state. It should be noted that it can also be specified that all the instances of a class are non-modifiable by using a flag (`instancesInvariant`) which appears in a class definition. In this case, an instance can only be manipulated during the transaction in which it was created. Once this transaction commits, the instance can no longer be modified.

In Gemstone, instances can only be migrated between classes if:

- A new class is a subclass of the old class.
- The new class has no instance attributes in addition to those of the superclass (however, it can have additional instance methods and additional class attributes).
- The new class has the same storage format as the old class.
- The new class has exactly the same domains as for the attributes of the old superclass.

Instances can be migrated only under very restrictive conditions. The purpose of these restrictions is to allow instance migration provided that there are no modifications to the instances involved. The message for requesting migration of an object is `changeClassTo`. This message has the class to which the object must migrate as its only argument. The following is an example of the migration of an object:

```
| tempVar |
tempVar := C new.            'Creates an instance of
                              class C'

.....................
tempVar changeClassTo: C1 'Converts the instance of
                              class C to the instance
                              of class C1'
```

O_2

Schema modifications in O_2 cannot be executed dynamically. Some proposals exist in the relevant literature but these have not yet been implemented in the system. A class can only be deleted in O_2, if that class has no instances and is not used in the definition of other classes. As far as instance evolution in O_2 is concerned, both the state and the structure of an instance can be modified, since exceptional instances are permitted.

Iris

Schema evolution in Iris is limited, in that only those functions which are not the properties of types can be added and deleted dynamically[3]. Therefore, modifications equivalent to deleting and adding attributes cannot be executed (see Figure 5.1). The functions representing properties of a type are automatically deleted, if the type is deleted. Functions which are not properties of a type can always be deleted. The system automatically deletes all those derived functions that are defined in terms of the deleted function. The following is the syntax for the instruction to delete a function:

DELETE FUNCTION function-name;

where `function-name` is the name of the function that is to be deleted.

There are no instructions for changing the ordering of the supertypes of a type. In fact, in Iris, such modifications do not make much sense, since the ordering of supertypes is not used to resolve conflicts; instead, it is requested that there should be no conflicts. The ordering of the supertypes thus has no effect on a type definition. A type can be deleted as an instruction for this exists in the user interface. The instruction has the following syntax:

DELETE TYPE type-name;

where `type-name` is the name of the type that is to be deleted. However, a type can only be deleted if it has no subtypes and is not used in defining other types. Deleting a type does not result in the deletion of its instances. They continue to belong to other types and, in any case, continue to belong to the type `UserTypeObject` which represents the root of the inheritance hierarchy to which all user-defined types belong.

---

[3] It should be recalled that, in Iris, the properties of a type are functions which represent the attributes of the instance objects of the type.

As far as the evolution of instances in Iris is concerned, objects can acquire and lose types dynamically with the following instructions:

```
ADD TYPE type-name [ [PROPERTIES] ( [ function-name-commalist] )]
TO add-initializer-commalist;
REMOVE TYPE type-name FROM host-variable-commalist;
```

The component `add-initializer-commalist` in the instruction `ADD TYPE` specifies one or more variables, one for each instance to which the type has to be added and, if necessary, the values which are to be assigned to the instances, in order to initialize the properties of the type which is added. As an example, suppose that the variable `doc` points to an object with the type `Document` and the type `Technical_Report` has to be added to that object by initializing the functions `argument` and `start_validity`. The following is the instruction for executing this operation:

```
ADD TYPE Technical_Report (argument, start_validity)
TO :doc ('CAD', '22-06-1992');
```

The following is an example of how the instruction for deleting a type is used:

```
REMOVE TYPE Technical_Report
FROM :doc;
```

which has the effect of deleting the type `Technical_Report` from the object pointed to by the variable `doc`.

5.4   Bibliographical Notes

One of the first works to deal with the problem of schema evolution in object-oriented databases is the article by Banerjee *et al.* (1987). This work discusses evolution within the context of ORION, on which part of the discussion in this chapter is based. Although some of the schema modifications proposed are specific to the ORION data model, most of the modifications can be applied generally. The article also focuses on the problem of consistency of the methods in schema modifications and proposes a solution which, however, has not been implemented in the system. As far as other systems are concerned, a discussion of schema evolution in GemStone and an option for implementation is discussed in Breitl *et al.* (1989). Schema evolution in O_2 is discussed in Zicari (1991).

Finally, Bertino (1992a) describes an approach to schema evolution based on the use of view mechanism; Kim and Chou (1988a) propose a mechanism based on schema versions in ORION.

No literature which looks comprehensively at instance evolution exists. The most relevant work is Zdonik (1990) which describes the various aspects of object evolution, including object migration between classes. Moreover, this article introduces certain integrity constraints which ensure that semantically correct object evolutions are obtained.

6 Authorization

Authorization mechanisms are a basic component of all DBMS. Authorization models, in particular, must be consistent with data models supported by DBMS. Existing authorization models have been defined mainly for the relational model (Griffiths and Wade, 1976) and they are not completely suitable for an object-oriented data model. Generally speaking, these models take a relation or an attribute of a relation as their authorization unit. In some cases, a view mechanism is used to select a subset of the tuple of a relation as an authorization unit. In OODBMS, however, a single object must be the minimum basic unit. An object is the logical unit of access, as it has an associated OID, which the user can use as a reference for accessing the object. An individual object must be treated as an authorization unit. And, an authorization model for an OODBMS must take into account other aspects of the model, for example, inheritance hierarchy, versions and composite objects.

Defining an authorization model which meets these requirements is rather complex and its implementation is crucial because of the impact that authorization controls can have on the system's performance. A sophisticated discretionary authorization model has been defined and implemented for ORION (Rabitti *et al.*, 1991). Other systems use a much simpler authorization model. For example the authorization unit in GemStone is the secondary storage segment. Defining *mandatory*

147

authorization mechanisms is even more complex. Preliminary proposals are presented in Thuraisingham (1989) and Jajodia *et al.* (1990). In this section, we will discuss discretionary authorization, which is the type of authorization of most interest as far as general-purpose OODBMS are concerned.

In the rest of this chapter, we describe the authorization model defined for the ORION system (see Rabitti *et al.*, 1991). Although the authorization model applies principally to ORION, it can be applied more generally. We will then discuss GemStone's authorization mechanism. The other systems, whose data model is described in Chapter 2, do not yet have authorization mechanisms.

6.1 Introduction to Authorization Mechanisms

Database authorization models have developed as extensions of models which were developed for resource protection in operating systems. An authorization consists of the following three basic components (Fernandez et al., 1981):

- A set O of *objects*
  these are the entities which are accessed and/or modified

- A set S of *subjects*
  these are active entities which require access to objects

- A set A of *authorization types*
  authorization types depend on the type of actions that subjects can execute on objects. The following are examples of the authorization types: reading, deleting, modifying.

An authorization can thus be defined as a triple – called an *authorization rule* – (s, o, a) where $s \in S, o \in O, a \in A$. A function f is also defined that determines whether an authorization is true or false:

$$f : S \times O \times A \to (\text{True, False}).$$

Given a triple (s, o, a), if $f(s, o, a) =$ True, then the subject s has an authorization of type a on the object o. If, instead, $f(s, o, a) =$ False, then the subject does not have the required authorization.

(Verdi, Document[i], R) is an example of an authorization rule. This rule establishes that the user, Verdi, can read the i-th instance of the class 'Document'. In the example, R denotes the 'Read' authorization type.

From now on, W will be used to denote the 'Write' or modification authorization type. It should be noted that, in reality, an authorization rule contains the object's OID. For the sake of clarity, we will use the term 'C[i]' to indicate the i-th instance of class C.

Implicit Authorization

One strategy for implementing the function f is explicitly to store all triples (s, o, a) for which f returns the value True. Although this strategy is simple to implement, it is somewhat inefficient. In fact, certain authorizations could be derived from others with rules and need not be explicitly stored. Some of them can be stored, while others can be derived using deduction rules, as is the case in deductive databases. For example:

- A user who is entitled to read a class can read all its instances; authorizations are derived with respect to domain O.
- A manager can access all the information that his employees can access; authorizations are derived with respect to domain S.
- A user entitled to modify an object, can also read it; authorizations are derived with respect to domain A.

In the model defined in Rabitti *et al.* (1991), authorization objects are organized in a granularity hierarchy (similar hierarchies are defined for sets of subjects and for authorization types). This hierarchy defines the way in which the objects in a system are arranged in terms of other objects. Given an object O, the hierarchy defines the composition of O in terms of objects on a lower level compared with the level of O. An example of such a hierarchy can be found in Figure 6.1. Access right to an object can be granted at any level of the hierarchy.

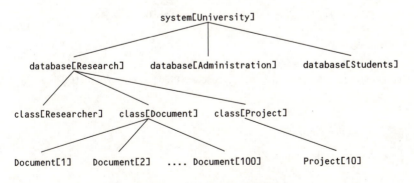

Figure 6.1 Granularity hierarchy.

For example, access right to the entire database or to an individual instance can be granted. The concept of implicit authorization is fundamental to the model. Given access right of type *a* on an object *o* to a user *s*, the user *s* implicitly has a type *a* authorization on all the objects of which *o* consists. For example, if a user has received the right to read the 'Document' class, then he or she will implicitly be granted the same right for all instances in the class. Obviously, if, on the other hand, a user has received the right to read an instance, this authorization does not imply that the user can read other instances in the class. The concept of implicit authorizations obviates the need explicitly to grant and store all those authorizations which can be derived from other authorizations and this allows for a certain level of efficiency in certain situations. If, for example, a user needs to access an instance of a class and the system determines that the user has a right of accessing the class, then further authorization controls are not required for subsequent access within the same transaction on instances in the same class. Figure 6.2 shows an example of explicit authorization and of authorizations deriving from this.

Fernandez *et al.* (1981) have already introduced the concept of implicit authorization. In the model defined in Rabitti *et al.* (1991), this concept has been extended to include the concepts of strong and weak and positive and negative authorization. A strong authorization does not admit exceptions to implicit authorizations, whereas a weak authorization does

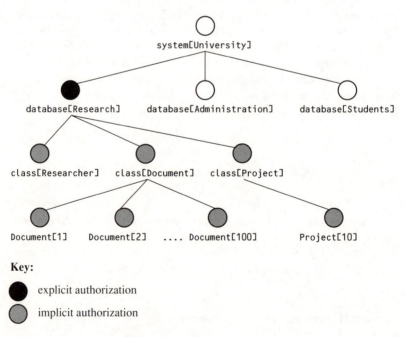

Figure 6.2 Implicit authorization.

admit those exceptions that are specified with negative or positive authorizations. If, for example, a user receives a weak authorization to read the `Document` class, and then a negative authorization to read the `Document[1]` instance of the `Document` class, the user can read all instances except this one. Obviously, since an exception can also be weak, exceptions to exceptions can thus be defined.

Positive and Negative Authorization

The authorization mechanism in a DBMS is often based on the assumption that a subject has no authorizations on an object unless it is explicitly authorized (Fernandez *et al.*, 1981). If there is no authorization for an object, this means that the object cannot be accessed. The model discussed by Rabitti *et al.* (1991) is based on the same assumption, but authorization can also be explicitly denied. Therefore, a subject *s* is denied access to an object *o*, if: (i) *s* has no authorization on *o*; or (ii) *s* has a negative authorization on *o*. As we will see later, explicit denial of authorization is useful for expressing exceptions to implicit authorizations.

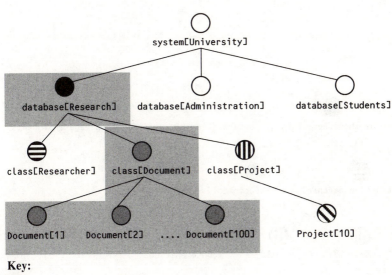

Key:

explicit weak authorization (write, positive)

implicit weak authorization (write, positive)

explicit weak authorization (read, negative)

explicit weak authorization (write, negative)

implicit weak authorization (write, negative)

Figure 6.3   Implicit authorizations with weak exceptions.

Strong and Weak Authorization

A strong authorization does not allow exceptions to implicit authorizations derived from it whereas a weak authorization does. For example, if a user *s* has a strong authorization on the database 'Research' (see Figure 6.1), then *s* has the same authorization on all the objects in that database.

Figure 6.3 illustrates an example of a weak authorization with exceptions which are also weak. In the example, user *s* is granted a weak authorization to write in the 'Research' database. Then, *s* is denied, in weak mode, the right to write the class 'Project' and to read the class 'Researcher'. The denials are executed by assigning to *s* a weak negative authorization to write the class 'Project' and a weak negative authorization to read the class 'Researcher'. These negative authorizations represent exceptions to the weak authorization granted to *s* on the 'Research' database. The implicit authorizations which *s* obtains to the 'Research' database are authorizations on the objects in the shaded area in Figure 6.3.

A weak authorization can also allow strong exceptions. Figure 6.4 illustrates an example of this. In the example, the authorization on the

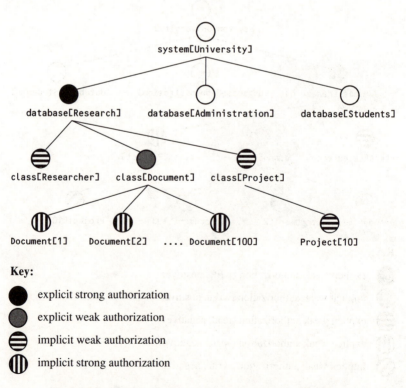

Figure 6.4 Implicit weak authorizations with strong exceptions.

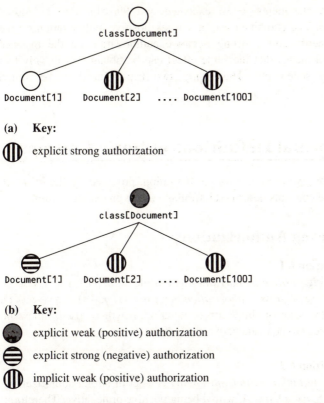

(a)   Key:

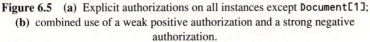

(III)   explicit strong authorization

(III)   implicit weak (positive) authorization

(b)   Key:

     explicit weak (positive) authorization

     explicit strong (negative) authorization

(III)   implicit weak (positive) authorization

Figure 6.5   **(a)** Explicit authorizations on all instances except `Document[1]`;
(b) combined use of a weak positive authorization and a strong negative
authorization.

'`Research`' database has a strong authorization to the '`Document`' class as
an exception. Implicit authorizations deriving from the latter authorization
do not, therefore, allow exceptions.

Combined Use of Positive and Negative, and Strong and Weak Authorizations

The combination of the various types of authorization discussed above
represents a concise and flexible way of satisfying various requirements
posed by authorization. It reduces the amount of storage space required
and the number of authorization statements which the user has to execute.
Let us consider, by way of example, the class '`Document`'. Let us assume
that a user has to be granted authorizations on all the instances of that
class, except on the instance `Document[1]`. Assuming that the class has
100 instances, a conventional authorization mechanism would require 99

authorization statements to be executed and 99 triples to be stored (Figure 6.5a). The combined use of a weak positive authorization on the class 'Document' and a strong negative authorization on the instance Document[1] means that the same effect can be obtained with only two authorization statements. Thus, only two triples need to be stored (Figure 6.5b).

6.2 Formal Definitions of Basic Concepts

In this section, we present a formal definition, provided by Rabitti *et al.* (1991), of the concepts described informally in the preceding section.

6.2.1 Strong Authorizations

Definition 6.1

A *strong positive authorization* is a triple $(s, o, +a)$, $s \in S$, $o \in O$, $a \in A$. A *strong negative authorization* is a triple $(s, o, -a)$, $s \in S$, $o \in O$, $a \in A$. For the sake of simplicity of notation, a will be used, unless no distinction needs to be made between $+a$ and $-a$.

Definition 6.2

A *strong authorizations base* (AB) is a set of strong authorizations (s, o, a), $s \in S$, $o \in O$, $a \in A$, with a being positive or negative. Therefore:

$$AB \subseteq S \times O \times A.$$

All authorizations in AB are *explicit strong authorizations*. And, if $(s, o, +a) \in AB$ then $f(s, o, a) = $ True; whereas if $(s, o, -a) \in AB$ then $f(s, o, a) = $ False.

The function $i(s, o, a)$, defined subsequently, determines whether the authorization (s, o, a) can be derived from the explicit authorizations in AB. In particular, $i(s, o, a)$ returns True (False), if the authorization $(s, o, +a)$ $((s, o, -a))$ can be derived from any authorization (s_i, o_j, a_k) present in AB. If, however, both $(s, o, +a)$ and $(s, o, -a)$ cannot be derived from AB, $i(s, o, a)$ returns *Undecided*.

Definition 6.3

The function $i(s, o, a)$ is defined as:

$$i : S \times O \times A \rightarrow \{\text{True, False, Undecided}\}.$$

Therefore, if $(s, o, +a)$ $((s, o, -a)) \in AB$, then $i(s, o, a) = $ True (False). Otherwise, if there is an authorization $(s_i, o_j, +a_k) \in AB$, such that

$(s_i, o_j, +a_k) \rightarrow (s, o, +a)$, then $i\ (s, o, a)$ = True. Otherwise, if there is an authorization $(s_i, o_j, -a_k) \in AB$ such that $(s_i, o_j, -a_k) \rightarrow (s, o, -a)$, then $i\ (s, o, a)$ = False. Otherwise, $i\ (s, o, a)$ = Undecided.

In the above definition, we used the concept of implications between authorization rules. Implication is based on a set of inference rules, called derivation rules which will be covered in the following section.

Let us consider, for example, the authorizations illustrated in Figure 6.2. In this example, $(s, \text{database[Research]}, +W) \rightarrow (s, \text{class[Researcher]}, +W)$ and thus $i\ (s, \text{class[Researcher]}, W)$ = True.

Given an authorization rule $(s, o, a) \in AB$, the set of rules deduced with the derivation rules is denoted by $P(s, o, a)$. For example, $P(s, \text{database[Research]}, +W)$ contains the authorizations for user s to modify classes 'Researcher', 'Project', 'Document' and all their instances.

Since there are negative authorizations, a condition of consistency must be defined, to avoid, for example, both a rule and its negation being derivable from the authorization base.

Consistency of AB

For each $(s, o, a) \in AB$ with a positive or negative, if there is a rule $(s_i, o_j, a_k) \in AB$, such that $(s, o, a) \rightarrow (s_i, o_j, a_k)$, then there should be no rule $(s', o', a') \in AB$, such that $(s', o', a') \rightarrow (s_i, o_j, \neg a_k)$ (where $\neg(+a) = -a$ and $\neg(-a) = +a$).

In addition to the condition of consistency, a further condition, known as the non-redundancy condition, is defined. This condition is used in AB to avoid the insertion of 'useless' rules, that is, rules that can be derived from those already in AB. However, this condition can be relaxed in some cases to improve performance. Other implementation strategies are discussed in Rabitti *et al.* (1991).

Non-redundancy of AB

For each (s_i, o_j, a_k), with a_k positive or negative, such that $(s, o, a) \in AB$ and $(s, o, a) \rightarrow (s_i, o_j, a_k)$ exist, then $(s_i, o_j, a_k) \notin AB$.

Let us consider the example in Figure 6.2 and explicit authorization (stored in AB) $(s, \text{database[Research]}, +W)$; an explicit authorization $(s, \text{class[Researcher]}, +W)$ would be redundant, as it can be derived from the authorization to the **Research** database. On the other hand, an explicit authorization $(s, \text{class[Researcher]}, -W)$ would be inconsistent with the authorization $(s, \text{database[Research]}, +W)$.

6.2.2 Weak Authorization

Definition 6.4

A *weak positive authorization* is a triple $[s, o, +a]$, $s \in S, o \in O, a \in A$.
A *weak negative authorization* is a triple $[s, o, -a]$, $s \in S, o \in O, a \in A$

Definition 6.5

A *weak authorization base* (*WAB*) is a set of weak authorizations (s, o, a), $s \in S$, $o \in O$, $a \in A$, with a positive or negative. Therefore:

$$WAB \subseteq S \times O \times A.$$

As with strong authorizations, the set of consequences of a given authorization rule (s, o, a) is defined as the set, denoted by $P[s, o, a]$, of the authorization rules that can be derived from it. However, unlike strong authorizations, only the authorizations which have not been modified from exceptions are present in $P[s, o, a]$.

Consider the example in Figure 6.3 and the explicit weak authorization [s, database [Research], +W]. The set $P[s$, database[Research], +W] contains authorization rules for the user s on all the objects belonging to the subtree having as root the database[Research] in the granularity hierarchy, except for those objects for which exceptions have been defined, and consequently, the objects class[Researcher] and class[Project] and all the instances of these classes.

Implication rules have been defined for weak authorizations. A weak implication is denoted by the symbol $\mapsto$ and is defined as follows:

$(s_i, o_j, a_k) \mapsto [s'_i, o'_j, a'_k]$ if, and only if $[s'_i, o'_j, a'_k] \in P(s_i, o_j, a_k)$.

This implication is called weak since it allows exceptions. A function d is defined which determines whether a weak authorization rule is true or false in *WAB*. Therefore, the function d is analogous to the function i, defined for *AB*, since it determines whether there is an authorization in *WAB* or can be derived from the rules present in the *WAB*. One difference between the function i and the function d is that, as will be discussed briefly later on, the latter does not return the value Undecided.

Definition 6.6

The function $d(s, o, a)$ is defined as:

$$d : S \times O \times A \to \{\text{True}, \text{False}\}.$$

If [s, o, $+a$]([s, o, $-a$]) $\in$ *WAB*, then d (s, o, a) = True (False); if there is an authorization (s_i, o_j, a_k) $\in$ *WAB*, such that (s_i, o_j, $+a_k$) $\mapsto$ [s, o, $+a$], then $d(s, o, a)$ = True. If there is an authorization (s_i, o_j, $-a_k$) $\in$ *WAB*, such that (s_i, o_j, $-a_k$) $\mapsto$ [s, o, $-a$], then $d(s, o, a)$ = False.

Two invariants are also defined for the *WAB*.

Completeness of WAB

For each authorization (s, o, a) with a positive or negative, there must be a rule (s_i, o_j, a_k) $\in$ *WAB* such that (s_i, o_j, a_k) $\mapsto$ [s, o, a].

This condition ensures that the entire space $S \times O \times A$ is completely covered by weak authorizations, so that function d is completely defined and cannot therefore return the value Undecided.

Consistency of WAB
For each $[s, o, a] \in WAB$ with a positive or negative, if there is a rule $[s_i, o_j, a_k] \in WAB$ such that $[s, o, a] \mapsto (s_i, o_j, a_k)$, then there must not exist a rule $[s', o', a']$ WAB, such that $[s', o', a'] \mapsto (s_i, o_j, \neg a_k)$ (where $\neg(+a) = -a$ and $\neg(-a) = +a$).

This condition ensures that there are no contradictions in the consequences of weak authorization rules. It should be noted that a condition of non-redundancy is not defined for the *WAB* since, in some cases, redundancy is necessary to resolve conflicts between the implications of two authorization rules. An example is given later when authorization for composite objects is dealt with.

Finally, as far as the co-existence of strong and weak authorizations is concerned, it is required that *WAB* should conform with *AB*. This means that if a modification is made to *AB* which is inconsistent with *WAB*, the *WAB* must be modified. Vice versa, a modification to the *WAB* it is not accepted if it is inconsistent with *AB*. Therefore a further condition of invariance is defined, which formalizes the co-existence of *AB* and *WAB*.

Co-existence of AB and WAB
For each $[s, o, a] \in WAB$ with a positive or negative, there must not exist any rule $(s_i, o_j, a_k) \in AB$ such that $(s_i, o_j, a_k) \rightarrow (s, o, \neg a)$.

6.2.3 Operations

The basic operations which an authorization must provide include checking, granting and revoking authorizations. The definition of these operations differs depending on whether *AB* or *WAB* is being considered. The operations for both types of authorization base are described below.

Authorization Control

In order to control an authorization (s, o, a) the function $f(s, o, a)$ must be evaluated. The function f is defined in terms of the functions i and d. Whether the authorization (s, o, a) is true or false in relation to *AB* is checked first. If this cannot be inferred from *AB* (remember that function i can return the value Undecided), *WAB* is used to decide whether the authorization is true or false.

> Function $f(s, o, a)$:
>> if $i(s, o, a) =$ Undecided,
>>> then $f(s, o, a) = d(s, o, a)$;
>> else $f(s, o, a) = i(s, o, a)$.

Grant Operation for Strong Authorizations

Granting an authorization (s, o, a) means inserting it in *AB*. This operation is executed by the function $g\ (s, o, a)$, which returns the Boolean value True as result, if the authorization is inserted in *AB*. If not, it returns False. An authorization is inserted in *AB* if it is not already in *AB* and cannot be derived in the authorizations which are already in *AB*. In addition, it must not be inconsistent with authorizations which are already in, or which can be derived in *AB*.

Grant Operation for Weak Authorizations

Granting an authorization $[s, o, a]$ means inserting it in *WAB*. This operation is executed by the function $gw\ (s, o, a)$ which returns the Boolean value True as result, if the authorization is inserted in *WAB*. If not, it returns False. An authorization is inserted in *WAB*, if it is not already present and cannot be derived from authorizations already present. It must not be inconsistent with the authorizations which are already in, or which can be derived in either in *AB* or in *WAB*.

Revoke Operation for Strong Authorizations

Revoking an authorization (s, o, a) means removing it from *AB*. This operation is executed by the function $r\ (s, o, a)$ which returns the Boolean value True as result, if the authorization is explicitly present in *AB*. If not, it returns False.

Revoke Operation for Weak Authorizations

Revoking an authorization (s, o, a) means removing it from *WAB*. This operation is executed by the function $rw\ (s, o, a)$ which returns the Boolean value True as result, if the authorization is explicitly present in *WAB*. If not, it returns False.

Authorizations to Execute Grant and Revoke Operations

When defining an authorization, rules for determining when a subject is authorized to execute grant and revoke instructions for access rights have to be defined. In the DB2 system (see Date 1985), for example, a user can grant other users access right only if he or she has this right with the Grant option. In other models, it is assumed, for the sake of simplicity, that if a subject s has an authorization on an object, it has the right to grant that authorization to other users. A Grant option is always implicit in authorizations in the model of Rabitti *et al.* (1991). However, this model can be extended by making a distinction between authorizations with and without a Grant option. This will be described in greater depth in Section 6.3.2.

6.3   Derivation Rules

As stated, authorizations can be derived in relation to any of the definition domains of function f. In this section we will deal with the specific rules of derivation for the three definition domains.

6.3.1 Authorization Subjects

The concept of role is used to reduce the number of authorization subjects. It enables users to be arranged on the basis of the specific functions they have within an organization. Users are grouped together according to *roles* which are used as authorization subjects. A user can belong to several roles. Roles are arranged in a *role lattice*: *RL*.

A node in this lattice represents a role. An arc from a node A to a node B indicates that authorizations of role A subsume (are greater than) those of role B. Figure 6.6 illustrates an example of a role lattice.

The rule for checking user authorization is the following:

A user has an authorization of type a on an object o, if there is a role s such that $f(s, o, a) =$ True and the user belongs to s.

Definition 6.7

Given $s_i, s_j \in S$, $s_i > s_j$ denotes that there is an arc from s_i to s_j in *RL*; $s_i > s_j$ denotes that: (i) $s_i = s_j$ or $s_i > s_j$; (ii) or that there is a number n of roles $s_1 S, ..., s_n \in S$, such that $s_i > s_1... > s_n > s_j$.

In other words, a role s_i is greater than a role s_j, if s_i is an ancestor of s_j in *RL*.

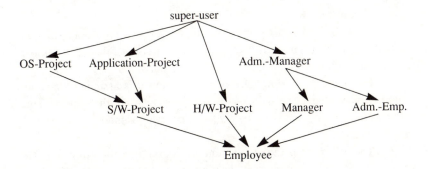

Figure 6.6   Example of Role Lattice.

The following is the first authorization implication rule. It allows implicit authorizations to be derived in the domain S of function f.

Rule 1. For each $o \in O$, and $a_i \in A$, if $s_i \geq s_j$, then $(s_j, o, +a_i) \to (s_i, o, +a_i)$.

From this rule, we obtain the following corollary for negative authorizations.

Corollary 1. For each $o \in O$, and $a_i \in A$, if $s_i > s_j$ then $(s_i, o, -a_i) \to (s_j, o, -a_i)$.

Corollary 1 is derived from Rule 1 by observing that, in the predicate calculus $(p \to p') \leftrightarrow (\neg p' \to \neg p)$ with predicates p and p'.

Rule 1 establishes that if a role has an authorization on an object, all the roles which precede that role in the partial ordering given by the role lattice are granted the same authorization. Conversely, if a role s is denied authorization, that authorization is denied to all roles following s in *RL*.

For example, given the lattice shown in Figure 6.6;

(S/W-Project, class[Document, +W) $\to$ (Application-Project, class [Document], +W) since the role 'Application-Project' precedes the role 'S/W-Project'. Conversely;

(Application-Project, class[Document], –W) $\to$ (S/W-Project, class [Document], – W.

6.3.2 Authorization Types

Like roles, authorization types are arranged in a lattice, called an *Authorization Type Lattice*: *ATL*. Each node on the lattice represents an authorization type. An arc from a node a_i to a node a_j indicates that the authorization type a_i implies type a_j.

Definition 6.8

Given a_i, $a_j \in A$, $a_i > a_j$ denotes that there is an arc from a_i to a_j in *ATL*; $a_i \geq a_j$ indicates that: (i) $a_i = a_j$ or $a_i > a_j$; (ii) or that there is a number n of authorization types a_1 A, ..., $a_n \in A$, such that $a_i > a_1 ... > a_n > a_j$.

For the sake of simplicity of presentation it is assumed that each authorization type $a \in A$ is valid for each type of the object. This assumption does not apply in the next section, where authorization objects are discussed.

The following is the second authorization implication rule. It states that implicit authorizations can be derived in respect of domain A of function f.

Rule 2. For each $s \in S$, and $o \in O$, if $a_i \geq a_j$ then $(s, o, +a_i) \rightarrow$ $(s, o, +a_j)$.

The following corollary can be obtained from this rule for negative authorizations.

Corollary 2. For each $s \in S$, and $o \in O$, if $a_i \geq a_j$ then $(s, o, -a_j) \rightarrow$ $(s, o, -a_i)$.

The authorization types considered in Rabitti *et al.* (1991) include: R (read), W (modify), G (create), RD (read definition). Therefore, $A = (R, W, G, RD)$. An authorization G is needed to create a new object (it is similar to the 'resource' authorization of DB2 (see Date, 1985)), while the authorization RD is needed to read the object definition. In object-oriented models, even the actual object definitions can contain information which is important in terms of privacy. Take a class of VLSI circuits as an example. The class describes the structure of its instances and thus defines the types of components used in the circuits. The class definition of such instances may thus contain important information which must be adequately protected.

There is a partial ordering of the authorization types in set A. The lattice is shown in Figure 6.7. Given the lattice in Figure 6.7, the following are some examples of implications of authorization types:

(S/W-Project, class[Document], $+W$) $\rightarrow$ (S/W-Project, class [Document], $+R$).

Conversely;

(S/W-Project, class[Document], $-R$) $\rightarrow$ (S/W-Project, class [Document], $-W$).

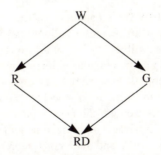

Figure 6.7 Example of an Authorization Type Lattice.

Note that the *ATL* illustrated in Figure 6.7 is not the only one that is possible. Let us assume that we want to extend the model to include specific authorization types for distinguishing between cases where a subject does or does not have the Grant option. In order to achieve this, we could introduce in A the following authorization types:

W-g, R-g, G-g, and RD-g. The implications for these new authorization types must also be specified. Figure 6.8 illustrates a possible extended *ATL*.

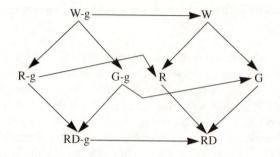

Figure 6.8   Example of extended Authorization Type Lattice.

6.3.3   Authorization Objects

Deriving authorizations in domain O of the function f is particularly important for reducing storage and access costs, since a database usually contains a large number of objects. In particular, we will use the concepts AOS (*Authorization Object Schema*) and AOL (*Authorization Object Lattice*) in dealing with the subject. AOS is the schema of authorization objects, whereas AOL is the instantiation of AOS in a specific database.

AOS and AOL

In a granularity hierarchy for a database, such as the one in Figure 6.1, each node represents at least two information types which can be a unit of authorization; the node itself and the set of the nodes on the lower level. In other words, each node in the granularity hierarchy can be associated with several authorization objects. For example, an authorization on a class can relate to the class itself intended as an object, or the set of its instances. As far as authorization is concerned, the node representing the class must be subdivided into two different authorization objects, with one node representing the class itself, and one node representing the set of its instances (*setof-Instances* node). Figure 6.9 illustrates the AOL relating to the granularity hierarchy illustrated in Figure 6.1. For example, in Figure 6.1, two nodes in the AOL in Figure 6.9: 'class[Document]' and '*setofInstances*[Document] correspond to the class Document in Figure 6.1. However, it is important to note that this authorization model has been defined for ORION, in which the extension of a class' instances is automatically associated with that class. The use of a data model with different hypotheses would result in a different AOS and AOL. If several extensions were associated with a class (for example, by means of predicates) then a 'class' node could potentially have several '*setofInstances*' nodes as children, and not just one, as is the case in ORION.

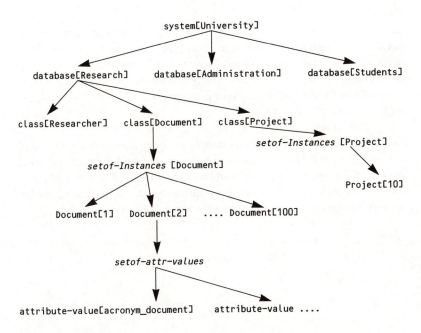

Figure 6.9   Example of Authorization Object Lattice.

The reason for the existence of several authorization objects for certain objects in a database is that, when the authorization model was developed, there was a preference for reducing authorization types to a minimum. For example, six authorization types would have had to be introduced for classes: reading and writing the class (understood as the class-object), reading and writing the class definition and reading and writing all the class instances. This could have meant increasing the complexity of implication rules. This is discussed in Bertino (1992), where the number of authorization objects is reduced and the number of authorization types increased.

An AOL, an example of which is illustrated in Figure 6.9, is a lattice in which each node represents an authorization object. An arc from a node *A* to a node *B* denotes that an authorization on *A* is propagated to *B*. Each node in an AOL belongs to one authorization object type and to one only.

Authorization object types constitute the schema for authorization objects. This schema is called the AOS. The AOS for the ORION system is shown in Figure 6.10. As discussed earlier, different hypotheses in the data model could result in a different AOS.

Association of Authorization Types with the Authorization Objects

The authorization model discussed so far must be refined to be able to model which authorization types are valid for which authorization object types. In fact, certain authorization types, R and W, for example, are applicable to all objects types, whereas others are not. For example, the type G is significant for the authorization object types 'Class' and 'Database', but not for 'Instance'.

The model can be refined by an AAM (*Authorization Association Matrix*). Figure 6.11 shows an example of such a matrix for the AOS shown in Figure 6.10. The matrix column shows the authorization types, whereas the rows represent the authorization objects. The entry $[AT_i, a_j]$ contains the value T (True), if the authorization type a_j is defined for the AT_i type of objects. Otherwise it contains the value F (False).

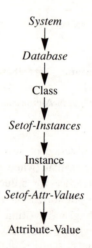

Figure 6.10   Example of schema for authorization objects

Therefore, all the authorization rules explicitly stored in *AB* and *WAB* must be semantically correct. This requirement is formalized by adding to the preceding rules and corollaries the following correctness constraint:

for each $(s, o, a) \in AB$ and for each $[s, o, a] \in WAB$, $c\,(o, a) = T$
where: c: $O \times A \rightarrow$ (True, False).

The function c for an object o is calculated by determining the authorization type of the object o and then accessing the AAM.

When defining the implications of the authorization objects, in what way the various authorization types are propagated along an AOL has to be taken into account. In fact, we can see that certain authorization types, R or W, for example, are propagated downwards in the AOL, whereas others, RD, for example, are propagated upwards (and thus in the opposite direction to that of the lattice).

For example, consider authorization R on an instance of a class C. The authorization R implies authorization RD (in fact, from the ATL in Figure 6.8, we have R > RD). Moreover, the object definition is contained in the class of which the object is its instance. Authorization RD on an instance of a class C implies an authorization RD on class C itself. Similarly, an authorization RD on a class implies an authorization RD in the database to which the class belongs. Thus, authorization RD is propagated in the opposite direction to that of the AOL.

Finally, an authorization R on an instance does not imply authorization R on the class, whereas an authorization R on a class implies the same authorization on all its instances. The authorization RD is propagated in the direction of the AOL. Finally, certain authorization types are not propagated at all. For example, a subject s which has the authorization G on a database D can create a new class in D. However, this authorization does not imply that s has the right to create instances of any class in D; s can generate instances only from classes which it has created or from classes for which it has received the appropriate authorizations.

The authorization types are grouped into three sets: $A.down$ – propagated downwards; $A.up$ – propagated upwards; and $A.nil$ – not propagated. Thus, in the ATL defined in Figure 6.8:

$A.down = $ (R, W)
$A.up = $ (RD)
$A.nil = $ (G).

	W	R	G	RD
System	T	T	T	T
Database	T	T	T	T
Class	T	T	F	T
Setof-Instances	T	T	T	T
Instance	T	T	F	T
Setof-Attr-Values	T	T	F	T
Attribute-Value	T	T	F	T

Figure 6.11   Example of authorization association matrix.

Implication Rules for Authorization Objects

In this paragraph we define the semantics of implication rules between authorization objects.

Definition 6.9

Given $o_i, o_j \in O$, $o_i > o_j$ denotes that there is an arc from o_i to o_j in AOL; $o_i \geq o_j$ denotes that: (i) $o_i = o_j$ or $o_i > o_j$; (ii) or that there is a number n of authorization objects $o_1 \in O$, ..., $o_n \in O$, such that $o_i > o_1 ... > o_n > o_j$.

The following is the third implication rule for authorizations; it means that implicit authorizations can be derived in relation to domain O of function f.

Rule 3. For each $s \in S$, and $a \in A.down$, if $o_i > o_j$, $c\,(o_j, a_n) = T$, and $c(o_i, a_n) = T$, then $(s, o_i + a) \rightarrow (s, o_j, +a)$.

For each $s \in S$, and $a \in A.up$, if $o_i \geq o_j$, $c\,(o_j, a_n) = T$, and $c\,(o_i, a_n) = T$, then $(s, o_j + a) \rightarrow (s, o_i, +a)$.

The following corollary for the negative authorizations can be obtained from this rule.

Corollary 3. For each $s \in S$, and $a \in A.down$, if $o_i \geq o_j$, $c\,(o_j, a_n) = T$, and $c\,(o_i, a_n) = T$, then $(s, o_j, -a) \rightarrow (s, o_i, -a)$.

For each $s \in S$, and $a \in A.up$, if $o_i \geq o_j$, $c\,(o_j, a_n) = T$, and $c\,(o_i, a_n) = T$, then $(s, o_i - a) \rightarrow (s, o_j, -a)$.

In Rule 3 and in Corollary 3, the preconditions $c\,(o_j, a_n) = T$, and $c\,(o_i, a_n) = T$ are used to ensure that only semantically correct authorizations for o_i and o_j are derived with the implication rules.

An Example

When determining whether a subject has an authorization type on a given object, a combination of all the various rules and corollaries seen earlier is used, since authorization of the subject can be determined after various inference steps have been executed along the three domains of function f.

Let us assume, by way of example, that the authorization (S/W-Project, database[Research], +W) is stored in AB, and that we have to check the authorization (OS-Project, Document[2], R). The following inference steps are executed:

- In domain S, 'OS-Project' > 'S/WProject'; therefore, (S/W-Project, database[Research], +W) → (OS-Project, database[Research], +W).

- In domain O 'database[Research]' > 'class[Document]' > 'Document[2]' and W $\in$ A.*down*; therefore (OS-Project, database [Research], +W) $\rightarrow$ (OS-Project, Document[2], +W).

- In domain A W > R; therefore (OS-Project, document[2], +W) $\rightarrow$ (OS-Project, document[2], +R).

Since the authorization (OS-Project, Document[2], +R) can be derived from AB, f (OS-Project, Document[2], R) = True.

To illustrate the use of negative authorization let us assume that the authorization (OS-Project, class[Document], −RD) is stored in AB, and that we must check the authorization (Employee, Document[2], W). The following inference steps must be executed:

- In domain S, 'OS-Project' > 'S/W-Project > 'Employee'; therefore (OS-Project, class[Document], −RD) $\rightarrow$ (Employee, class[Document], −RD).

- In domain O, 'class[Document]' > 'Document[2]' and also RD $\in$ A.*up*; therefore (Employee, class[Document], −RD) $\rightarrow$ (Employee, Document[2], −RD)

- In domain A, W > R > RD; therefore (Employee, Document[2], −RD) $\rightarrow$ (Employee, Document[2], −W).

Since the authorization (Employee, Document[2], −W) can be derived from AB, f (Employee, Document[2], W) = False.

6.4   Application to the Object-Oriented Model

The previous model must be broadened, if further characteristics of the object data model are to be modelled. In the rest of this section, we will discuss extensions relating to various aspects of classes, inheritance hierarchies, composite objects and versions. The extensions involve introducing new authorization object types in the AOS, along with the corresponding entries in the AAM matrix. Figure 6.12 illustrates an AOS. Below, we focus on ORION's data model, but the main concepts of the authorization model are almost directly applicable to other models.

6.4.1   Properties of a Class

The first extension to be introduced is the authorization of reading and writing an attribute for all the instances of a class. This extension is modelled by introducing two new authorization object types, *Setof-Attributes* and Attribute. An authorization R (or W) on a specific instance

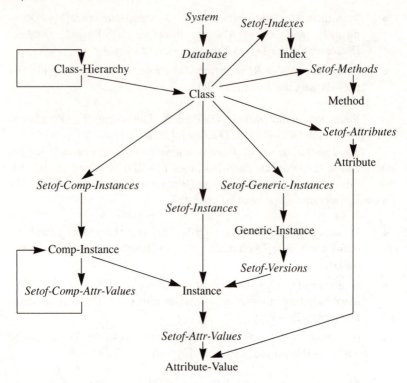

Figure 6.12 Extended schema of authorization objects.

attribute of a class for a subject means that the subject can read (or modify) this attribute for all the class' instances. An attribute which is an authorization object can also be a class attribute. If this is the case, the authorization is not propagated to the instances of the class, since they do not have that attribute. Therefore, an authorization R (or W) on a specific class attribute for a subject means that the subject can read (or modify) this attribute. Thus, authorizations on classes understood as objects can also be supported.

The authorization W on attributes (whether instance or class attributes) concerns only modifications of their values. Intentional modifications, such as removing an attribute or modifying its domain, are possible only if there is a W type authorization on the object representing the class. For example, under the authorization rule (*s*, class[Researcher], W), the subject *s* can modify the structure of the class and therefore, he or she can add and delete attributes and modify their domain. Under the rule (*s*, *setof-Attributes*[Researcher], W), however, subject *s* can modify the values of all attributes of all instances of the class 'Researcher' but he or she cannot modify the structure of this class.

The second extension concerns methods. An R type authorization on a method for a subject *s* allows *s* to execute the method. All access executed by the method while it is being executed are, however, checked later. In Bertino (1992), an extension of the authorization model is described in which methods can be executed in *protected mode*. When methods in protected mode are executed, authorization control is not performed on subject *s* who has activated the execution of the method, but on another subject, often the subject who has granted *s* the authorization to execute the method. Thus, we can ensure that specific subjects access or modify one or more objects only by using specific methods. Finally, adding, deleting or modifying a method are considered as modifications to a class. A W type authorization must be granted on the class for them to be executed.

The third extension concerns indices. A user can be granted authorization to add indices to and remove them from a class. This authorization is modelled on the W authorization type. Obviously, a user cannot read or modify the contents of an index, since such operations can only be executed by the system.

Figure 6.13 shows the AAM matrix for the various authorization object types for a class.

	W	*R*	*G*	*RD*
Class	T	T	F	T
Setof-Instances	T	T	T	T
Setof-Indexes	T	F	T	T
Index	T	F	F	T
Setof-Methods	F	T	F	T
Method	F	T	F	T
Setof-Attr-Values	T	T	F	T
Attribute-Value	T	T	F	T

Figure 6.13   Authorization association matrix for class authorization objects.

6.4.2 Inheritance Hierarchies

Inheritance poses the problem of whether authorizations granted to a subject on a class must be inherited by the subclasses of that class. There are two possible approaches. In the first, users who are authorized to access all of a class' instances have no implicit authorization on subclasses' instances. Authorization on a class concerns only its instances and not its members. The main problem with this approach is that a query involving all of a class' members requires multiple authorization checks. Under the second approach, authorizations are inherited. Therefore, a user who has a right to read and write on all of a class' instances implicitly has the same right on the subclasses' instances. Generally speaking, the first approach is preferable since it allows for reusage without reducing data privacy, and it is this approach which is used in ORION. Using the second approach, a user wanting to create a class by reusing the definition of another class would have no privacy in terms of its instances. Therefore, when privacy is required, a user would not be able to reuse the definition of another class to define his/her own class.

Moreover, in the authorization model, a specific authorization type is provided for generating subclasses. This type, denoted with the letters SG, allows a subclass of a given class to be defined. SG ∈ *A.nil* and the following is the ordering of SG with respect to other types in *A*: W > SG and SG > RD.

The first inequality establishes that a user with an authorization W on a class *C* implicitly receives the right to derive subclasses from it. The second establishes that a user receiving the authorization to derive a subclass from a class *C* implicitly receives the right RD on *C*, since, obviously a user cannot define a subclass of *C* if he or she cannot read its definition.

Let us assume that a subject *s* wants to create a subclass of the 'Researcher' class. The authorizations required of it for this operation are:

(*s* database[Research], G) (*s*, class[Researcher], SG).

Upon the definition of the new class, *s* receives the explicit authorization W on that class. This authorization implies all the others. Users with access rights on superclasses of the new class are not implicitly granted rights on that class, which have to be explicitly authorized by *s*.

6.4.3 Composite Objects

In the authorization model for composite objects, a whole composite object can be used as the authorization unit. The extension of the model for composite objects involves the introduction of certain new types of authorization objects: *setof-Comp-Instances*, Comp-Instance, *setof-Comp-Attr-Values*. Figure 6.14 illustrates an example of AOL for a composite object. It is assumed in the example that the 'Document' class is, in reality, a composite class, having a list of bibliographical references as a text component.

An authorization on a composite class *C* implies the same authorization on all the instances of *C* and on all the objects (including those in other classes) which are components of objects of *C*. For example, consider the 'Document' composite class. This class has 'Text' and 'Bibliography' as component classes. If a subject *s* receives authorization

R on 'Document', it implicitly receives the same authorization on the instances of the 'Text' and 'Bibliography' classes which are components of the instances of 'Document'.

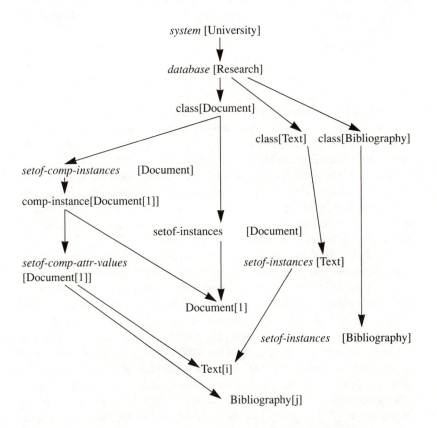

Figure 6.14   Example of AOL for composite objects.

If a subject *s* receives authorization R on the 'Document', it implicitly receives the same authorization on the instances of 'Text' and 'Bibliography' which are components of the instances of 'Document'. However, this subject receives no implicit authorization on the instances of 'Text' and 'Bibliography' which are not components of instances in 'Document', since not all the instances in these classes are necessarily components of instances in the latter class.

If some components are shared, a weak negative authorization can result in conflicts. For example, consider the composite objects and the weak authorizations [*s*, comp-instance[1], +W] and [*s*, comp-instance[2], −W] shown in Figure 6.15a. Since the authorizations are propagated to the components, there are two authorizations with corresponding sets of derived authorizations which are not disjoint. The derived authorizations in common are shown by the shaded area in Figure 6.15b. Conflict arises because one authorization is the negation of the other. This means that if the authorization on comp-instance[1] is issued before the authorization on comp-instance[2], the latter is denied by the system as it would make the *WAB* inconsistent.

One way of resolving the conflict and permit authorization on comp-instance[2] to be granted is for the user to issue an explicit weak authorization on the composite object which has the object comp-instance[4] as its root. In other words, the user explicitly resolves the conflict. Thus, the set of consequences of the authorization on comp-instance[4] is removed from the sets of consequences of the authorizations on comp-instance[1] and comp-instance[2]. The sets of consequences of authorizations on comp-instance[1] and comp-instance[2] are disjoint. Let us assume, therefore, that the following positive weak authorization is issued: [s, comp-instance[4], +W]. This authorization is redundant in relation to the authorization [s, comp-instance[1], +W]. However, it is needed to avoid conflict between the authorization [s, comp-instance[2] and the subsequent issue of the authorization [s, comp-instance[2], –W]. Figure 6.15c shows the sets of derived authorizations of these three weak authorizations.

Note that, if a subject s receives an authorization on an 'instance' type authorization object, it receives no implicit authorization on the components of that object. Therefore, it can only read (or modify) the values of the attributes. If there are attributes referencing component objects, the subject can only read the OID of the component objects or assign a new component, but it cannot read or modify the component object. For example, with the authorization (s, comp-instance [Document[1]], +R), a user can read the objects Document[1], Text[i], Bibliography[j]. However, with the authorization (s, Document[1], +R), s can only read the object Document[1]. Being able to read Document[1] s can obtain the OIDs of the components of Document[1], but implicitly it receives no authorization to access the objects Text[i] and Bibliography[j].

6.4.4 Versions

An important requirement for versions is that authorizations can be granted both on a whole hierarchy of versions and on an individual version of a given hierarchy. As is the case with composite objects, versions also require new types of authorization objects (see Figure 6.12). The authorization types R and W are defined for these new authorization object types. An authorization on a *setof-generic-instances* type node implies the same authorization on all the generic instances in the class. With a W type authorization on a generic instance, the user can modify the generic

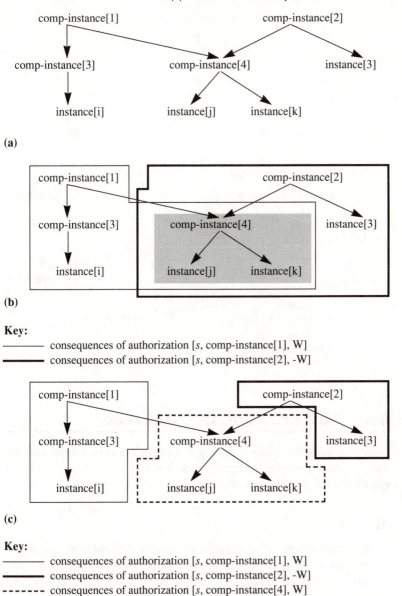

Figure 6.15   Composite objects with shared components.

instance itself – change the default version, for example. A W type authorization on a *setof-versions* type object implies a W type authorization on all the versions belonging to the same hierarchy and, moreover, it allows new versions to be created. Figure 6.16 is an example of *AOL* for an object with versions.

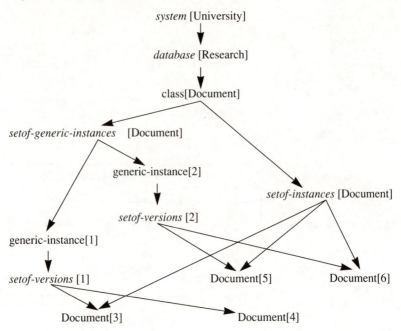

Figure 6.16 Example of AOL for objects with versions.

6.5 **Authorization in GemStone**

GemStone provides a very simple authorization model compared with the model shown above. In particular, it does not support variable levels of granularity for authorization objects.

Segments

Segments are the only type of authorization unit in GemStone. A segment groups together a set of objects. A segment has only one owner who can authorize other users to read from and write to his/her own segments. All objects within a segment have the same level of protection. Therefore, if a subject *s* has the authorization to read a segment, he or she can read all the objects in the segment.

Default Segments

All users are given a default segment in GemStone. The segment identifier is stored in the user *profile*. Normally, an object created by a user is stored in the default segment given to the user. A user can determine which is his default segment with the `defaultSegment` message. The following is an example of how this message is used:

```
| mySegment |
mySegment := System myUserProfile defaultSegment.
```

Only the system administrator can grant a user the right to change default segment. The following is an example:

```
System myUserProfiile defaultSegment: ASegment.
```

When the message above has been executed, the user will have as default the segment specified in the message by the variable `ASegment` the next time he or she connects with the system.

A user can transfer objects from one segment to another and can create new segments, given the appropriate authorization. By doing this, he or she can change an object's accessibility. For example, if an object is transferred from a segment which all users can access, in order to read and write, to a segment which no user, except the owner, can access, only the owner will be able to access the object.

Read and Write Authorizations

There are two types of access rights in GemStone which can be granted on a segment: `#read` and `#write`. Finally, there is a special type, called `#none` which, when granted to a user, deletes authorizations.

In GemStone, groups can be defined and authorizations to groups can be assigned. An example is shown in the following instruction which assigns to the group `#Engineering` the write authorization on its default segment:

```
System myUserProfile defaultSegment group: #Engineering
                             authorization: #write.
```

The authorization granted with the preceding instruction can be revoked with the following instruction:

```
System myUserProfile defaultSegment group: #Engineering
                             authorization: #none.
```

Having been granted the appropriate authorization from the system administrator, a user can add a group to his or her own profile, by implicitly obtaining all the authorizations granted to the group.

There is a special message, called `worldAuthorization` with which all the GemStone system users are assigned an authorization on a given segment. The following is an example:

```
mySeg worldAuthorization: #read.
```

Procedural Authorization

In GemStone, as in other OODBMS, an appropriate code can be inserted in methods to execute authorization checks. This approach is useful in several situations. Its main disadvantage is that authorization rules are not expressed declaratively and are distributed in the various methods. Modifying an authorization rule can become a very complex operation. And this approach requires that all access to objects' attributes should be with methods, whereas, as previously discussed, this is not always the case in OODBMS.

Let us consider, for example, the class `Researcher` and the attribute `salary` and let us assume that only specific users can read this attribute. Therefore, the read method of 'salary' must check that the user who activated the execution of the method belongs to the set of authorized users. The following is one way of implementing this method:

```
Salary
    | currentID |
    currentID := System myUserProfile useridID.
    (currentID in: OK_Users)
            ifTrue: [^salary]
            ifFalse:[ self securityViolation:
                        'access not authorized'].
```

The method above first determines the identifier of the user who activated the method. This identifier is determined by the user profile with the `useridID` message. The second step is to check that this identifier belongs to the set called `OK_Users`. This set contains the identifiers of all authorized users. If the check is positive and the user belongs to the set of authorized users, the value of the salary is returned. If the result of the check is negative, an error message is returned.

6.6 Bibliographical Notes

Problems relating to authorization models for object-oriented databases have not yet been researched in great depth and there are few works dealing with them. There are also considerable problems involved in the design and implementation of authorization models, some of which have not yet been resolved and almost all systems supply somewhat simple authorization mechanisms, or provide none at all.

Works on the subject fall into two categories; those which deal with non-discretionary type authorization and those which deal with discretionary type authorization. Works on the first type of authorization include an article by Thuraisingham (1989), one of the first on the subject, and the more recent article by Jajodia, Kogan and Sandhu (1990) who extend multi-level authorization models to include object-oriented models.

The most recent work to date on the second type of authorization is the authorization model developed for ORION discussed in an article by Rabitti *et al.* (1991), a large section of which has been considered in this chapter. Certain extensions to this model are discussed by Bertino (1992), who proposes a different approach to authorization in the context of methods, and by Bertino and Weigand (1992), who deal with content-based authorization and who propose some modifications concerning authorization on versions and on inheritance hierarchies. They also take a more extensive look at the authorization administration. Finally, a recent article by Ahad *et al.* (1992) discusses a possible authorization model for Iris. This model has not yet been incorporated in the current version of Iris.

7 Query Processing

The greatest innovation of the relational model compared with models of previous generations of DBMS, such as Codasyl and hierarchical DBMS, was declarative queries and associated techniques for automated evaluation. Optimization problems have been the focus of a great deal of theoretical and applications research. Much research is still being carried out in this field. The same cannot be said for OODBMS. The greatest problem is that the object-oriented data model does not yet have a formal theoretical framework, and so there is no model on which to base development of the theory and architecture which would provide the basis for optimization. Most OODBMS designers have not invested a great deal of time in the design and development of appropriate techniques for optimizing object-oriented queries. For the most part, techniques developed for the relational model have been used, for OODBMS as well, very often with a lower degree of sophistication than the technique used in some relational DBMS on the market today.

In this chapter, we shall look at some aspects of object-oriented query optimization and we shall provide some of the elements of a cost model. However, the definition of an appropriate mathematical model is still largely being researched.

7.1   Introduction

Evaluating a relational query is essentially carried out in two phases. The first phase involves possible optimizations. The second phase consists of the actual execution. This organization in two phases can be applied to OODBMS as well (Kim, 1990). Straube and Oszu (1990) define a more detailed subdivision, shown in Figure 7.1, of the activities performed during the first phase. An analysis of the steps required for optimization reveals that the query language does not require the programmer (and, to a lesser extent, the database user) to know the details of the database implementation. The first step in this process has the main purpose of eliminating redundancies and producing a standardized version of queries. The phase of optimization which we will be looking at in this chapter and which this section introduces is shown in Figure 7.1. It includes generating an execution plan and the choice of the best option.

A set of reasonable execution plans is produced by the optimization phase for a given query. One plan is chosen as the best, on the basis of the anticipated costs for each plan generated. The chosen plan is then executed in the next phase.

At the moment, considerable research is needed to deal with optimization and execution of object-oriented queries. However, it is generally thought that such research does not so much require a fundamental shift of emphasis, but rather a few, small changes to the techniques that have been used successfully for relational queries.

In this section, we shall first highlight why all essential techniques for relational queries are directly applicable to objects. We shall also describe these techniques. Then we shall look at the changes which have to be made to take into account features typical of object-oriented models.

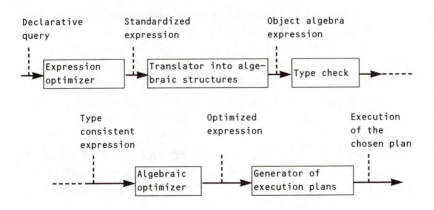

Figure 7.1   Query processing: front-end.

7.1.1 Query Graphs

The concept of *query graphs*, a subset of the *schema graph* defined in Chapter 2, is useful in discussing query strategies. The terminology associated with it, which we shall use throughout the rest of the book, is introduced in this section.

In relational databases, the schema graph for a relation is the relation itself. The selection operation applied to a relation identifies the tuples which satisfy the predicates in the query, and the predicates are evaluated on the only node in the graph in terms of the schema graph. In an object-oriented database, a query can be seen as a combination of *simple* and *complex* predicates. A *simple predicate* is a predicate of the form <name-attribute operator value>. The value can be an instance of a primitive class or an OID of an instance of another class. The latter is important because the equality of the objects referred to can be tested with it. A *complex predicate* is a predicate of an adjacent sequence of attributes on a branch of the aggregation hierarchy of a class.

A query graph must, therefore, include all the classes (and the hierarchies rooted in such classes) to which any one of the attributes indicated in a simple or complex predicate refers.

The following is a precise definition of the query graph (QG) for a single operand query on a class C (Kim, 1990):

(1) QG is a connected subgraph of the graph in the schema SG for C. C is the root of QG. Thus, QG and SG for C have the same root. Moreover, C must be a non-primitive class.

(2) QG only includes those nodes of the corresponding SG on which at least one predicate of the query is specified.

(3) An arc from an attribute of a class to the domain in SG can be changed in QG into an arc from that attribute to a subclass of its domain. Only the inheritance hierarchy rooted in the new domain is then included in QG.

(4) The set of arcs from the class root C to the direct and indirect domains of the attributes of C included in the QG form a direct graph rooted in C. Thus, the hierarchy of classes of QG is a direct rooted graph in which certain branches form cycles and others do not.

(5) The leaf nodes of an acyclic branch correspond to simple predicates, whereas the non-leaf nodes of a branch, whether cyclic or acyclic, can have simple or complex predicates defined on them.

Figure 7.2 is an example of a query graph referring to the query:

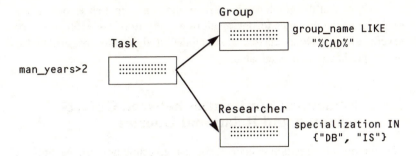

Figure 7.2 Example of a query graph.

```
Find all tasks with a number of man years greater
than two, whose leader is a researcher with a
specialization in databases or information
systems, and with a participating group whose name
contains the word 'CAD'
```

Note that a single operand query is significantly more powerful than a query on a single relation in a relational database, since it involves the joins of the classes along the aggregation hierarchy rooted in the target class, and the inheritance hierarchy is automatically included in the evaluation of it.

However, compared with the relational model, the single operand query has the limitation of not being able to extract attributes other than those of the target class. Moreover, an implicit join establishes statically that only classes (C_i, C_j), such that C_j is the domain of an attribute of C_i, are classes that can be joined. This excludes joins between arbitrary pairs of classes which share a domain, that is, explicit joins.

To express this type of query, the model and, thus, the definition of the query graph (QG), must be extended. Below, we define an explicit join between two classes. The extension to include N classes is immediate. The attributes on which the join is made in C_i and C_j are denoted by S_i and S_j and it is assumed that S_i is a superclass of S_j or that $S_i = S_j$.

(1) C_i and C_j are both roots of the QG that corresponds to a single operand query on C_i and C_j, respectively.

(2)   The QGs for C_i and C_j partially overlap (if they did not, the two join attributes would not be compatible). S_i and S_j are both the root of a hierarchy of classes; if $S_i = S_j$, the entire hierarchy is shared by C_i and C_j. If S_i is a superclass of S_j, the hierarchy rooted in S_i is the domain of the join attribute of C_i and the hierarchy rooted in S_j is the domain of the join attribute of C_j.

Note that the graph can have more than one target class, only if the query language provides for the result of a query to be the explicit join of several classes. Other classes are included if they must be visited for nested predicates to be evaluated.

7.1.2   Structural Similarities between Object-oriented and Relational Queries

The reason why relational query processing techniques can be applied directly to the new model is that, if the existing hierarchical structure between classes is not considered, the structure of queries is essentially the same in both paradigms. This ought to be sufficiently clear from the description of the SQL-like language described in the previous chapter. In fact, extensions to SQL in an object-oriented language OSQL have indeed been proposed (Beech and Mahbod, 1988). Banerjee *et al.* (1988) propose an algorithm for the transformation of queries from an object-oriented query language to semantically equivalent relational queries.

As we have seen, the attribute/domain link between a pair of classes is effectively the join of those classes. Generally speaking, the attribute/domain link between a class C and the domain D of one of the attributes A of C creates the join between the classes C and D, in which the attribute A of class C and the identifier OID, which is defined by the system and which can be considered an attribute of class D, are the join attributes.

On the basis of these observations, a single operand query, which involves N classes along a hierarchy composed of classes rooted in the query target class, is equivalent to a relational query, which requires the join in N relations corresponding to N classes. This statement applies as well to multiple operand queries, an example of which has been given. If the dimension due to the inheritance hierarchy is suppressed, the QG obtained is effectively an explicit join of the two target classes of the multiple operand query, in which the join attributes are those defined by the user.

In the same way that joins can be made of N relations in $N!$ possible permutations, N classes in an aggregation hierarchy can be visited in one of the $N!$ permutations. For example, the three classes shown in the example in Figure 7.2 can, in principle, be visited in **3!** modes. In the relational model, some of these permutations involve the Cartesian product as the result and they are therefore omitted from the list of proposed plans for the evaluation of a query. This approach is a perfectly sensible one even for the object-oriented model. For example, of the **3!** permutations resulting from the example above, those in which a join is made between the *Group* and *Researcher* classes should be rejected since they do not present implicit or explicit joins in the query. Therefore, a join between these two classes would be reduced to a Cartesian product.

The following are the techniques which have been developed for relational query processing:

(1)   Determination of all reasonable permutations between the relations involved in a query. Therefore those resulting in a Cartesian product are excluded.

(2)   Generation of an execution plan for each permutation obtained in step 1. An execution plan specifies the access method used (index, hash, table, etc.) for retrieving tuples from each relation and the methods used to join tuples of one relation with tuples of the next relation in a given permutation (nested-loop, sort-domain, etc.). We shall looking at this in greater depth later.

(3)   Evaluation of the cost of each execution plan generated in step 2. Cost formulae and statistics on the database are used.

(4)   In distributed databases, generation of a global query plan as a collection of local plans executed on each database.

The various ways in which the class instances are logically linked to those in the subsequent classes in a given permutation in an object-oriented query should now be considered.

Given a pair of classes C and D, such that D is the domain of an attribute A of C, the values of that attribute A are identifiers of the instances of class D.

If classes C and D are in this order, in a given permutation, the join between these classes is obtained by iterating the following operations:

```
for c in C do
  begin
    retrieve c.A;
    retrieve d in D such that
    OID(d)=c.A if A is single-valued
    OID(d) ∈ c.A if A is multi-valued;
    evaluate the predicate on d
  end.
```

If, however, the permutation involves retrieving the instances in class D before the retrieval of the instances in C, then the following schema will apply:

```
for d in D do
  begin
    retrieve u=OID(d);
    evaluate the predicate on d
    retrieve c in C such that
```

```
c.A=u if A is single-valued
u ∈ c.A if A is multi-valued;
end.
```

These operations are repeated to retrieve instances of other classes.

The ideas presented informally here can be formalized and specified with appropriate notations. Definitions supporting the description of the strategies in an object-oriented query are given in the following paragraphs.

7.2 Traversal of Nodes in a Query Graph

This section is mostly dealt with by Kim *et al.* (1988). The main methods of visiting the nodes in a query graph are: *forward traversal, reverse traversal* and *mixed traversal*.

In the following definitions, the terms *class* and *node* are used synonymously. Which of the two is meant will be clear from the context.

Definition 7.1

A *forward traversal* is a visit of the class in the order $C_1,...,C_n$ which includes all the classes in the query graph QG such that for $1 < i \leq n$:

(1) C_1 is the root class of QG;

(2)   The other classes are visited in any depth-first order in QG.

There are two forward traversals in the example in Figure 7.2: (Task Group Researcher) (Task Researcher Group).

Definition 7.2

A *reverse traversal* is a visit of the class in the order $C_1,...,C_n$ which includes all the classes in the query graph QG such that for $1 < i \leq n$:

(1) C_1 is a leaf-node class of QG;

(2) C_i can be a leaf-node class of QG;

(3)   All the classes which are children of C_i must be visited before C_i, that is, they must be in $C_1,...,C_{i-1}$.

There are two reverse traversals in the example in Figure 7.2: (Group Researcher Task) (Researcher Group Task).

Definition 7.3

A *mixed traversal* is a visit of the classes in the order $C_1,...,C_n$ which includes all the classes in the query graph QG such that for $1 < i \leq n$:

(1) C_1 is any class of QG;

(2) C_i is connected to one of $C_1,...,C_{i-1}$ by a direct arc towards C_i;

(3) C_i and one of $C_1,...,C_{i-1}$ must have a common parent in QG;

(4)   one or more classes which are children of C_i in QG must be in $C_1,...,C_{i-1}$.

There are two mixed traversals in the example in Figure 7.2: (Group Task Researcher) (Researcher Task Group).

In these definitions, the visit of nodes is restricted such that the nodes representing subclasses in QG are not explicitly included in the visit. It is assumed that, when a node is visited, its subclasses are visited at the same time.

The traversal methods used in conventional systems with links are the forward traversal and the mixed traversal without the property (3). Reverse traversal and mixed traversal with the property (3) are specific to object-oriented databases. However, it is clear that efficient use of the reverse traversal is often subordinate to the presence of *reverse* references and thus to the presence of links between each object and the objects of which they are components.

7.2.1 Access Algorithms to Instances of Classes

In addition to the order of class visits in a query graph, strategies for retrieving the class instances visited must also be selected. Ways of retrieving instances from the visited classes must be chosen, as well as the order of class visits. In most systems that use pointers, be they logical or physical, access to data results in one record being created at a time (such access methods being known as *nested-loop methods*). In other systems, access creates several records at a time, and this is known a a *sort-domain* method. An accurate evaluation of the optimum execution strategy for a query will take both access methods into account and will select the one that involves the minimum cost.

Nested-loop

In a nested-loop access method, each class object is taken into consideration and processed separately. The attributes (simple and nested) of an instance are evaluated with respect to the predicates of the query, if there are any which involve other attributes. If the instance passes this test, then it is passed to the parent node (in reverse traversals) or to the child node (in forward traversals) of the query graph.

Sort-domain

By contrast, a sort-domain (or *sort-merge*) method involves instantiating all class instances at the same time, evaluating them with respect to the predicates and passing them all to the proper node in the query graph. The advantage of the sort-domain method over the nested-loop method is that the storage pages containing class instances of the class are never accessed more than once, resulting in considerable savings in terms of response times.

7.2.2 Query Execution Strategies

By appropriately combining the strategies for traversing query graphs with the strategies for accessing instances, we obtain four basic query strategies. Given a branch of length n, and a path defined starting from the root of the branch $P = C_1.A_1...A_m$, $(1 \leq m \leq n)$, these strategies are described below (Kim *et al.*, 1988).

(1)   *Nested-loop forward traversal (NLFT)*
       The following steps are involved in this strategy. An instance of class C_1 is retrieved and the value of its attribute A_1 is determined. Given this identifier, a first access is executed on the system's tables to identify the object's address; access must then be executed again to access the object so that the value of attribute A_2 can be determined. These steps are repeated until attribute A_m is reached, on which the predicate is evaluated. The operations are then repeated for all instances of class C_1.

(2)   *Sort-domain forward traversal (SDFT)*
       This strategy differs from the above in that all the instances of class C_1 are traversed and all the values of attribute A_1 are retrieved before visiting instances of other classes. The addresses for all OIDs obtained are found and these are ordered in such a way that the same page does not have to be accessed twice. The process is repeated until the instances of class C_m are accessed.

(3)   *Nested-loop reverse traversal (NLRT)*
       This strategy is similar to *NLFT*, except for the fact that C_m is the first class that is visited. An instance I of C_m is accessed and the predicate is evaluated. If the predicate is verified, then a search on the instances of class C_{m-1} is executed to determine which instance has the instance I as the value of the attribute A_{m-1}. This is repeated until class C_1 is reached. It is obvious that, when there are reverse references from the instances of C_i to the instances of C_{i-1}, the instances of C_{i-1} do not need to be examined. Instead, the objects are accessed directly by following these references.

(4)   *Sort-domain reverse traversal (SDRT)*

This strategy is similar to *NLRT*, in that the search starts from the instances of class C_m. All the instances of C_m are accessed, the predicate is evaluated and a list of the OIDs of the instances qualifying the predicate is generated. The instances of class C_{m-1} are then selected to determine which instances have an identifier in the generated list as the value of the attribute A_{m-1}. The process is repeated until C_1 is reached.

An estimate can be made of the costs, in terms of accesses to storage pages, with respect to more significant parameters, in order to evaluate which is the best of each of these strategies for each configuration. See the next section for an in-depth account of cost models and formulæ.

The spectrum of possible strategies is extended if index techniques are taken into account, in that some of the strategies described above, in particular those using reverse traversal operations, can be replaced by auxiliary structures such as hash tables and indices. The use of index techniques is, generally speaking, extremely important for efficient query execution, not only because they have a significant impact on query execution times, but also because they lead to new query execution strategies. This matter merits a separate section and the use of indices in execution strategies will be described in the next chapter. Suffice it to say here that the use of the indices in object-oriented databases is particularly suitable for increasing the efficiency of implicit joins, and thus for ease of retrieval of the nested objects of an objects' composition hierarchy.

A query execution strategy can thus be seen as the decomposition of a query into a set of basic operations, among which a partial order is established. Basic operations include:

[P]   *projection*. This operation extracts one or more attributes from an instance. It is assumed that projection removes duplicates. A special attribute name, OID, preceded by the class name, indicates that the projection must return the OIDs of the instances of the class. A class name in a projection means that all the attributes of the instances of the class in question must be returned by the projection operation.

[S]   *selection*. This operation applies one or more simple predicates to a set of objects.

[∩]   *intersection*. This operation intersects two sets of objects and removes duplicates.

[I]   *index scanning*. Given a key, this operation accesses a given index and returns the objects which appear in the index.

[NJ] *nested-loop join*. This is the first strategy for accessing the instances described in the preceding paragraph.

[SJ] *sort-domain join*. This is the second strategy for accessing instances described in the preceding paragraph.

[O] *arrangement*. Given a set and an ordering relation, this operation orders the elements in the set.

It is useful to represent query execution strategies by means of QEG (*Query Execution Graph*).

Query Execution Graph

A node of a QEG represents one of the operations in the preceding list and is labelled with the name of the operation and other information which may be necessary for executing the operation. A node representing the selection is given a selection predicate. Similarly, the node representing the index scanning operation is given with the predicate solved by the index search. A node representing the ordering operation is given the attribute on which the ordering is based. Nodes in a QEG also denote the classes to which the query is applied, in which case the label is simply the name of the class. The arcs of a QEG are directed. An arc from a node N to a node N' means that the result of the operation denoted by node N (if N denotes an operation) or the instances of the class (if N denotes a class) are the input to the operation denoted by N'. This notation reinterprets the concept of an execution graph for relational queries described by Yao (1979).

Using this graphic representation, Figure 7.3 shows some of the possible execution strategies for the query:

```
Find all the tasks with a number of man_years
greater than two, whose leader is a researcher
with a specialization in databases or information
systems, and with a participating group whose name
contains the word 'CAD'.
```

A node which represents a nested-loop or sort-domain join is given the join predicate. It can also have a conditional arc labelled with the name of a class and represented in the graph by a thick arrow. Conditional arcs mean that, as soon as the join is executed, the instance in the class which labels the *conditional arc* is passed to the node which follows the arc, and the predicate corresponding to the node is evaluated on that. If the instance satisfies the predicate, the join's result is passed to the non-conditional arc which follows the join's node.

For example, in the strategy illustrated in Figure 7.3(a), an instance I of the Task class is accessed. If the man_years attribute of I has a value greater than two, then the join is executed, that is, the object referred to by

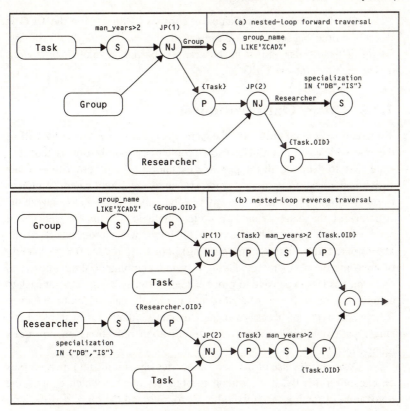

JP(1):Task.participant=Group.OID
JP(2):Task.leader=Researcher.OID

Figure 7.3 Examples of query execution graphs for nested-loop strategies

the **participant** attribute of **I** (node **NJ**) is returned. This object is an instance **J** of the **Group** class. Then, the **group_name** attribute of **J** is considered. If the name contains the string 'CAD', the result of operation **NJ**, that is, the pair (**I, J**), is passed to the node following **NJ**, via the non-conditional arc. The latter node represents the projection operation which only retains the instances of the class **Task**, **I**. Then the object referred to by the **leader** attribute of instance **I** is looked for, object K of the class **Researcher**; if **K** has the value '**DB**' or '**IS**' for the **specialization** attribute, then, as before, the pair (**I, K**) is passed to the node following the non-conditional arc. Here, the final projection is executed, returning the instances of the class **Task** which satisfy the query. Note that, when the query also involves classes in the inheritance hierarchy rooted in those classes involved in the QEG, then the instances of such classes are also accessed along with the instances of the root class.

Given a QEG, query execution consists of linearizing the QEG in which the ordering relations are preserved, that is, a topological ordering. Given that the order shown in the graph is partial, several linearizations can be obtained for one QEG.

7.2.3 Query Optimization

There can be several QEGs for the same query and the least costly will be the one which is chosen. The main problem in optimization is that it is expensive to generate all the possible execution plans in order to evaluate which is the best, in particular when strategies are complicated by indices or other similar structures. One way to solve this problem is to analyze the structure of the database and to collect statistics on the frequencies of access to each class (which can be obtained, when required, by using appropriate forms of system monitoring) in order to reduce the complexity of choosing the best strategy, taking it from a combinatorial complexity to one which is less expensive to process. Generally speaking, it is not easy to achieve this result for generic situations but results can indeed be achieved for specific types of access to data. This can be done, for example, for a single path involving queries and modification operations on any class along this path.

Note that the use of methods in queries has significant repercussions on execution. Firstly, it is difficult to optimize queries which contain the invocation of methods. A method is a program and therefore it is difficult to make an estimate of the cost and of its selectivity. One strategy, which is used in most systems, consists in restricting the set of objects to be processed before invoking a method; therefore a method is executed as late as possible during query execution. However, this strategy is inefficient in many situations. Therefore other approaches require the user to provide relevant information as input to the system. The obvious disadvantage is that this forces the user to make a considerable evaluation effort which, in general, he or she should not have to do.

Secondly, methods with side-effects can cause the result of a query to depend on the order of evaluation of the various predicates. Therefore, certain systems do not permit the use of methods with side-effects in queries, whereas other systems leave it up to the user, as forbidding the use of methods with side-effects may be too restrictive.

7.2.4 Differences in Query Processing compared with the Relational Model

Despite the similarities between object-oriented queries and relational queries, there are certain important semantic differences. In this section, we summarize the main differences (Kim, 1990).

Indices

Aggregation and inheritance hierarchies call for the use of indices defined on nested attributes and on classes along the inheritance hierarchy. The use of such indices has an impact on the processing of object-oriented queries, albeit primarily on cost evaluation of strategies.

Multiple-valued Attributes

Multiple-valued attributes require the introduction of existential quantifiers, such as **each** and **exists**, which are associated in queries with attributes whose values are sets of objects. Again, this variation from the relational form has repercussions primarily on the evaluation of costs associated with these quantifiers.

Methods

As stated in the previous paragraph, the use of methods in the conditions of a query can make it difficult, if not impossible, to compile or evaluate the query using traditional approaches.

Database Statistics

As is the case in the relational model, database statistics, such as the number of tuples in a relation or the number of different values for each attribute, are helpful in query processing. In object-oriented databases, these statistics must be extended to include information, such as the number of instances in each class along the inheritance hierarchy and the number of pages containing such instances.

7.3 Cost Model

The cost model presented in this section is taken from Bertino and Foscoli (1992b). The model provides mathematical functions which determine the cost of the various types of traversal discussed in the sections above. Below, we refer to the concept *path*. A path is essentially a branch in a query graph and is thus a branch in an aggregation hierarchy, given that a query graph is part of the aggregation hierarchy originating in the target class of the query. More formally, a path is defined as follows:

Definition 7.4
Given an aggregation hierarchy H, a *path* P is defined as $C_1.A_1.A_2.....A_n$ $(n \geq 1)$ where

- C_1 is a class in H;
- A_1 is an attribute of class C_1;
- A_i is an attribute of class C_i in H, such that C_i is the domain of attribute A_{i-1} of class C_{i-1} $(1 < i \leq n)$.

And

- length$(P) = n$ denotes the length of the path;
- classes$(P) = C_1 \cup \{C_i / C_i$ is the domain of attribute A_{i-1} of class C_{i-1}, $1 < i \leq n\}$ denotes the set of classes along the path. The number of classes along the path is equal to the length of the path;
- dom(P) denotes class C, domain of attribute A_n of class C_n.

With reference to Figure 2.3 of Chapter 2, the following is an example of path P:

P_1 : Project.task.leader.name
length$(P_1) = 3$
classes$(P_1) = \{$Project, Task, Researcher$\}$
dom$(P_1) = $ STRING

7.3.1 Model Parameters

The model estimates the evaluation cost of a nested predicate denoted by a path. Therefore, it determines the cost of a sequence of implicit joins for the four types of basic strategies discussed in the preceding sections. The parameters of the model have been subdivided into four categories.

Logical data parameters

Given a path $P = C_1.A_1.A_2...A_n$, the following parameters describe the characteristics of the classes along the path. Most of the parameters introduced are needed accurately to model the topology of references between objects, which are instances of classes in the database.

- nc_i Number of classes in the inheritance hierarchy having class C_{i-1}, $1 \leq i \leq n$ as their root.
- D_{ij} Average number of distinct values for attribute A_i of class $C_{i,j}$, $1 \leq i \leq n$, $1 \leq j \leq nc_i$.
- D_i Average number of values for attribute A_i, evaluated with respect to all the members of class C_{i-1}, $1 \leq i \leq n$.
- $N_{i,j}$ Cardinality of class $C_{i,j}$, $1 \leq i \leq n$, $1 \leq j \leq nc_i$.

- Nh_i Cardinality of the set of members of class $C_{i,1}$, $1 \leq i \leq n$, $Nh_i = \sum_{j=1}^{nc_i} N_{i,j}$

- $fan_{i,j}$ Average number of references to members of class $C_{i+1,1}$ contained in attribute A_i of an instance of class $C_{i,j}$, $1 \leq i \leq n$ and $1 \leq j \leq nc_i$.

- fan_i Average number of references to members of class $C_{i+1,1}$ contained in attribute A_i of a member of class $C_{i,1}$, $1 \leq i \leq n$. The difference between this parameter and the one above is that this parameter is obtained as the average evaluated on all the instances of all the classes in the inheritance hierarchy with the root $C_{i,1}$, whereas in the parameter above the average is for each class.

- $d_{i,j}$ Average number of instances in class $C_{i,j}$, with a value other than the null value for attribute A_i, $1 \leq i \leq n$ and $1 \leq j \leq nc_i$.

- d_i Average number of members of class $C_{i,1}$ with a value other than the null value for attribute A_i, $1 \leq i \leq n$; $d_i = \sum_{j=1}^{nc_i} d_{i,j}$

- $k_{i,j}$ Average number of instances in class $C_{i,j}$, with the same value for attribute A_i, $1 \leq i \leq n$ and $1 \leq j \leq nc_i$; $k_{i,j} = \lceil (d_{i,j} * fan_{i,j})/D_{i,j} \rceil$

- kh_i Average number of members of class $C_{i,1}$ with the same value for attribute A_i, $1 \leq i \leq n$.

Physical Data Parameters

This category of parameters models certain physical aspects concerning the storage of instances of classes in a path.

- $P_{i,j}$ Number of pages of secondary storage for the instances of class $C_{i,j}$ for $1 \leq i \leq n$, $1 \leq j \leq nc_i$.

- Ph_i Number of pages of secondary storage for the members of class $C_{i,1}$ for $1 \leq i \leq n$.

- r_i Binary variable which assumes the value: equal to 1, if the members of the class $C_{i,1}$ have reverse references to the members of class $C_{i-1,1}$ in the path; equal to 0, if not, $2 \leq i \leq n$.

Query Parameters

- NI_i Number of members of class $C_{i,1}$ on which the nested predicate must be evaluated, $1 \leq i \leq n$.
  (Note that NI_i coincides with the number of members of class $C_{i,1}$ for queries containing a single nested predicate. For complex queries which contain Boolean combinations of predicates, the number of members of class $C_{i,1}$ on which the nested predicate is to

be evaluated may have been reduced with respect to the total number of members of the class, due to the evaluation of the other predicates.)

- AP_i Number of pages effectively accessed to find the members of class $C_{i,1}$ in order to evaluate the nested predicate, $1 \leq i \leq n$.

Derived parameters

Certain parameters which are derived from parameters in the preceding categories are used in the remainder of the discussion. The mathematical formulation of these parameters is given in Appendix B.

- *RefBy(i, s, y, k)* Average number of values contained in the nested attribute A_y for a set of k instances of class C_i whose position in the inheritance hierarchy is equal to s, $1 \leq i \leq y \leq n$.

- *RefByh(i, y, k)* Average number of values contained in the nested attribute A_y for a set of k members of class $C_{i,1}$, $1 \leq i \leq y \leq n$.

- $\overline{k}_{i,j}$ Average number of instances of class $C_{i,j}$ with the same value for the nested attribute A_n ($1 \leq i \leq n$, $1 \leq j \leq nc_i$)

- $\overline{kh}_i$ Average number of members of class $C_{i,1}$ with the same value for the nested attribute A_n ($1 \leq i \leq n$)

- *Ref(i, y, s, k)* Average number of instances of class $C_{i,s}$ with a value in a set of k elements, $1 \leq i \leq y \leq n$, as the value of the nested attribute $A_{y,}$.

- *Refh(i, y, k)* Average number of members of class $C_{i,1}$ with a value in a set of k elements, $1 \leq i \leq y \leq n$, as the value of the nested attribute A_y.

Assumptions

The cost model is formulated on the basis of certain assumptions which are typical of cost models for databases. It is assumed that the distributions of values of the various attributes are not correlated and that the values of each attribute are distributed uniformly. It is further assumed that the cardinality of the instances of a class is not correlated with the cardinality of the other classes belonging to the same inheritance hierarchy.

7.3.2 Cost Functions

The cost formulae below relate to the evaluation of a nested predicate of the form

$$C_1.A_1...A_n \ op \ \exp$$

where *op* is a relation operator for comparison and *exp* an expression. This predicate can be evaluated with a forward traversal, or a reverse traversal according to the execution strategies described in the previous sections. The costs presented below are expressed in terms of number of disk accesses.

The evaluation of the parameters D_i and kh_i depends on the type of distribution of the values of the attribute A_i, among the various classes of the inheritance hierarchy which have class $C_{i,1}$ $(1 \leq i \leq n)$ as their root. This distribution takes the form of one of two extremes: *disjunctive distribution* and *inclusive distribution*. In the former, each value of attribute A_i is used in a single class and the total number of different values is given the sum of the $D_{i,j}$s of all classes in the hierarchy; $D_i = \sum_{j=1}^{nci} D_{i,j}$.

For this distribution, the parameter kh_i is equal to the greater of all the $k_{i,j}$s of the classes in the hierarchy which have class $C_{i,1}$ as their root; therefore, $kh_i = \text{MAX}(k_{i,1},.....,k_{i,nc_i})$. In contrast, D_i assumes in the inclusive distribution the highest of the $D_{i,j}$s of the classes in the hierarchy which has $C_{i,1}$ as its root; therefore: $D_i = \text{MAX}(D_{i,1}.....,D_{i,nci})$. Moreover, the value of kh_i is given as the sum of the $k_{i,j}$s of all the classes in the hierarchy. Therefore: $D_i = \sum_{j=1}^{nci} k_{i,j}$

Forward Traversal

The nested-loop access strategy for accessing the instances in a class is considered first. The value of the parameter NI_1 is determined as follows:

- $NI_1 = N_{1,1}$ if class $C_{1,1}$ has no subclasses or the query only has $C_{1,1}$ as the target class
- $NI_1 = Nh_1$ if class $C_{1,1}$ has some subclasses and the query has all the classes in the inheritance hierarchy with the root $C_{1,1}$ as its target.

Note that queries with a single predicate are being considered here. If the queries contain Boolean combinations of predicates, then NI_1 can be replaced in the formulations above by a value S, which is less than $N_{1,1}$ or by Nh_1, depending on the order in which the predicates are evaluated. The parameter NI_k, $1 < k \leq n$ is determined as follows:

$$NI_k = \begin{cases} NI_{k-1} * fan_{k-1,1} & \text{if k = 2 and the query has } C_{1,1} \text{ as its target} \\ NI_{k-1} * fan_{k-1} & \text{otherwise} \end{cases}$$

Assume that the total number of instances accessed is equal to the number of pages; $AP_k = NI_k$ is obtained. The total cost is given by the following expression:

$$C = \sum_{k=1}^{n} AP_k$$

Let us now consider the sort-domain. The parameter NI_1 is determined as above whereas parameter NI_k, $1 < k \leq n$, is determined as follows:

$$NI_k = \begin{cases} D_{1,1} & \text{if } k = 2 \text{ and } C_{1,1} \text{ is the query's target} \\ D_1 & \text{if } k = 2 \text{ and the set of classes in the} \\ & \text{inheritance hierarchy with } C_{1,1} \text{ as} \\ & \text{its root is the query's target} \\ RefBy(1, 1, k - 1, NI_l) & \text{if } k > 2 \text{ and } C_{1,1} \text{ is the query's target} \\ RefByh(1, k - 1, NI_l) & \text{otherwise} \end{cases}$$

Assume that the instances of some classes are clustered. By applying the Yao function (Yao, 1977), we find that the number of pages AP_k, $1 \leq k \leq n$ containing a number NI_k of accessed objects is

$$APk = \begin{cases} H(NI_k, Ph_k, Nh_k) & \text{if } k > 1 \\ P_{k,1} & \text{if } k = 1 \text{ and the target of the query is } C_{1,1} \\ Ph_k & \text{otherwise} \end{cases}$$

If $NI_1 = S$ then the Yao function must also be applied to $k = 1$, since the number of pages accessed is less than $P_{1,1}$ or Ph_1. Thus, the total cost is represented by the following expression:

$$C = \sum_{k=2}^{n} \text{SORT}(NI_k) + \sum_{k=1}^{n} AP_k$$

The number of page accesses which is needed to sort a list of OIDs of instances can be determined in the following way. Let n be the number of OIDs on the list. Also, let s and d be the dimensions in terms of bytes of an OID and a page respectively. The number of page accesses to sort a list of OIDs with n elements is $D_p * (log_2 D_p)$ where D_p, the number of pages needed to store the list, is $(n/(d/s))$. It is assumed that a *two-way* sorting is executed.

Reverse Traversal

The nested-loop access strategy for accessing the instances of a class is considered first. The value of the parameter NI_n is determined as follows:

$$NI_n = Nh_n$$

In fact, all the instances of the classes with position n must initially be accessed. Thus, only those objects, which have the value of attribute A_n equal to the value given in the query, are considered in reverse traversal. The average number of accesses for these objects is kh_n, if the predicate in the query is an 'attribute=value' type, or $c * kh_n$, if the predicate is an 'attribute op value' type, where op $\in \{<, >, \leq, \geq\}$, and c is the cardinality of the set of values which satisfy the predicate and which can be contained in attribute A_n. Note that the same object can be accessed repeatedly in the nested-loop strategy. The value of the parameter NI_k, $1 \leq k \leq n{-}1$ is determined as follows:

$$NI_k = c * \prod_{j=k+1}^{n} kh_j * (r_k * V1_k + (1 - r_k) * V2_k)$$

where $V1_k$ and $V2_k$ are two auxiliary parameters whose value is given by the following expression:

$$V1_k = \begin{cases} k_{k,1} & \text{if } k = 1 \text{ and } C_{1,1} \text{ is the query's target} \\ kh_k & \text{otherwise} \end{cases}$$

$$V2_k = \begin{cases} N_{k,1} & \text{if } k = 1 \text{ and } C_{1,1} \text{ is the query's target} \\ Nh_k & \text{otherwise} \end{cases}$$

If the objects which are members of a class $C_{i,1}$ have reverse references of the members of the class which precedes $C_{i,1}$ in the path, not all the instances of the class in position $i - 1$ in the path need to be accessed.

The average number of pages accessed is equal to the number of objects accessed. Thus:

$$AP_k = NI_k$$

is obtained. The total cost is:

$$C = (1 - r_1) * AP_1 + \sum_{k=2}^{n} AP_k$$

If the members of class $C_{2,1}$ have reverse references of the members of class $C_{1,1}$, no instances of the class in position 1 in the path need to be accessed since the reverse references, which are OIDs, contained in the members of class $C_{2,1}$, are the solution to the query.

Now consider the sort-domain strategy. The parameter is NI_n as in the case above, whereas the parameter NI_k, $1 \leq k < n$, is given by the following expression:

$$NI_k = r_k * V3_k + (1 - r_k) * V2_k$$

where $V2_k$ is the auxiliary variable defined previously. $V3_k$ is determined as follows:

$$V3_k = \begin{cases} \overline{k}_{k,1} & \text{if } k = 1 \text{ and } C_{1,1} \text{ is the query target} \\ \overline{kh}_k & \text{otherwise} \end{cases}$$

The definition of $V3_k$ is valid for 'attribute = value' queries. However, if the predicate is based on a set of c values, then $Ref(k, 1, n, c)$ is replaced with $\overline{k}_{k,1}$ in the definition of $V3_k$, and $Refh(k, n, c)$ with $\overline{kh}_k$. Assuming that the instances of the same class are clustered, by applying the Yao function (Yao, 1977), the number of pages to be accessed for a given number of objects is obtained:

$$AP_k = r_k * H(NI_k, Ph_k, Nh_k) + (1 - r_k) * V4_k$$

where $V4_k$ is a binary variable whose value is given by the following expression:

$$V4_k = \begin{cases} P_{k,1} & \text{if } k = 1 \text{ and } C_{1,1} \text{ is the query's target} \\ Ph_k & \text{otherwise} \end{cases}$$

Therefore, the total cost is

$$C = (1 - r_1) * (AP_1 + \text{SORT}(NI_2)) + \sum_{k=2}^{n} AP_k + \sum_{k=3}^{n} \text{SORT}(NI_k)$$

7.4 Bibliographical Notes

The problem of optimization of object-oriented queries has not yet been very widely researched. One of the reasons for this is that the techniques developed for relational DBMS can be adapted to developing optimizers for OODBMS. Most OODBMS designers have adopted this approach. However, better results are achieved in query processing by using optimizers developed specifically for the object-oriented data model. This is the only way of ensuring that the best results are obtained, since the specific characteristics of this model are taken into account.

One of the first works to deal with the problem of optimization in object-oriented databases is an article by Kim *et al.* (1988), which covers optimization for ORION. The article makes an interesting comparison with techniques developed for relational and network databases. An article by

Jenq *et al.* (1990) extends optimization techniques for the distributed version of ORION. There are no articles on the optimization techniques used in other OODBMS. A recent article by Cluet and Delobel (1992) introduces the problem of optimization in O_2. An article by Bertino and Foscoli (1992b) presents cost formulae for the various types of traversals described above. The cost model is characterized by a set of parameters for accurately modelling different database 'topologies'; for example, the model considers null references and multiple-value attributes, as well as reverse references. Finally, an article by Gardarin and Lanzelotte (1992) describes an approach based on rewriting techniques. The various transformations executed on queries are checked by means of cost functions. However, the cost functions described in this article are based on a very small set of parameters, which means that database 'topology' cannot accurately be modelled.

8 Storage Management and Indexing Techniques

Performance is a basic requirement in any database management system. In an object-oriented database system it is influenced by a large number of factors, mainly stemming from the complexity of object-oriented data models (e.g. inheritance, complex objects). Thus, appropriate storage techniques for objects, as well as adequate indexing techniques, are needed to provide a good performance level.

In this chapter, after taking a brief look at storage and indexing techniques on relational DBMS, we shall discuss techniques for storing, indexing and clustering complex objects which have so far been proposed for OODBMS. In the final section of the chapter, we shall discuss another important aspect of performance, namely the choice of OID structure and the transformations to which these OIDs are subject when objects are transferred from mass storage to central storage and vice versa.

8.1 Storage Techniques for Relational DBMS

A disk is divided into a set of *partitions*, each consisting of a number of *segments*. Each segment consists of a number of *pages* or *blocks*. A specific portion of the disk, called the *header*, contains information including the number of partitions, the address and the size of each partition and a *log* for recovery in case of a system crash. Segments are described by tables in which page addresses for each segment are stored.

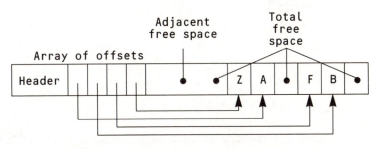

Figure 8.1 Organization of a page of storage.

Figure 8.1 shows the organization of a page which contains objects. Each page contains a *header* for holding information on the page, an array containing the offsets of the objects within the page and the objects themselves. An object offset can change when the object grows or when the page is compacted to make space for other objects (Kim, 1990).

In relational DBMS, records that represent the tuples of a relation are normally stored contiguously on the disk. If the attributes of the relation are fixed in length, these are stored within the corresponding record as adjacent fields, in which case the records of a relation can be stored in a single file.

For managing records of varying length, most relational DBMS store records directly on disk pages and simultaneously assign an identifier (ID) to each record. The structure chosen for IDs plays a significant role in the speed at which tuples can be retrieved. For example, in System R (Astrahan *et al.*, 1976), IDs consist of two parts:

(1) The high order bits in an ID identify the segment and the page of the file where the record is stored. Segments can be assigned to different portions of one or more files by means of a segment table. These bits provide a physical address and so the page containing a given record can be retrieved with one access to disk.

(2) The low order bits identify a record within a page. These bits are an index to a *slot* vector, which is stored at the start of a page (or in any fixed position), containing the addresses of the records within the pages.

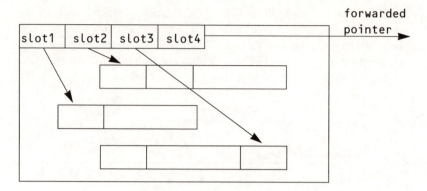

Figure 8.2   Addressing records with a slot vector.

Figure 8.2 shows the organization of a page where the address of the records on the page is contained in a slot vector.

This technique of identifying records has the following advantages:

- In terms of accesses to disk, this is as fast as a system which uses the complete address of the record (page and byte), but it allows to change the length of records and to relocate them either on the same or on different pages, since it is easy to change the element of the *slot* vector that corresponds to the record, by inserting in it the new address of the record.

- This is often faster than a system using a purely logical ID (called a surrogate ID). In fact, the use of a surrogate ID requires another addressing level, since a hash table has to be used – the table associates the physical addresses of records with surrogate IDs; consequently, one or more accesses to disk are required to scan the hash table.

8.2   Storage Techniques for Objects

Since an object-oriented database model is more complex than a relational database model, memory organization in OODBMS must be able efficiently to support:

- objects with both atomic and complex attributes;
- objects with multi-valued attributes, in which the attributes can, in turn, be either atomic or complex;
- objects with variant attributes;
- objects with 'long field' attributes.

The last requirement stems from the need to manipulate multimedia information, texts, images and voice, for example, which are essential in advanced applications such as the management of office documents.

Moreover, the efficiency of storage organization depends not only on the structure of objects and their relations, but also on the *way* in which the application programs access the objects, which shall be denoted as *access pattern* from here onwards.

Access patterns fall mainly into one of the following two categories:

- Access based on the whole object.
  This access pattern is appropriate for applications which execute complex manipulations of objects by means of specialized programs. In these cases the whole object is copied onto the application's virtual memory.

- Access based on the attributes of the object.
  This access pattern is used to retrieve attributes of objects placed at a given level along the aggregation hierarchy (see Chapter 7) and it is appropriate when large objects need to be accessed.

Storage techniques for OODBMS proposed up to date stay between two main approaches:

- the direct model;
- the normalized model.

In the direct model, objects are stored in the same way in which they are defined in the conceptual schema, that is, the unit of storage is the same as the semantic unit. More specifically, objects which belong to the same class are stored in the same file and each file record is an object instance of the class. The greatest advantage of this approach is that transferring of a whole object is a very efficient process, since join operations are not required to reconstruct objects which have been previously decomposed. The disadvantage consists of the fact that accesses to a set of attributes of an object can be very expensive, especially if the object has fields with large dimensions.

In the normalized model, the objects are decomposed into atomic components which are stored in different files. The relation between the various components is maintained by means of OIDs.

Generally speaking, an intermediate approach between these extremes can be adopted; complex objects are decomposed, but components are grouped together according to access patterns and the components that are accessed contemporaneously are stored in the same file. The problem with this approach is that its efficiency depends on having prior knowledge of the exact access pattern for applications.

The direct model of storage organization presented earlier is the simplest method of storing the attributes of objects and it is the same as the one used in relational DBMS. This is an efficient method, but suffers from a number of drawbacks in situations such as the following:

- When attributes of varying sizes have to be managed, for example, character strings of varying length, lists, sets and collections. In this case, it is better to use the normalized approach, storing the attribute as a separate object in a separate area; the object can be found by means of its OID.

- When new attributes have to be created, for example, if the schema is modified. In fact, if a space of a fixed size is reserved for the attributes of an object, new attributes cannot be added, unless an additional area at the end of the object has been reserved for this purpose.

- If the majority of attributes have the value null (these are known as *sparse attributes*). In fact, allocating a space of a fixed size for these attributes can be a waste of space.

In the latter two cases, that is, the creation of new attributes and of sparse attributes, a *property list* is used. A property list consists of a sequence of triples <*identifier, size, value*> for each attribute of the object. *Identifiers*, which should not be confused with OIDs, indicate which attribute of the object is stored. The *size* contains the number of bytes stored (which can be omitted for attributes of fixed size) and the *value* is the value (of varying size) of the attribute.

Property lists are particularly flexible. In fact, the same type of attribute can have values of different lengths in different objects, or the attributes can be stored in different physical locations, or not all the objects in the same class need necessarily have the same set of attributes. And property lists are useful even if there are sparse attributes, since attributes which have null values need not be stored. Space and time can thus be saved.

The main disadvantage of property lists is that, in order to retrieve or store the value of a given attribute, the whole property list needs to be scanned for the desired attribute to be found. Another disadvantage is that the representation format of property lists must be transformed to suit the representation format used by the application programming language.

The inheritance hierarchy is another factor influencing the way attributes are stored. In fact, if there is inheritance (single or multiple), not only must the attributes of a given class be stored, but also those of its superclass (or of its superclasses, if there is multiple inheritance).

In the case of single inheritance, the object can be stored by first storing the attributes of its father class and then those of its subclasses, respectively. This method of storing attributes, which is used alongside property lists discussed earlier, is suitable even for storing attributes of varying sizes. It should also be noted that, for fixed-sized attributes, the offset of a field in this form of representation is always the same, even for the field which represents the attribute of the subclass. This is due to the fact that the attributes of the subclass are concatenated to those of the superclass.

For OODBMS which support multiple inheritance, the storage technique described earlier cannot be used. In this case property lists can be used; or objects can be stored separately, each of them containing the fields associated with a superclass, and linked to one another.

Finally, as far as storing attributes of varying sizes and large attributes (images or text, for example) is concerned, these can be managed as attributes of varying sizes as illustrated earlier. This method of storage is combined with a *stream* or *demand-page* mechanism such that portions of the object can be transferred in increments to the central memory, instead of the whole object.

8.3 Clustering Techniques

The problem of *clustering* in database management systems focuses on 'partitioning' objects in the database and placing these partitions on disk. The aim is to reduce the number of I/O operations on disk necessary for retrieval.

Generally speaking, in order to define these clusters, both for relational DBMS and OODBMS, two main factors must be taken into consideration, namely the *structure of the objects* and the *access pattern* of applications. The latter can be defined in advance on the basis of the known characteristics of the applications involved, but it would also be useful to be able to analyse its evolution over time. In order to be able to do this, statistics could be gathered not only in respect of the frequency of access to 'individual' objects but also the frequency with which, when an object *a* is accessed, an object *b* is also accessed. However, gathering such statistics would involve additional high costs and large correlation matrices would be needed to store them.

Relational DBMS use two clustering techniques. The first involves storing the tuples of a relation in the same page segment on disk, on the basis of the value of an attribute or of a combination of attributes of a relation. The second technique is to store the tuples of more than one relation in the same segment, if the relations have one or more attributes in common and they have equal values. The system's performance is improved when there is a query requiring the execution of a join.

Clustering techniques for OODBMS, compared with relational DBMS, must take into consideration the existence of complex objects, as well as inheritance (single or multiple) and the presence of methods. The structure of a complex object can be represented as a hierarchy or a direct acyclic graph (DAG). Operations on such a structure are navigation through the OIDs and retrieval of ancestors and descendants of a given node.

A good clustering strategy involves placing the nodes of an aggregation hierarchy or of a DAG in a *linear clustering sequence*. The nodes in the aggregation hierarchy can be stored in depth-first order, so that all the descendant nodes of each node *p* in the hierarchy are stored immediately after *p*. This strategy is efficient if an object and all its descendants have to be retrieved. In (Kim, 1990), five basic options for clustering are explained.

The first two alternatives are the same as those presented earlier for relational databases.

The third alternative involves clustering all object instances of classes which belong to an aggregation hierarchy of classes. This strategy can be seen as a variation of the second option, in that it involves storing objects of different classes in adjacent positions in the memory.

The fourth clustering option consists of storing contiguously all the object instances of the classes belonging to the inheritance hierarchy of a given class.

The last clustering strategy is the result of a combination of the two previous strategies. It is an attempt to find a convenient arrangement for retrieving instances of any connected subgraph of the graph of the schema rooted in a particular class. In fact, a given class is, generally speaking, the root of an inheritance hierarchy and of an aggregation hierarchy of any given class.

The clustering strategies discussed above are *static*, in that once the cluster has been defined, this cannot be changed at *run-time*. This creates two potential problems:

(1) A static clustering schema does not take into consideration the dynamic evolution of objects (creation and deletion of objects). For example, in applications such as design databases, objects are updated frequently during the first stages of the design cycle. These updates can destroy the structure of the initial cluster. This may mean that the clustering structure has to be reorganized to maintain the performance level.

(2) Objects can be connected by means of several relations, which can generate aggregation hierarchies or independent DAGs. For example, in a design database, a design evolves through various stages, such as initial creation, checking of design rules, extraction of design parts and simulation. Design tools used in the various

stages may have access patterns which are not the same as those chosen for the initial definition of the cluster. Therefore, it is difficult for a unique clustering schema to be adequate for all the possible access patterns of the application, in which case it would be preferable to use a different clustering schema for each stage (Maier, 1989). Moreover, several users can access the same objects with different access patterns at the same time; thus the use of a clustering schema based on the requirements of an individual application (or of an individual class of users) can jeopardize the performance of other applications and user classes.

Also, many clustering techniques use the disk page as clustering units, the aim being to reduce the number of pages accesses required to retrieve a complex object. These techniques assume that each access to a page requires an I/O operation on disk and that the total access time is obtained by multiplying the number of pages accessed by the mean time of access to the page; but they do not take into account the effect of not having the pages adjacent to one another which may result in a non-uniform access time for the various pages. Moreover, these techniques group the objects together on the basis of a single access pattern.

8.3.1 Dynamic Clustering

With regard to the effects of the dynamic evolution of objects on a clustering schema, significant operations include the creation and deletion of objects. Whereas deletion may not be a problem, since deleted objects can be marked and the space made available to them can be reused later, when a new object is created, a new space must be allocated immediately on disk. Regardless of the clustering strategy used, it is unlikely that the sequence of creation of objects of the aggregation hierarchy would be the same as the desired clustering sequence. For example, objects could be created in a breadth-first sequence, whereas instead the clustering sequence chosen is depth-first; in this case the pages on which the objects are stored have to be 'connected' in order to maintain the validity of the desired clustering sequence. However, the pages will, in general, be *sparse*, that is, not adjacent to one another. This may have a considerable impact, since to retrieve a set of sparse pages from disk requires more time than would be required if the pages were adjacent to one another, because of the mechanical characteristics of disk drives. In fact, reading a block of data from disk involves seek, latency and transfer time. For a set of blocks stored in sequence, only one seek and one latency time are needed, whereas for access to n blocks stored randomly, a time equal to the sum of the seek time and the latency time for each block is required.

Reorganizing and recompacting pages in a cluster after modification operations is similar to the problem of reorganizing files. There are two types of file reorganization techniques; *on-line* (Soderlund, 1981; Omiecinsky, 1985) and *off-line* (Sockut, 1979; Batory, 1982). Optimal on-line reorganization is a NP-complete problem (Omiecinsky, 1985), whereas the problem with off-line reorganization involves determining the best point of reorganization, that is, the frequency with which this must be done. In Chen and Hurson (1991), an on-line reorganization technique is described which is based on the use of *chunks* (a set of pages stored adjacent to one another on disk) as the unit of allocation for clusters and a cost model is proposed for evaluating the gains and the overheads of on-line dynamic reorganization. The main result presented in the work is that the on-line dynamic reorganization is justified in cases where the ratio between the reading and writing operations is high, whereas, if the opposite is true, off-line reorganization is more suitable.

8.3.2 Clusterings for Multiple Relations

We have already seen that there can be several relationships between objects which result in different aggregation hierarchies and DATs. For example, in a database for CAD, one thinks of a set of objects constituting a configuration, or a version of a design. Because of the characteristics of the algorithms used in application programs such as CAD tools, certain relationships can be used more frequently than others. This situation can be represented in a direct graph, in which the nodes represent the objects and the arcs represent the relationships between objects. The different access patterns for the various relationships can be represented by giving a *weight* to the arcs, making those for the more frequently used relations heavier. In other words, an arc with a weight w which goes from a node a to a node b means that the conditional probability of accessing b, once a has been accessed, is given by w. In Chen and Hurson (1991), a clustering algorithm with levels is proposed. The algorithm arranges all the nodes of the graph in a linear sequence, where nodes connected by means of 'heavier' arcs are nearer than others. The results of simulation reported have shown that, in the case of the proposed clustering with levels, access time is around half that required for objects stored randomly.

8.4 Indexing Techniques for OODBMS

Indexing techniques for object-oriented databases must take the following factors into consideration:

- *Nested predicates*
  Because of objects' nested structures, most object-oriented query languages allow objects to be restricted by predicates on both nested and non-nested attributes of objects. Nested predicates are often expressed by means of *path-expressions*.

- *Inheritance*
  A query may apply only to a class or to a class and all to its subclasses.

- *Methods*
  Methods can be used in queries as *derived attribute methods* and as *predicate methods*. A derived attribute method has a function comparable to that of an attribute, in that it returns an object (or a value) to which comparisons can be applied. A predicate method returns the logical constants True or False. The value returned by a predicate method can therefore be used in the evaluation of a Boolean expression which determines whether or not the object satisfies the query.

In the remainder of the presentation, it is assumed that queries are made against classes. This assumption considers classes as having the extensional notion of the set of their instances. In several systems (for example GemStone and O_2), classes do not have their extensions associated. Therefore, instances of the same class are grouped by means of collections, or sets, and queries are made on them. The techniques and results presented in this chapter apply to cases in which the concept of class also denotes extensions. Their validity in cases where collections are used is a research area which has yet to be fully investigated.

In the following discussion, we shall also refer to the concepts of *aggregation graph, query graph, forward traversal* and *reverse traversal* which were described in previous chapters.

8.4.1 Indexing Techniques for Aggregation Hierarchies

In this section, we present various indexing techniques that support efficient evaluation of implicit joins along aggregation paths. We discuss, for each index organization, how read and update operations are carried out; moreover, some results taken from Bertino and Kim (1989) on the efficiency of the different index organizations are provided. We will refer to the schema shown in Figure 8.3 which is a variation on Figure 2.3 in Chapter 2 to make it easier to follow the subject which is being described.

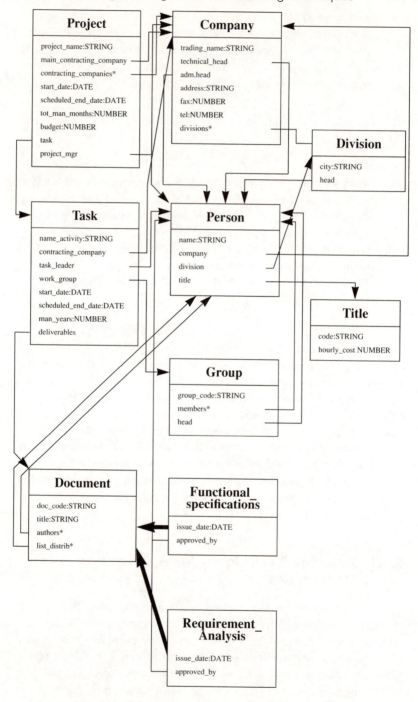

Figure 8.3 Example of a schema.

First, we introduce some preliminary definitions:

- *Path*: this is a branch in an aggregation hierarchy. It starts with a class C and ends with a nested attribute of C.
- *Path instantiation*: this is a sequence of objects obtained by instantiating the classes belonging to the path.
- *Nested index:* this is an index which establishes a direct connection between the object at the start of and the object at the end of the path instantiation. The index key is the object at the end of the path instantiation.
- *Path index*: This is an index which stores instantiations of a path (that is, sequences of objects). The index key is the object at the end of the path instantiation, as in the nested index.

Definition 8.1[1]
Given an aggregation hierarchy H, a *path* P is defined as $C_1.A_1.A_2.....A_n$ $(n \geq 1)$ where

- C_1 is a class in H;
- A_1 is an attribute of class C_1;
- A_i is an attribute of class C_i in H, such that C_i is the domain of the attribute A_{i-1} of class C_{i-1} $(1 < i \leq n)$.

And

- length(P) = n denotes the length of the path;
- classes(P) = $C_1 \cup \{C_i / C_i$ is the domain of attribute A_{i-1} of class $C_{i-1}, 1 < i \leq n\}$ denotes the set of classes along the path. The number of classes along the path is equal to the length of the path;
- dom(P) denotes class C, the domain of attribute A_n of class C_n.

With reference to Figure 8.3, the following is an example of path P:

- P_1 : Project.main_contracting_company.divisions.head.name
  length(P_1) = 4
  classes(P_1) = {Project, Company, Division, Person}
  dom(P_1) = STRING
- P_2: Person.division.city
  length(P_2) = 2
  classes(P_2) = {Project, Division}
  dom(P_2) = STRING

---

[1] This definition, already introduced in Chapter 7, is repeated here to make the explanation easier to follow.

- P_3: Project.main_contracting_company.divisions
length(P_3) = 2
classes(P_3) = {Project, Company}
dom(P_3) = Division

The classes along the path are ordered and the order is determined by the path definition itself. For example, in P_1, Project occupies position 1, Company occupies position 2, Division occupies position 3 and Person occupies position 4. In the discussion below, it is assumed that an OID consists of the class identifier and the identifier of the object within the class. For example, Project(i) denotes the ith instance of the class Project. Primitive objects (numbers, Boolean, characters, strings, for example) are identified by their value.

Definition 8.2
Given the path $P = C_1.A_1.A_2....A_n$, a *complete instantiation* of P is defined as a sequence of $n + 1$ objects, denoted as $O_1.O_2....O_{n+1}$, where:

- O_1 is an instance of class C_1;
- O_i is the value of the attribute A_{i-1} of object O_{i-1} (that is, $O_{i-1}.A_{i-1} = O_i$, or $O_i \in O_{i-1}.A_{i-1}$ if A_{i-1} is multi-valued) ($1 < i \le n + 1$).

The objects in Figure 8.4 represent (some) instances of some of the classes in the schema shown in Figure 8.3. Note that the multi-valued attributes are shown by a rectangle with its sides in bold type-face.

With reference to Figure 8.4, the following examples are complete instantiations of the path:

P_1 = Project.main_contracting_company.divisions.head.name
(classes(P_1) = {Project, Company, Division, Person}
dom(P_1) = STRING):

- Project[i].Company[k].Division[k].Person[x].Jones
- Project[j].Company[i].Division[h].Person[y].Smith

In practice, a complete path instantiation contains an instance of any of the classes which belong to the path and ends with an instance of the class which is the domain of the path. Note that the instances of a path need not necessarily end with primitive objects. The following is an example of an instantiation which does not end with a primitive object:

Project[i].Company[k].Division[k].

On the other hand, a partial instantiation is an instantiation starting with an object which is not an instance of the first class along the path, but

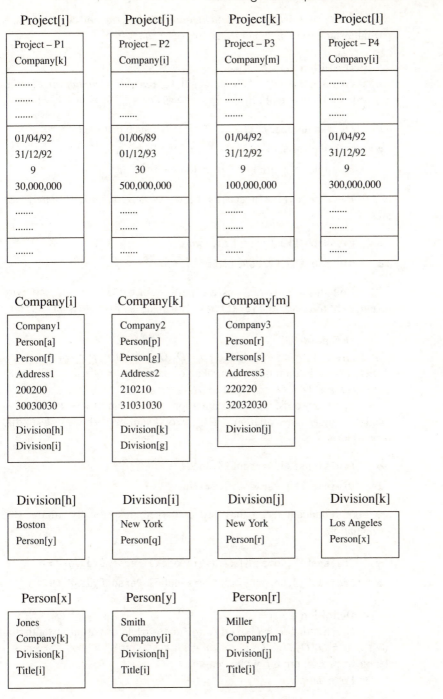

Figure 8.4 Instances of classes in a schema.

which is the instance of some other class of the path. In other words, a partial instantiation of a path P instantiates a *subpath* of P.

Definition 8.3

Given a path $P = C_1.A_1.A_2....A_n$ a *partial instantiation* of P is defined as a sequence of objects, denoted as $O_1.O_2....O_j$ $j < n + 1$, where:

- O_1 is an instance of class C_k in Class(P) such that $k + j - 1 = n + 1$;
- O_i is the value of attribute A_{i-1} of an object O_{i-1}, $1 < i \leq j$.

Examples of partial path instantiations

P_1 = Project.main_contracting_company.divisions.head.name

are:

- Divisions[k].Person[x].Jones
- Division[h].Person[y].Smith.

Both these instantiations are partial since they do not start with instances of the class `Project`, but with instances of the class `Division`.

Definition 8.4

Given a partial instantiation $p = O_1.O_2....O_j$ of P, p is *not redundant* if there are no instantiations (complete or partial) $p' = O'_1.O'_2....O'_k$ of P, $k > j$, such that $O_i = O'_{k-j+i}$ $(i = 1,....,j)$.

In other words, a path instantiation is redundant if it is contained in another longer instantiation. The two examples above of partial instantiations:

- Divisions[k].Person[x].Jones
- Division[h].Person[y].Smith.

are both redundant since they are contained, respectively, in the two instantiations:

- Project[i].Company[k].Division[k].Person[x].Jones
- Project[j].Company[i].Division[h].Person[y].Smith

Definition 8.5

Given a path $P = C_1.A_1.A_2....,A_n$, a complete or partial instantiation of it is $p = O_1.O_2.O_3....O_j$ $(j < = n + 1)$, $\pi_{<m>}(p) = O_1.O_2....O_m$ $m < j$ denotes a projection of p with a length m.

For example:

$\pi_{<2>}$ (Project[i].Company[k].Division[k].Person[x].Jones) = = Project[i].Company[k].

Multi-index

This organization (Maier and Stein, 1986) is based on the allocation of an index to each of the classes constituting the path. Therefore, given a path $P = C_1.A_1.A_2....A_n$ which crosses n classes $C_1 C_2....C_n$, a *multi-index* is defined as a set of n simple indices (called index components) $I_1, I_2,....I_n$ where I_i is an index defined on $C_i.A_i$, $1 \leq i \leq n$. All the indices $I_1, I_2,....I_{n-1}$ are *identity indices*, that is, they have OIDs as key values. The last index can be either an identity index or an *equality index*, depending on the domain of A_n. An equality index is an index whose key values are primitive objects, such as integers and characters. Operators including '=' (equal to), '~' (different from), ' < ', '$\leq$', '$\geq$' ' > ' can be applied to an equality index, whereas only the operators '==' and '~~' (not identical to) apply to an identity index.

Consider, for example, the path:

P = `Project.main_contracting_company.divisions.city.`

For this path, 3 indices will be allocated and the value of each is shown below. Remember that the value of each index is represented as a pair, whose first element is the key value and whose second element is the set of OIDs of the objects holding this key value for the indexed attribute.

- First index I_1 on Project.main_contracting_company
    - `(Company[k], {Project[i]}`
    - `(Company[i], {Project[j],Project[l]})`
    - `(Company[m], {Project[k]})`

- Second index I_2 on Company.divisions
    - `(Division[h], {Company[i]})`
    - `(Division[i], {Company[i]})`
    - `(Division[k], {Company[k]})`
    - `(Division[j], {Company[m]})`

- Third index I_3 on Division.city
    - `(Boston, {Division[h]})`
    - `(New York, {Division[i], Division[j]})`
    - `(Los Angeles, {Division[k]})`

Under this organization, solving a nested predicate requires scanning a number of indices equal to the length of the path. For example, in order to select all the projects with a main contracting company which has a division in Los Angeles, the following steps must be taken:

(1) Scanning index I_3 with the key-value = Los Angeles; the result is {Division[k]}

(2) Scanning index I_2 with the key-value = Division[k]; the result is {Company[k]}

(3) Scanning index I_1 with the key-value = Company[k]; the result is {Project [i]}, which is the result of the query.

Therefore, under this organization, the retrieval operation is performed by first scanning the last index allocated on the path. The results of the scan are used as keys for a search on the index preceding the last one in the path and so on until the first index is scanned. Thus, this organization only supports reverse traversal scanning strategies. The greatest advantage of this organization, compared with other organizations which will be described later, is the low updating cost.

Join Index

Join indices were introduced to perform joins in the relational model efficiently (Valduriez, 1987). They have also been efficiently used to implement complex objects.

Given two relations R and S and the attributes A and B belonging to R and S, respectively, a *binary join* index is defined as

$$BJI = \{(r_i, s_k) \mid f(\text{tuple } r_i.A, \text{tuple } s_k.B) \text{ is True}\}, \text{ where}$$

- f is a Boolean function which defines the join predicate;
- r_i denotes the surrogate of a tuple of R;
- s_k denotes the surrogate of a tuple of S;
- tuple r_i (tuple s_k) refers to the tuple which has r_i (s_k) as its surrogate.

An index *BJI* is implemented as a binary relation and two copies may be kept, one clustered on r and the other on s, respectively. Each pair is implemented as a $B+$ tree. In aggregation graphs, a *BJI* sequence can be used in a multi-index organization to implement the various index components along the given path. With reference to the path P in the example above, we would have, in this case:

- First binary join index BJI_1 on Project.main_contracting_company – copy clustered on OIDs of instances of Company

```
(Company[k], {Project[i]})
(Company[i], {Project[j],Project[l]})
(Company[m], {Project[k]})
```

– copy clustered on OIDs of instances of Project

```
(Project[i], {Company[k]})
(Project[j], {Company[i]})
(Project[l] {Company[i]})
(Project[k] {Company[m]})
```

- Second binary join index BJI_2 on Company.divisions
  – copy clustered on OIDs of instances of Division

```
(Division[h], {Company[i]})
(Division[i], {Company[i]})
(Division[k], {Company[k]})
(Division[j], {Company[m]})
```

  – copy clustered on OIDs of instances of Company

```
(Company[i], {Division[h]})
(Company[i], {Division[i]})
(Company[k], {Division[k]})
(Company[m], {Division[j]})
```

- Third binary join index BJI_3 on Division.city
  – copy clustered on OIDs of instances of Division

```
(Division[i], {New York})
(Division[h], {Boston})
(Division[j], {New York})
(Division[k], {Los Angeles})
```

  – copy clustered on OIDs (values) of instances of STRING

```
(Boston, {Division[h]})
(New York, {Division[i], Division[j]})
(Los Angeles, {Division[k]})
```

In a BJI-multi-index organization, both a forward traversal strategy and a reverse traversal strategy can be used to traverse the classes in the path if, for each BJI, both copies are allocated. Reverse traversal can be used to solve queries such as 'Select all projects which have a main contracting company with a division in New York'. Forward traversal is used when it is necessary to identify all objects referenced by a given object; for example: 'Determine the cities where divisions of the main contacting company of Project[i] are located'. Forward traversal can be executed by directly accessing the objects, since these store the references to other objects in their attributes. However, the use of *BJI* indices can result in a faster traversal in cases of costly accesses to objects (for example, where large objects are involved).

The use of the join index in the optimization of complex queries is discussed in (Valduriez, 1987a). The most significant conclusion drawn in the work referred to is that the most complex part of a query (that is, the joins) can be executed using join indices without having to access the database. However, there are cases where conventional indices (selection indices on join attributes) are more efficient, for example, when the query simply involves a join preceded by a high-selective selection. The major conclusion is that join indices are more suitable for complex queries, that is, queries involving several joins.

Nested Indices

When solving a nested predicate, both previous indexing techniques require to access a number of indices proportional to the path length. Other index organizations have been proposed which aim to reduce the number of indices to be accessed. The first of these organizations is the *nested index* (Bertino and Kim, 1989). This provides a direct association between an object of a class at the end of the path and the corresponding instance of the class at the beginning of the path. For example, in the case of the path:

P = `Project.Main_contracting_company.divisions.city.`

the nested index has the following values:

- `(Boston, {Project[j]})`
- `(New York, {Project[j], Project[k], Project[l]})`
- `(Los Angeles, {Project[i]})`

More formally, a nested index can be defined as follows:

Definition 8.6

Given a path $P = C_1.A_1.A_2....A_n$, a *nested index* on P is defined as a set of pairs (O, S) where:

$S = \{O'$ such that there is $O_1.O_2.......O_{n+1}$, a complete instantiation of P where $O' = O_1$ and $O = O_{n+1}\}$.

The first element of the pair (O, S) is the key of the index.

In the definition above, the equality between non-primitive objects is based on object identity (Khoshafian and Copeland, 1986), whereas equality between primitive objects is based on value. Note that, in the case that primitive objects also have an identifier (OID), the user can choose between indices based on identity (Maier and Stein, 1986) and indices based on value. The difference between the two types of index is that an index based on identity contains object identifiers as key values, whereas in the other case, the keys are constituted by the values of primitive objects. It should also be noted that, except for the difference in operators which can be applied, the organization of the indices remains the same in both cases. In this index organization, retrieval is quite fast, since a query, for example, 'Select all the projects of a main contracting company which has a division with head office in New York' is resolved by scanning only one index. The most important problem with this index technique concerns update operations which require several objects to be accessed, in order to determine which index entries must be updated. For example, assume that we want to remove Division [h] from the set of divisions of the Company [i]. To execute this update operation, the following steps must be taken:

(1) Access Division[h] and determine the value of the 'city' attribute. The result is: New York.

(2) Determine all Project instances which have Company[i] as main_contracting_company; the result is: Project[j], Project[l].

(3) Remove {Project[j], Project[l]} from the index entry with the key value 'New York'; after this operation, the index entry is (New York, {Project[k]}).

As can be seen from the above example, both the forward traversal and the reverse traversal of objects are required for an update operation. The forward traversal is required to determine the value of the indexed attribute (that is, the value of the attribute at the end of the path) for the modified object. The reverse traversal is necessary for determining all instances at the beginning of the path. Reverse traversal is very expensive when there are no inverse references between the objects. In such cases, it may not be possible to use the nested index.

Path Index

A path index (Bertino and Kim, 1989) is based on a single index, like the nested index. It can be defined more precisely as follows:

Definition 8.7

Given a path $P = C_1.A_1.A_2....A_n$, a *path index* on P is defined as a set of pairs (O, S) where:

$S = \{\pi_{<j-1>}(p_i)$ such that:

(1) $p_i = O_1.O_2....O_j (1 \le j \le n + 1)$ is a complete instantiation or a partial non-redundant instantiation of P;

(2) $O_j = O\}$

For example, in the case of the path:

P = Project.main_contracting_company.divisions.city

the path index has the following values:

- (Boston, {Project[j].Company[i].Division[h]})
- (New York, {Project[j].Company[i].Division[i], Project[k].Company[m].Division[j], Project[l].Company[i].Division[i]})
- Los Angeles, {Project[i].Company[k].Division[k]})

Therefore, a path index differs from a nested index in that, given a key value, all the path instantiations, whether complete or partial, which end with the key, are stored in the index, whereas in a nested index, only objects at the beginning of the complete path instantiation are stored.

It should also be noted that nested indices and path indices are identical (and are the same as normal indices, used in most relational DBMS), when $n = 1$, that is, when the attribute on which they are defined is not nested.

A further difference between nested indices and path indices is that the latter can be used directly to solve nested predicates in all classes along the path, whereas this is not possible for a nested index.

Updates of a path index are expensive, as forward traversals are required, like in the case of nested indices. However, a reverse traversal is not necessary. Thus, path indices can be used even when there are no inverse references between the objects in the path.

Access Relations

Access relations (Kemper and Moerkotte, 1990) are organizations very similar to path indices, in that they consist of calculating all instantiations along a path and storing them in a relation. With reference to path P, used as an example, the access relation will contain the following tuple:

```
< Project[i], Company[k], Division[k], Los Angeles >
< Project[j], Company[i], Division[h], Boston >
< Project[j], Company[i], Division[i], New York >
< Project[k], Company[m], Division[j], New York >
< Project[l], Company[i], Division[h], Boston >
< Project[l], Company[i], Division[i], New York >
```

A path can also be split into several subpaths and different access relations can be allocated for each subpath. Likewise, incomplete path instantiations can be stored using null values in the relations.

8.4.2 Index Structures and Operations

The data structure used to model the various index organizations is the binary tree *B+tree* (Bayer and McCreight, 1972; Comer, 1979). The structure of the internal nodes is the same both for nested indices and for path indices. An internal node consists of f records, where each record is a triple < *key-length, key, pointer* >. The pointer contains the address of the next node in the index. The format of leaf nodes is, however, different in the two organizations. A record of a leaf node in a nested index consists of:

- record-length;
- key-length;
- key-value;
- number of elements of the list of OIDs associated with the key;
- list of OIDs.

Assume that the list of OIDs is ordered. Assume also that, when the size of the record exceeds the size of the page, a small directory will be kept at the beginning of the record. This directory contains, for each page containing the record, the address of the page and the identifier of the greatest value contained in the page. When an OID is deleted or added to that record, the page which has to be modified can be directly identified. A record of a leaf node in a path index consists of:

- record-length;
- key-length;
- key-value;
- number of elements of the path instantiations associated with the key;
- list of path instantiations.

The structure of this record is shown in Figure 8.5.

Each path instantiation is implemented by a an array having the same length as the path. The first element of the array is the OID of an instance of class C_1, the second element is the OID of the instance of class C_2 referred by attribute A_1 of the instance identified by the first element of the array and so on.

Now let us examine the operations which can be executed with the two index organizations discussed, in order to evaluate their cost.

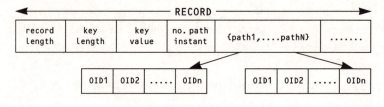

Figure 8.5   Leaf node in a path index.

Nested Index

Consider queries first. Given a path $P = C_1.A_1.A_2....A_n$ and a nested index defined on this, to evaluate a predicate against a nested attribute A_n of class C_1, a single index must be scanned. Therefore, the cost of solving a nested predicate is equivalent to the cost of solving the predicate on a simple attribute of C_1.

Now, consider an update operation applied to an object O_i, an instance of a class C_i belonging to Class(P) where $P = C_1.A_1.A_2....A_n$. Now assume that attribute A_i of object O_i has the object O'_{i+1} as value and that O_i is modified, so that a new object O'_{i+1} is assigned to attribute A_i. In order to execute this operation, a reverse traversal is executed on the path starting from object O_i to determine the identifiers of the instances of class C_1 which contain a direct or an indirect reference to object O_i. The structure which implements the index can then be modified.

Generally speaking, to update a nested index after a modification, the path must be forward traversed twice and reverse traversed once. If O_i is the modified object, then the forward traversal has the length $l_f = n - i$, where n is the length of the path. The reverse traversal has the length $l_r = i - 2$ if $i > 2$, $l_r = 0$ if $i \leq 2$. If objects do not contain reverse references, a nested index organization cannot be used.

Insertion and removal operations are similar to modification operations, except that only one forward traversal operation is required.

Path Index

Given a path $P = C_1.A_1.A_2.....A_n$ and a path index defined on this, in order to solve a predicate against the nested attribute A_n of a class C_i, $1 \leq i \leq n$, only one index needs to be scanned. Once the path instantiations associated with the value of the key have been determined, the OIDs occupying the i-th position of each array are extracted. However, note that it may be necessary to access more leaf nodes in respect of the corresponding nested index, due to redundancy of records in a path index.

To analyze modification operations, we consider the previous case, that is when an object O_i, $1 \leq i \leq n$, instance of class C_i belonging to

Class(P) is modified by replacing O_{i+1}, the value of A_i, with a new object O'_{i+1}. In order to make the change, two forward traversal operations are required, as for nested indices. However, unlike the nested index, a path index does not require a reverse traversal operation, since the complete path instantiations are stored in the leaf nodes. Therefore, as we have already seen, this organization can be used even if the objects do not contain reverse references.

8.4.3 Comparison of Index Organizations

In this section, we give a brief presentation of the results, taken from Bertino and Kim (1989), of a comparative evaluation between the various index organizations discussed earlier. For an in-depth discussion, see Bertino and Kim (1989).

An important parameter in evaluating an index organization is the *degree of reference sharing*. Two objects share a reference when they refer to the same object and this parameter models the topology of references between objects.

The major results of the analysis presented in Bertino and Kim (1989) can be summarized as follows. For retrieval, the nested index has the lowest cost; the path index has, in general, a lower cost than the multi-index. Note that the nested index has a better performance than the path index in retrieval, because the path index contains the OIDs of instances of all the classes along a path, whereas the nested index contains only the OIDs of instances of the first class in the path. Furthermore, a single path index allows predicates to be solved for all the classes along a path, whereas a nested index does not. In updating operations, the multi-index has the lowest cost. For paths with a length 2, the nested index has a slightly lower cost than the path index. For paths with a length greater than 2, the nested index involves a slightly lower cost than the path index if the updates are executed on the first two classes in a path. In other cases, the nested index involves a significantly higher cost than the path index. However, note that the update costs for the nested index have been calculated on the basis of the assumption that there are reverse references between the objects. Otherwise, update operations for the nested index become very much more expensive.

For paths with a length greater than 2, intermediate solutions can be based on splitting a path into shorter subpaths and on allocating a nested index, path index or a simple index on each of the subpaths.

An algorithm determining an optimal index configuration on paths was proposed in Bertino (1991a). The algorithm receives as input the frequency of retrieve, insert and delete operations for the classes along the path. Moreover, it also takes into account whether reverse references exist between objects, as well as logical or physical data characteristics. The algorithm determines the optimal way of splitting a path into subpaths and the index organization to be used for each subpath (including the option of not allocating any index). An interesting result obtained with this algorithm is that, when the degrees of reference sharing along a path are very low (that is, close to 1), and reverse references between objects are allocated, the best index configuration is one which allocates no index on the path. This result shows how reverse references between objects can be an access technique which in some situations can be used as an alternative to indices.

8.4.4 Indexing Techniques for Inheritance Hierarchies

As has been discussed earlier (see Chapter 3), object-oriented query languages offer the option to declare whether the scope of a query is only a given class C, or the class C and the inheritance hierarchy rooted in class C. Since a given attribute of C is inherited into all its subclasses, the first issue concerns how to evaluate efficiently a predicate against such an attribute, when the scope of the query is the inheritance graph rooted in C.

A solution, based on conventional indexing techniques, requires to construct an index on such an attribute for each of the classes of the subgraph and then to scan all these indices and to perform the union of their results.

In Kim *et al.* (1989b), a different approach was proposed, known as the *inherited index*, which directly supports queries against an inheritance subgraph. This approach consists of maintaining one index on the common attributes for all classes of the inheritance graph. Therefore, an index entry contains the identifiers of the instances of all the classes in the hierarchy. As described in Kim *et al.* (1989b), a leaf node on an inherited index has a different format than a traditional non-inherited index. A leaf node of an inherited index contains: the value of the key, a key directory and, for each class in the inheritance graph, the number of elements in the list of OIDs for instances of this class that hold the key value of the indexed attribute and the list of OIDs. The key directory contains one entry for each class which has instances with the key value of the indexed attribute.

Figure 8.6 shows the format of a leaf node in an inherited index.

Thus, an inherited index allows to obtain, with a single index look-up, all the instances which satisfy the predicate for which the index is used, but it does not prevent the evaluation of queries having as scope only one or some of the classes included in the index. In fact, this simply requires to access the index, and then to scan the key directory for the pointers to the instances of the class to be retrieved.

In general, an inherited index is more efficient for all queries whose access scope involves a significant subset of classes belonging to the

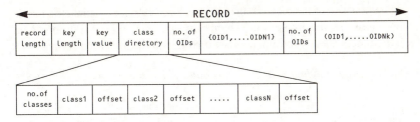

Figure 8.6   Leaf node in an inherited index.

inheritance graph, whereas a non-inherited index is more efficient for queries against a single class. The results from a quantitative evaluation of the performance of these indexing techniques are given in Kim et al. (1989b). The distribution of key-values across the classes in the inheritance graph has proved to be an important parameter in this evaluation. Generally speaking, if each key-value is taken from instances of one class *C* only (called disjoint distribution), an inherited index is less efficient than a non-inherited index. On the other hand, if each key-value is taken from the instances of several classes, the inherited index may perform better. The most important conclusion from the work of Kim *et al.* (1989b), is that, for predicates with a single key, an inherited index is more efficient than a non-inherited index, in cases where the query involves at least 2 classes of the inheritance graph. For 'range-key' predicates, an inherited index is more efficient if the query involves at least three classes.

8.4.5 Precomputing and Caching

The indexing techniques presented thus far are based on the structure of objects, that is, on their attributes. Another possibility (Breitl *et al.*, 1989) is to define indices on the basis of the behaviour of objects, that is, on results of methods. Techniques based on this approach have been proposed in Bertino and Quarati (1992), Bertino (1991b), Jhingram (1991) and Kemper *et al.* (1991). Most of these techniques are based on precomputing (caching) the results of method invocation. These results are stored in an index or another access structure, so that queries containing method invocations can be efficiently evaluated. A major issue of this approach is how to detect when the computed method results are no longer valid. In order to do this, in most of the approaches proposed, *dependency information* is kept. This keeps track of which objects, and, possibly, which attributes of objects, have been used to compute a given method. When an object is modified, all the precomputed results of the methods which have used this object are invalidated. Various solutions have been proposed for the problem of dependency information, also in terms of the characteristics of the method. In Kemper *et al.* (1991), a special structure is proposed which is implemented by means of a relation. In this proposal, an item of dependency information is a record with the following format:

$$< oid_i, method-name, < oid_1, oid_2, ..., oid_k >>.$$

This record keeps track of the fact that the object identified by oid_i was used to compute the method *method–name* with input parameters $< oid_1, oid_2, ..., oid_k >$. The input parameters also include the identifier of the object to which the message invoking the method was sent. A more sophisticated approach is proposed in Bertino and Quarati (1992) and Bertino (1991b). If a method is *local*, that is, if it uses only the attributes of the object upon which it was invoked, all the dependency information will be stored in the object itself. This information is coded in the form of bit-strings, resulting in a minimum overhead. If the method is not local, that is, if this uses attributes of other objects, all the dependency information is stored in a special object. All the objects whose attributes have been used in the precomputation of a method have a reference to this special object. The main advantage of this approach, compared with the one proposed in Kemper *et al.* (1991), is that this allows for greater flexibility in allocating and clustering objects. For example, a 'special object' may be clustered together with one of the objects used in the precomputation of the method, depending on the expected update frequency. In order further to reduce the need for invalidation, it is important to determine the attributes that are actually used in the precomputation of a method. Two basic approaches can be identified. The first approach is called *static* and is based on inspecting the method implementation. Therefore, for each method, the system keeps the list of attributes used in this method. In this way, when an attribute is modified, the system has only to invalidate a method if this uses the modified attribute. Note, however, that an inspection of method implementations actually determines *all* attributes that can possibly be used when the method is executed. Depending on the method execution flow, some attributes may never be used in computing a method on a given object. This problem is solved by the *dynamic approach*. Under this approach, the attributes used by a method are actually determined only when the method is precomputed. Therefore, the same method precomputed on different objects may use different sets of attributes for each one of these objects.

8.5   Object Identifiers

It should be recalled that OIDs are used both by application programs for referencing objects and for representing relations between objects. The choice of the type of representation of OIDs can also influence the performance of an OODBMS.

OIDs can be represented in different ways (for a review of the different approaches proposed, see Khoshafian and Copeland (1986).

An OID can be physical or logical. The former contains the actual address of the object, whereas the latter is an index from which the address of the object is obtained.

Different approaches have been proposed for the representation of both physical and logical OIDs, thereby producing at least four types of OID.

- *Physical address*
  The OID is the physical address of the object. This representation, normally used by programming languages, has the advantage of being very efficient, but it is rarely used in OODBMS since, if a given object is moved or deleted, all the objects containing its OID must be modified.

- *Structured address*
  The OID consists of two parts – the first contains the segment number and the page number, thus making it possible to obtain quickly the address on the disk to be read, whereas the second part contains a logical slot number, which is used to determine the position of the object within the page. With this representation, the object can be relocated within the page simply by changing the slot array, or it can be moved to another page by inserting its forward address in the slot array.

- *Surrogate*
  The OID is generated by using an algorithm which guarantees its uniqueness (for example, the time and date, or a monotonically increasing counter). Surrogate OIDs are then transformed into the object's physical addresses, normally by using an index.

- *Typed surrogates*
  A variant of the surrogate for representing OIDs involves having both a type identifier (type ID) and a portion of the object identifier. A different counter generates the object identifier portion for each type. Thus, the address space is segmented. Moreover, the type identifier in the object's OID allows to determine the object type without retrieving the object from the disk.

As we have already seen, the choice of representation of OIDs can be a critical factor in determining performance, since an object is retrieved by its OID.

It is possible to retrieve an object which has a structured type OID with a single page access. In the worst case, a structured OID requires two disk reads to retrieve the object. This second case arises when the object has been moved to another page (for example, if the object had become too large). And, depending on how references to objects are implemented, all references to the relocated object can be identified and they can be made to point directly to the new page, thus avoiding the need for the second page look-up. This technique is used in ONTOS, Objectivity/DB and other OODBMS.

Surrogate OIDs are not very efficient in object retrieval. In fact, these are often transformed into an address by means of a hash function. However, in the best case, a well-balanced hash function which uses the pages themselves as buckets of the hash function enables most of the objects to be retrieved with a single disk access. Surrogate OIDs are used in GemStone and POSTGRES.

Typed surrogate OIDs, for example those used in ORION and ITASCA, allow a performance level similar to that of surrogate OIDs. However, it should be noted that having a type identifier in an OID makes it more difficult to change the type of an object.

Another factor which affects performance is the length of the OIDs. OIDs with a length ranging between 32 and 48 bits can have a significant effect on the overall size of a database, above all when the database contains a large number of interrelated complex objects. Whereas, with 32 bit long OIDs, up to 4 thousand million objects can be managed, 64 bit long OIDs are needed in the following situations:

- When OIDs must be unique for the entire life of the object, so that dangling references can be identified. This is the case in systems where it is not feasible to find all references to an object.

- When OIDs are represented by means of surrogates generated by a monotonically increasing function, it is not feasible to reuse OIDs which have already been generated and are no longer used ('holes').

- In a distributed environment where OIDs must be unique. In this case, it may be necessary to prefix the OID with a machine or database identifier.

8.6   Swizzling

As we have already seen, OIDs are used to represent references between objects. In many implementations, OIDs are converted into memory addresses, when the objects are retrieved from disk and transferred to the central memory. This transformation, known as *swizzling*, is executed to increase the speed at which one can 'navigate' between objects using OIDs and it can be applied to the various OID representations.

The advantage of swizzling is the increased speed with which references can be navigated between objects. In fact, addressing the central memory is often faster than scanning OIDs. Moreover, if the working set of objects can be contained in virtual memory, object access speed will be comparable to the speed at which programming languages access data structures.

Furthermore, it should be noted that transforming OIDs into memory addresses and vice versa is a costly process and that the advantages of faster navigation between objects may not be justified by the cost of swizzling. In Moss (1990), an analytical model is proposed for evaluating the conditions under which swizzling is appropriate. The principal result indicates that, rather than using swizzling, it would be better to use tables which map OIDs to object memory addresses (as in Objectivity/DB), when objects have a high probability of being swapped out from main memory and when the references are not used a significant number of times. Swizzling is often used in combination with an object storage approach called disk imaging. In this approach the main memory address is physically written over the field of the object which contains the OID. This over-writing operation is usually possible, since an OID is often longer than a central memory address. However, it should be noted that, when an object that has been modified has to be written back to disk, all the 'swizzled' OIDs which are contained in the object must be identified and transformed back into OIDs. As to when to execute swizzling, the following approaches can be followed:

(1)   The first time an application retrieves an object from disk.

(2)   The first time a reference has to be 'followed'.

(3)   Under application request, by an explicit call to the OODBMS at run-time.

It may also be possible (as in ObjectStore) to maintain the OIDs in the swizzled format. In particular, ObjectStore assigns database objects to fixed addresses in adjacent segments of virtual memory, when the objects are created. When a segment of objects is brought into main memory, ObjectStore tries to 'map' the objects to the same virtual memory addresses. If this is not possible, the objects on the page (and the references to these) are transformed again, so that they can be placed in another virtual memory address.

In general, none of the methods presented above is better than any of the others and it is thus appropriate to use more than one method, especially if the application can give some 'hints' as to when to use swizzling. Swizzling on application demand clearly requires a further programming effort, whereas swizzling when the object is in the central memory may not be the best solution in cases where objects are not frequently referenced. Finally, keeping references in a swizzled format at all times limits the total number of objects in the database to the maximum size of the virtual memory.

8.7 Bibliographical Notes

Storage techniques for storing complex objects are dealt with in a chapter of the book by Cattell (1991), which also discusses in detail representations of OIDs and swizzling techniques. The latter are also addressed in the work of Moss (1990); the paper discusses options for representing OIDs in a memory cache and describes an analytical model to determine the number of references to objects required to justify the additional cost of transforming OIDs into pointers.

Clustering techniques are dealt with in an article by Banerjee *et al.* (1988a), which discusses linear clustering sequences and the efficiency of operations executed on these, an article by Kim *et al.* (1987a) which discusses the impact of the size of the objects, compared with the size of the page, on clustering efficiency and finally an article by Chen (1991) which discusses dynamic clustering and proposes a clustering algorithm with levels for multiple clustering. In addition, there is the work by Benzaken (1990) (within the context of the O_2 project), which proposes a clustering strategy which also considers the presence of methods and, consequently, page faults which can be caused by the execution of methods. The work referred to proposes an algorithm for the automatic derivation of optimal clustering and the corresponding cost model.

Most of the articles which discuss indexing techniques for object-oriented databases address the issue only in relation to aggregation hierarchies or inheritance hierarchies. The articles by Bertino and Kim (1989) present specific techniques for evaluating nested predicates along aggregation hierarchies and introduce the concepts of nested index and path index. The articles by Kemper and Moerkotte (1990) describe a relational structure which is very similar to the path index described in Bertino and Kim (1989). The use of the techniques described by Bertino and Kim (1989) and by Kemper and Moerkotte (1990) have also been discussed in the context of queries containing Boolean combinations of predicates. The articles by Bertino (1990) present some results for nested index; results for path index are presented in the articles by Bertino and Guglielmina (1992a, 1992b); results for access relations are presented in the article by Kemper and Moerkotte (1990a). The article by Kim *et al.* (Kim 1989b) discusses in-depth indexing techniques for inheritance, and presents an evaluation based on the simulation of two different index organizations. Finally, a recent article by Bertino and Foscoli (1992a) describes an integrated organization which can solve a nested predicate against a set of classes in an inheritance hierarchy. This organization integrates the functionalities of a path index (Bertino and Kim, 1989) and of an inherited index (Kim et al., 1989b).

Finally, articles by Bertino and Quarati (1992) and Kemper *et al.* (1991) describe techniques for an efficient evaluation of methods when invoked by queries. The approaches described in the two articles differ in that, in the former, (Bertino and Quarati 1992), the result of method precomputation is stored in those objects upon which methods are invoked, whereas in the latter (Kemper *et al.*, 1991), a separate structure is used.

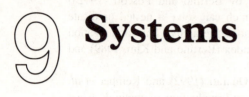

Systems

In this chapter, we describe briefly some of the systems currently available as commercial products, completed prototypes, or prototypes still under development. Aspects of some of these systems have already been discussed in previous chapters. In this chapter, we summarise the characteristics of some of the systems and describe their general architecture. This is not an exhaustive summary. We will describe those systems which, in our opinion, are the most complete or the most interesting, from the point of view of the solutions they propose, even though they may be at proposal or partial prototype stage. For each of the systems, we will present the significant characteristics from the viewpoint of their language and data models, as well as their most important operational characteristics. As for architecture, almost all the systems we shall be covering are based on the client-server approach, with the server usually supporting the DBMS functions. Almost all the systems have interactive environments and tools based on graphic interfaces to facilitate user interaction. The systems described include GemStone, Iris, ObjectStore, O_2, ORION, and Vbase.

9.1   GemStone

The GemStone system (Maier and Stein, 1986; Breitl *et al.*, 1989) was developed by Servio Logic Development Corporation with the aim to provide a DBMS characterized by a very powerful data model, and, hence, to reduce the time required for developing complex applications. The system is based on the Smalltalk-80 environment, extending it to include the functions of DBMS environments. It has a distributed architecture, and consists of a set of IBM-PC and/or Smalltalk-80 workstations and of an Object Server, implemented on the VAX/VMS file system, connected through a local network (Figure 9.1).

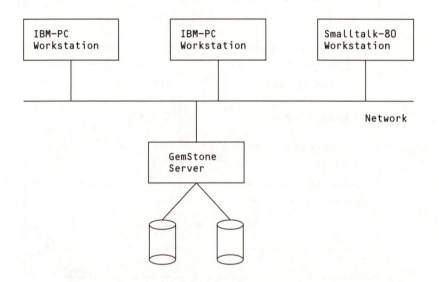

Figure 9.1   GemStone Systems Architecture.

The Server is also currently available for UNIX environments. The GemStone model is almost completely identical to the Smalltalk-80 model, and is based on concepts of object, class and message. Classes are organized into hierarchies with single inheritance. Applications can be written in the following languages: OPAL, C, C++ and PASCAL. OPAL is an extension of Smalltalk-80. It is used to define and manipulate data (DDL/DML), as the language for general computations and as the System Command Language. The OPE (OPAL Programming Environment) is a set of Microsoft Windows compatible applications, which include (see Figure 9.2):

- A Class Browser, which enables the user to inspect, add to and/or modify definitions of GemStone classes.
- A Bulk Loader/Dumper, with which the user can transfer formatted data (records of fixed length) between PC files and the GemStone server.
- A Workspace Editor, with which the user can create, edit and execute OPAL expressions.

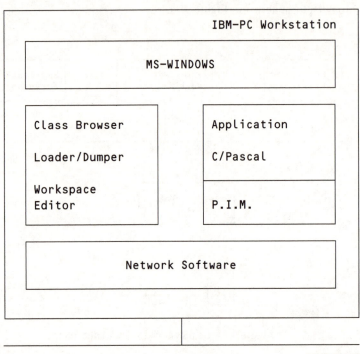

Figure 9.2   GemStone Client Architecture.

In order to support applications written in a procedural language, the system provides object modules which can be called from C, C++ and PASCAL, called PIM (Procedural Interface Modules), which the user 'latches on' to the applications which he/she executes on the PC. These modules implement remote procedure calls to the function provided by the GemStone Server.

In the (centralized) Server, the following two components can be identified (Figure 9.3):

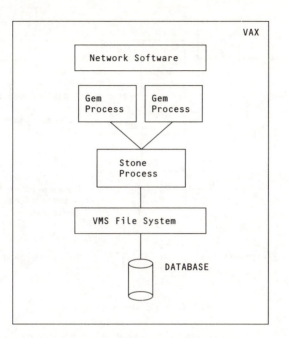

Figure 9.3   GemStone Server Architecture.

- Gem implements the object memory and the standard Smalltalk 'virtual machine'. Gem compiles and executes methods written in OPAL and it manages session control and authentication.

- Stone supplies the management of secondary storage, concurrency control, authorizations, transactions, crash recovery, and support for associative access. It also manages work areas associated with sessions.

9.2   Iris

The Iris system (Fishman *et al.*, 1989) was developed at the Hewlett-Packard laboratories. The current prototype is implemented in C language on HP-9000/320 UNIX workstation. The system is proposed specifically for supporting applications for office systems, knowledge bases and hardware and software design. Figure 9.4 shows the general architecture of the system. The data model is based on the concepts of object, type and function. A type in Iris is the equivalent to a class, since a type is defined as a collection – which has a name – of objects. The types are organized in hierarchies with multiple inheritance. In the model, there is no distinction between attributes and methods, since both are seen as functions. A function is a computation defined on a type. Therefore, this function can be

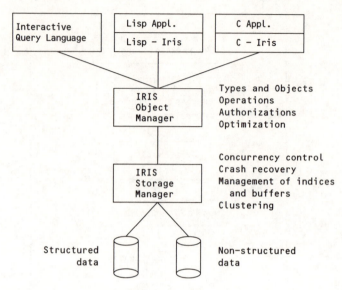

Figure 9.4 Iris Systems Architecture.

applied to all the instances of the type. A fundamental difference between the Iris data model and other object-oriented models is that the functions do not, in fact, 'belong' to the types. For the sake of simplicity, the functions defined on a single type are grouped together with that type when the schema is defined.

The functions which define the attributes of a type are thus associated with that type. However, functions can be specified which are defined in relation to several types and which are not, therefore, associated with a single type. All functions defined in relation to a type are inherited by their subtypes (as is the case with attributes and methods of classes). Inherited functions can be overridden. Therefore, the definition of a function inherited from a supertype can be redefined in a subtype, so the two types have a function with the same name but with different definitions.

The system can be accessed by means of both interactive and programming interfaces. The system provides an object-oriented SQL (OSQL) extension and an extension of the LISP 'structure browser' (called Iris Inspector) as the interactive interfaces and front-ends for the C languages, and LISP as programming interfaces. All interfaces are based on a set of C subroutines which implement the object manager interface.

The architecture consists of:

- An object manager which implements the Iris object-oriented model, providing support for the definition and manipulation of schema and query management.

- A secondary storage manager currently implemented on a relational manager, the HP DBMS All-base (similar to R System's RSS) (Astrahan *et al.*, 1976). This supports transactions, with save points and rollback to save points, concurrency control, filing and index management. Research is being carried out into extensions for supporting long transactions and multimedia data.

9.3 ObjectStore

ObjectStore was designed to simplify conversion of existing applications and for application areas such as interactive modelling, computer-aided analysis and design. One of the system's specific objectives has been to provide high performance levels. In order to achieve this, an architecture based on virtual memory with page-fault was adopted. Essentially, when an application refers to data which are not in the main memory, a page-fault occurs. ObjectStore intercepts the page-fault and loads the segment of the database containing the required data into main memory. It should be noted that this solution means that the system is highly portable since an interaction is required with the 'lower' layers of the operating system.

ObjectStore is based on a client/server architecture. The clients are high-level PCs and workstations, whereas the server can support different architectures on the same network.

The system consists of:

- ObjectStore DBMS
- ObjectStore run-time
- Schema Designer/Browser
- a DML built as a C++ preprocessor

ObjectStore is accessible by programs written in C and C++ with an interface library, whereas no direct support is provided for SQL. ObjectStore is currently available on Sun-3, Sun-4 and Sparcstation platforms.

9.4 O_2

O_2 (Deux *et al.*, 1990) is a system which was developed by the Altair consortium. The current system was implemented in C with some components developed in a dialect of LISP on Sun workstations. The system is based on a client/server architecture. The O_2 database model is quite flexible. For example, not only objects, but also complex values can be defined; the latter by using constructors, lists, tuples and sets. Class instances can be given additional methods and attributes. This means that objects with 'exceptional' behaviours with respect to the class to which they belong are available. The language provided for implementing methods is CO_2, an extension of C with constructs belonging to the O_2 object-oriented model. Persistence of objects in O_2 is orthogonal to the mechanism of classes. The instances of a class are not necessarily persistent. Conversely, complex values can be transformed into persistent values. Applications can be programmed in both CO_2 and Basic O_2. The latter is an extension of the Basic language and includes O_2's primitives.

The system's architecture, shown in Figure 9.5, is organized on three levels:

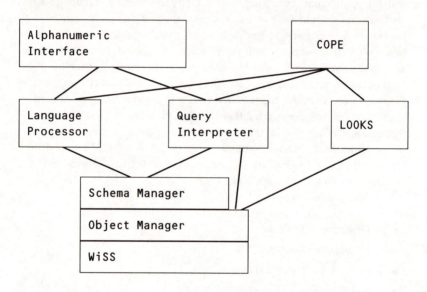

Figure 9.5 O_2 System Architecture.

- The highest level is the Schema Manager level. Functions provided by this level include creation, access, modification and deletion of classes, methods and global names. The schema manager is also responsible for controlling the consistency of the schema and for checking subtyping rules on inheritance hierarchies.

- The intermediate level is the Object Manager level. This component manages objects and complex values irrespective of their persistence. The object manager supports message exchange and client/server configuration. Moreover, it implements all functions relating to persistence, garbage collection, access mechanisms, such as indices, and clustering. Finally, it provides all functions for transaction management.

- The lowest level is the WiSS level (Wisconsin Storage Subsystem (Chou *et al.*, 1985)), which manages secondary storage. WiSS provides functions for persistence, disk management and concurrency control for records (it is the responsibility of the object manager to 'translate' complex objects into WiSS records).

In addition to these levels, O_2 provides a number of environments and tools for the user:

- The Language Processor manages all language instructions for data definition and program compilation.
- The Query Processor manages all query functions.
- The interface generation environment (LOOKS) provides a number of tools for developing and managing database interfaces. LOOKS supplies all the primitives for evaluating objects and values in the user interface and manages the interactions of these with the object manager.
- The programming environment (OOPE) provides a number of tools for application development. It uses the services provided by LOOKS for managing interfaces.
- The Alphanumeric interface provides direct access to the system's various languages, without the need to use graphic tools.

9.5   ORION

The ORION system was designed and developed within the framework of the Advanced Computer Architecture program at the Microelectronics and Computer Corporation (MCC). Advanced functions for applications including CAD and CAM, AI, and information systems were also developed. ORION has been used to provide persistence to the Proteus expert system which was developed in the same research program (Ballou *et al.*, 1988). Some of the more advanced functions supplied by ORION include version support and change notification, dynamic evolution of schemas, composite objects and multimedia data support.

The first version of ORION was a single-user system, implemented in Common LISP (Steele, 1984) on a Symbolic 3600 LISP machine, and subsequently ported on Sun under the UNIX operating system. Figure 9.6 shows the system's architecture:

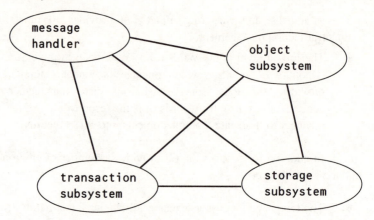

Figure 9.6 ORION System Architecture.

- The Message Handler module is responsible for handling all messages sent to the ORION system. These messages are used for invoking methods defined by the user, methods defined by the system and also access methods. Access methods are for searching for, or modifying the values of attributes. The system's methods provide all functions for data management, such as schema definitions, creation and deletion of instances, and transaction management.

- The Object Subsystem module provides the highest level of functions, for example, schema modifications, version control, query optimization and multimedia information management.

- The Storage Subsystem provides the management of objects on disk. It manages the allocation and deallocation of segment pages on disk, determines the location of objects in pages and transfers pages from disk to main memory and vice versa. It also supports index mechanisms to increase efficiency of query processing.

- Finally, the Transaction Subsystem provides all functions for transaction management, including concurrency control and crash recovery.

The second version of ORION is multi-user and is characterized by a distributed architecture. Two types of database are identified in distributed architecture; a public database, which is shared by several users and several private databases. The public database can be distributed on several nodes in the local network. However, applications do not see the distribution of the public database, as this is performed only for reasons of efficiency, load balancing and node capacity. A private database is owned by a user and can only be accessed by this user. The user can retrieve data from the public database and store it in his own private database, and vice versa – using check-in and check-out operations. Consequently, applications see the distinction between the private and public databases.

9.6   Vbase

The Vbase system (Andrews and Harris, 1987), developed at Ontologic Inc, is an object-oriented development environment which combines an object-oriented procedural language with persistent object management. It is currently implemented on the Sun OS 3.2 UNIX system. Figure 9.7 shows the system's logical architecture. The Vbase database model is based on the concept of Abstract Data Types. The classes are organized in a direct acyclic graph, supported by multiple inheritance. The system provides two interface languages:

- TDL (Type Definition Language). This is a proprietary language used to specify the database schema. It is used to describe both the structure of data and operations identified on such data. The TDL is a block-structured language which performs type checking of programs at compile time, so that increased efficiency is achieved at run-time. However, if type checking cannot be executed at compile time, it is executed at run-time so that the same expressive capacities of an object-oriented system with dynamic type checking are achieved.

- The COP (C Object Processor) is a strict superset of C and is used both for writing the code which implements operations identified in schemas, and for writing the applications programs. Moreover, all programs that can be compiled in C can also be compiled in COP.

The system also provides a mechanism for managing exceptions. Anomalous situations arising during the execution of an operation result in an exception and the transfer of control to predetermined procedures for managing them. Exceptions are typed, so that the user can define a hierarchy of exceptions to manage anomalous situations which can be refined gradually. Finally, the system provides a number of tools for application development: a debugger, an interactive object editor and a program which checks the consistency of the physical structure of the object space.

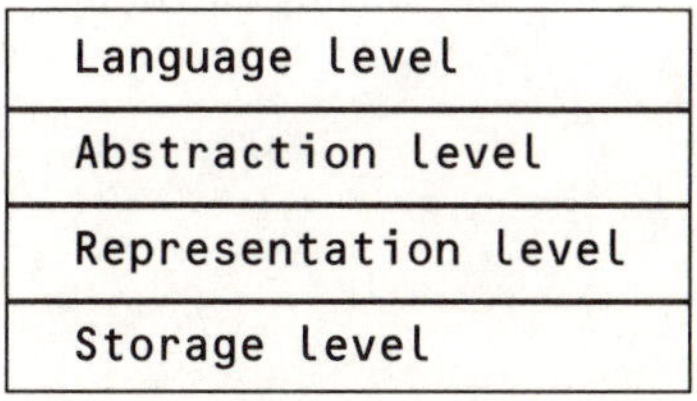

Language level
Abstraction level
Representation level
Storage level

Figure 9.7   VBASE Systems Architecture.

The system provides the following DBMS functions:

- Clustering a set of objects in the secondary storage and in the main memory.

- Defining the inverse of a given attribute. This means automatically modifying the inverse of an attribute whenever the attribute is modified.

- Customizing access to an attribute, by replacing the standard operations (set and get) which are defined by the system. For example, the user can read and write a bitmap using a compression algorithm.

9.7   Bibliographical Notes

Some introductory aspects of the architecture of OODBMS are described in a book by Cattell (1991) and in an article by Joseph et al. (1991). A recent article by Cattell and Skeen (1992) presents a benchmark used to compare the respective performance of relational DBMS and of OODBMS. The benchmark considers operations including the traversal of aggregation hierarchies between objects and access to an object, given its OID.

The architectures of the systems described in this chapter are dealt with in various articles. An article by Purdy et al. (1987) and a more recent article by Breitl et al. (1989) describe the architecture of the GemStone system. Certain issues relating to querying and indexing techniques are discussed in Maier and Stein (1986). The architecture of the O_2 system is described in an article written by all the designers of the system (Deux et al., 1990). An article by Fishman et al. (1989) and a more recent article by Wilkinson et al. (1990) describe the architecture of the Iris system. The architecture of the ORION is described in many articles including one by Kim et al. (1989a), which provides an overview of the various characteristics of the system, an article by Kim et al. (1989b) which discusses certain aspects of the system's performance and a more recent article by Kim et al. (1991) which describes various aspects of the distributed version of the system. Finally, an article by Andrews and Harris (1987) describes the architecture of the Vbase system.

Definition of Covariance and Contravariance

We give here a definition of relationships, established by America (1990) within the framework of the POOL language. The purpose of this definition of subtype is to ensure the property of substitutability, that is that an instance of a subtype can be replaced in any context in which an instance of the supertype can legally be used. This definition specifies rules of variance and contravariance that are often used in the definition of type systems.

A type τ is a subtype of a type σ if:

(1)   The properties of σ are a subset of those of τ.

(2)   For each method m_σ of σ, there is a corresponding method m_τ of τ, such that

(a) m_σ and m_τ have the same name.

(b) m_σ and m_τ have the same number of arguments.

(c)   The i-th argument type of m_σ is a subtype of the i-th argument type of m_τ (*rule of contravariance in arguments*).

(d)   Both m_σ and m_τ have a result, or neither of the two have a result.

(e)   If there is a result, then the type of the result of m_τ is a subtype of the type of the result of m_σ (*rule of covariance in results*).

The use of rules of contravariance in arguments and of variance in the result is due to the requirement that an instance of the type τ must be able to respond, without causing type errors, to all invocations of methods to which an instance of the type σ responds. Consider the following example. Assume that τ and σ are two types, both with a method with the name m. Assume also that the signatures of the two methods in the two types are defined as follows:

$$\sigma\, m(t_i) \rightarrow t$$
$$\tau\, m(t_j) \rightarrow t'$$

Consider the following fragment of a program which contains the declarations of three variables, s, v_i and v_j, respectively, of the type σ, t_i and t, and a method invocation:

$$...s : \sigma$$
$$v_i : t_i$$
$$v : t$$
$$...v = s \leftarrow m(t_i)...$$

The last statement in the program assigns the result of the invocation of method m to the variable v. For the property substitutability to be valid, it must be possible to assign an instance of a subtype of σ to s, without this causing type errors. Suppose that, at run-time, an instance of τ is assigned to s. Since the method look-up mechanism determines which method is to be executed dynamically (because of the property of late binding) on the basis of the class of the receiver, the method executed for the invocation $s \leftarrow m(t_i)$ is, when executed, in fact the method defined in τ. This method expects the input of an argument of type t_j, but instead, while execution is happening, it receives an argument of type t_i. To prevent type errors during the execution of the method m defined in τ, it must be ensured that for all the operations that can be executed on an object of type t_j can be executed on an object of type t_i. This condition is met if t_i is a subtype of t_j. This example demonstrates why the rule of contravariance in arguments is necessary.

The method m defined in τ returns an object of type t' once the method has been executed. The object is assigned to a variable which is of type t. To ensure that there are no type errors in the relevant statements after its assignment to the variable, all operations that can be executed on an object of type t should be able to be executed on an object of type t'. This condition is met if t' is a subtype of t. This example demonstrates why the rule of covariance in the result is necessary.

APPENDIX 2

Formulation of Derived Parameters for the Cost Model

The first parameter to be evaluated is $RefBy(i, s, y, k)$ $(0 \leq i \leq y \leq n,$ $1 \leq s \leq nc_i$ and $1 \leq k \leq D_y)$ which denotes the average number of values contained in the nested attribute A_y for a set of k instances of class $C_{i,s}$. It should be recalled that the average number of members of the class $C_{i,1}$ $(i > 1)$ referred to by at least one member of the class $C_{i-1,1}$ is given by the parameter D_{i-1}. Similarly, the average number of members of the class $C_{i,1}$ $(i > 1)$ referred to by at least one instance of class $C_{i-1, j}$, is given by the parameter $D_{i-1, j}$. The probability P_{A_i} that an object O_i, a member of the class $C_{i,1}$, has a value other than null as the value of attribute A_i is:

$$P_{A_i} = \frac{d_i}{Nh_i}$$

We now determine the probability that, given an object O_i, which is the instance of the class $C_{i,j}$, none of the $fan_{i, j}$ which are references contained in attribute A_i points to a given object O_{i+1}, which is a member of class $C_{i+1,1}$. This probability is obtained by first determining the number of possible subsets of $fan_{i,j}$ elements of a set containing a number $D_{i,j}$ of objects, which are members of class $C_{i+1,1}$. The number of possible subsets is given by the binomial coefficient:

$$\binom{D_{i,j}}{fan_{i,j}} = \frac{D_{i,j}!}{fan_{i,j}! * (D_{i,j} - fan_{i, j})!}$$

Therefore, the probability that a given object O_{i+1}, which is a member of class $C_{i+1,1}$ and which belongs to the domain (with a cardinality $D_{i,j}$) of definition of attribute A_i, is not pointed to by a given instance of class $C_{i,j}$ is:

$$\frac{\left(\begin{array}{c} D_{i,j} - 1 \\ fan_{i,j} \end{array}\right)}{\left(\begin{array}{c} D_{i,j} \\ fan_{i,j} \end{array}\right)} = \frac{D_{i,j} - fan_{i,j}}{D_{i,j}} = 1 - \frac{fan_{i,j}}{D_{i,j}}$$

By extending the above derivation the following is obtained; if $k_{i,j} > 1$, the probability that O_{i+1} is not pointed to by any object belonging to the set of instances of class $C_{i,j}$ a set of references $\{O^1_{i,j}, O^2_{i,j}, ..., O^k_{i,j}\}$, which has as the value of attribute A_i is:

$$Pr(i, j, k) = \left(1 - \frac{fan_{i,j}}{D_{i,j}} \right)^k$$

If $k_{i,j} = 1$, the above formulation is obtained as a probability without repetitions. Thus:

$$Pr'(i, j, k) = \prod_{y=0}^{k-1} \left(1 - \frac{fan_{i,j}}{D_{i,j} - y * fan_{i,j}} \right)$$

The above formulation is based on the observation that, when $k_{i,j} = 1$, any object among those belonging to the set of $D_{i,j}$ elements is pointed to by one object only. Therefore, given an instance of class $C_{i,j}$, the objects pointed to by that instance must be considered only once, and, after they have been considered, they must be removed from the set of $D_{i,j}$ elements. Thus, we have:

$$RefBy(i, s, y, k) = \begin{cases} \begin{array}{l} D_{i,s} * (1 - v(i, s) * Pr(i, s, k) - \\ (1 - v(i, s)) * (Pr'(i, s, k)) \end{array} & \text{if } y = i \\[2em] \begin{array}{l} D_y * (1 - v(i, s) * Pr(i, s, E'(i, s, y - 1, k)) - \\ (1 - v(i, s)) * (Pr'(i, s, E'(i, s, y - 1, k))) \end{array} & \text{if } y > i \end{cases}$$

where

$$v(i, s) = \begin{cases} 1 & \text{if } k_{i,s} > 1 \\ 0 & \text{if not} \end{cases}$$

where

$$E'(i, s, y, k) = RefBy(i, s, y, k) * P_{A_y}$$

The parameter $RefByh(i, y, k)$ is evaluated using a similar approach. This parameter represents the average number of values contained in the nested attribute A_y for a set of k members of the inheritance hierarchy in the n-th position in the path. The formulation $RefByh(i, y, k)$ is obtained by replacing D_i with $D_{i,j}$, kh_i with $k_{i,j}$ and fan_i with $fan_{i,j}$ in the expression $RefByh(i, y, k)$.

For the formulations $\bar{k}_{i,j}$ and $\overline{kh}_i$, two other parameters must be derived; $Ref(i, j, y, k)$ and $Refh(i, y, k)$. These parameters represent, respectively, the average number of instances of class $C_{i,j}$ which have a value in a set of k elements ($1 \leq i \leq y \leq n$ and $1 \leq j \leq nc_i$) as the value of the nested attribute A_y, and the average number of members of class $C_{i,1}$ which have a value in a set of k elements ($1 \leq i \leq y \leq n$) as the value of the nested attribute A_y. The formulation of these parameters follows the same approach as the formulation of the parameters $RefBy(i, j, y, k)$ and $RefByh(i, y, k)$ and is omitted for the sake of brevity. It should be noted that the parameters k and d replace, respectively, fan and D. A detailed description of the formulations of these parameters is given in Bertino and Foscoli (1991). The following is therefore obtained; $\bar{k}_{i,j} = Ref(i, j, n, 1)$ whereas $\overline{kh}_i = RefByh(i, n, 1)$, $a \leq i \leq n$ and $1 \leq j \leq nc_i$.

SUMMARY

Conclusions and Future Developments

Various aspects of OODBMS have been dealt with in this book. An attempt has been made to show how the conventional functions of a DBMS – such as authorization and access structures – are supported in an OODBMS, as well as describing new functions which are not available in conventional DBMS – such as version management mechanisms. Another aim was to highlight those areas which, in our opinion, are still open to research.

It can be seen from the whole of the book that OODBMS are, technologically speaking, highly sophisticated since they supply the functional capability of both programming languages and DBMS and also have additional functions including version management mechanisms and various types of evolution. Obviously, OODBMS technology has not yet reached a degree of maturity comparable with that of the current relational DBMS. The reasons for this are the increased complexity of the database model as well as the fact that more functions are supplied. Moreover, little research has been carried out in a number of areas, especially OODBMS architecture. It has taken a decade of research and development to bring relational database technology to its current level. One can envisage OODBMS reaching a comparable degree of maturity towards the end of the 1990's.

The future of OODBMS technology in industry is clearly an important issue and, as discussed in Cattell (1991), a variety of scenarios can be outlined. One possibility is that conventional DBMS will continue to be used in conventional managerial and administrative applications, whereas OODBMS will be used for new applications, including those discussed in Chapter 1. Another possibility is that systems will be developed which will succeed in efficiently supporting both conventional and advanced applications. However, developing such systems would appear to be somewhat difficult and is, undoubtedly, a long way off. For example, a system of this kind would have to support efficiently both very large volumes of short-duration transactions (as is the case in many managerial and administrative applications) and long cooperative transactions (as is the case in design applications). Moreover, this type of system would undoubtedly be very complex to use. The former is thus the most probable short-term scenario, with different data management systems being used for different applications, but with the possibility of using gateways for transferring data from one system to another, when required.

There are still many aspects of OODBMS which have yet to be investigated. Some of them have been highlighted in this book: the formal definition of the object-oriented database model and the corresponding query and manipulation languages, the definition of integrity constraints and the determination of efficient query processing strategies when methods are invoked in queries. There are also other areas of research which were not discussed in the preceding chapters but which are of great interest.

Integration Between the Object-Oriented Paradigm and Logic Programming

This trend is of considerable interest today, both from an academic and an industrial point of view. Generally speaking, current OODBMS are characterized by the fact that the behaviour of objects is defined by means of methods, expressed in imperative languages. Logic programming, on the other hand, provides a high-level declarative language, characterized by formal semantics. However, one significant limitation of logic programming is that it does not provide adequate structuring and modularization mechanisms. One can anticipate the integration of these two paradigms which would produce highly declarative database languages and systems and at the same time they would be characterized by structuring and modularization mechanisms, including classes, aggregation and inheritance hierarchies. Some proposals along these lines are discussed in Cacace *et al.* (1990) and Bertino and Montesi (1992).

Logical and Physical Design

OODBMS are a very much more complex systems to use than relational DBMS. This difficulty is due to the greater complexity of the model and the greater number of available options which the user has for modelling a given entity of the application domain and for carrying out specific operations. Such complexity can result in increased number of problems encountered in the process of designing databases. However, it should be noted that the logical design of an object-oriented database is simplified because, in contrast with relational DBMS, there is no need first to define a conceptual schema and then translate it into the DBMS model. In fact, the object-oriented model is of a sufficiently high level that it can be used to model the schema of the database directly from user requirements. This removes the distinction, which applies to conventional methodologies, between conceptual schemas and logical schemas. Thus, the user requirements can be 'executed' quite quickly. Moreover, since, in some OODBMS, even complex modifications to schemas are possible, the schemas can be used, tested and modified 'in the field'. Obviously, this simplification of the logical design process goes hand in hand with the problem of designing methods. This problem has been experienced to a lesser degree in relational DBMS, since the design of the database has essentially involved the structuring of data. However, in order to design methods, it would have to be possible to use approaches which have been proposed in software engineering (in particular, object-oriented methods), combined with the use of visual programming techniques.

As to physical design, few proposals have so far been made. The problem is more complex than in the case of relational DBMS and there are various reasons for this. First of all, OODBMS support various types of access – in particular, access to a single object by means of navigation and access to sets of objects by means of query languages. This means it is difficult, if not impossible, to obtain an optimum physical design for both access methods. Moreover, a wider spectrum of indexing techniques has been proposed – and some of these have been implemented – for OODBMS. For example, the ORION system provides both normal indices and indices allocated on inheritance hierarchies. The problem of allocating indices must be looked at again, since it must be determined on which classes the indices are to be allocated and also which type of index is to be used for each class.

Distribution and Parallelism

The various OODBMS described in previous chapters are based on client-server type architectures and distribution is therefore principally of the functional type. In these systems, the server is centralized, but there can be multiple clients. One interesting option is to make the server distributed. This would take advantage of potential parallelism and would inherit all the advantages provided by distributed database management systems. Problems connected with distributed management of objects have not been widely researched, although they have recently generated a certain amount of interest.

Integration of Dissimilar Systems

The problem of integrating databases which are different to one another is always very pressing, since it crops up time and again in many applications. The more conventional approaches to this problem are based on techniques of translating schemas between models and on identifying and solving semantic conflicts, in cases where schemas are semantically different. The use of an object-approach for integration has also recently begun to emerge. See, for example, the approach proposed in Bertino *et al.* 1989. In fact, the object-oriented paradigm itself, due to the encapsulation, appears to be the most natural approach for solving those problems of integration which have remained unresolved by more traditional approaches. As discussed in Bertino *et al.* (1989), the object-oriented approach appears the most suitable when one wants to integrate non-conventional type of data, such as images and texts, or when the schema of the data to be integrated is not visible, in public databanks, for example. There is considerable interest in the integration of heterogeneous systems using the object-oriented approach.

References

Abiteboul, S. and Bidoit, N. (1984). Non first normal form relations to represent hierarchically organized data. In *Proc. ACM Symposium on Principles of Database Systems*, Waterloo, Canada, March 1984

Abiteboul, S. and Beeri, C. (1988). *On the power of languages for manipulation of complex object*. INRIA Res. Report N.846. Inst. Nat. de Recherche en Informatique et en Automatique, Le Chesnay Cedex, France

Ahad, R. *et al.* (1992). Supporting access control in an object-oriented database language. In *Proc. 3rd International Conference on Extending Data Base Technology* (EDBT), Vienna, Austria, March 1992

Ahmed, S., Wong, A., Sriram, D. and Logcher, R. (1991). *A comparison of object-oriented database management systems for engineering applications*. IESL-MIT Technical Report No.IESL-90-03, 91-03, Cambridge MA

Albano, A. and Orsini, R. (1985). *Basi di Dati*. Torino: Boringhieri

Albano, A., Cardelli, L. and Orsini, R. (1985). Galileo: a strongly typed interactive conceptual language. *ACM Trans. on Database Systems*, 10(2), 230-260

Albano, A., Ghelli, G. and Orsini, R. (1991) A relationship mechanism for a strongly typed object-oriented database programming language. In *Proc. of 17th International Conference on Very Large Databases (VLDB)*, Barcelona, Spain, August 1991

Alasqhur *et al.* (1989). OOQL: a query language for manipulating object-oriented databases. In *Proc. of 15th International Conference on Very Large Databases (VLDB)*, Amsterdam, Holland, August 1989

Altair – INRIA (1989). *The O_2 Programmer's Manual*, Prototype Version 1.0, December 1989

America, P. (1990). A parallel object-oriented language with inheritance and subtyping. In *Proc. of International Conference on Object-Oriented Programming Systems, Languages, and Applications (OOPSLA) and European Conference on Object-Oriented Programming (ECOOP)*, Ottawa, Canada, October 1990

America, P. (1991) A behavioural approach to subtyping in object-oriented programming languages. In *Inheritance Hierarchies in Knowledge Representation and Programming Languages* (Lenzerini, M., Nardi, D. and Simi, M., eds.), New York, Wiley

Andrews, T. and Harris, C. (1987). Combining language and database advances in an object-oriented development environment. In *Proc. 2nd International Conference on Object-Oriented Programming Systems, Languages, and Applications (OOPSLA)*, Orlando FL, October 1987

Astrahan, M. *et al.* (1976). System R: a relational approach to database management. *ACM Trans. on Database Systems*, 1(2), 97-137

Atkinson, M., Bancilhon, F., DeWitt, D., Dittrich., K., Maier, D. and Zdonik, S. (1989) The object-oriented database system manifesto. In *Proc. of 1st International Conference on Deductive and Object-Oriented Databases (DOOD)*, Kyoto, Japan, December 1989

Atzeni, P., Batini, C. and De Antonellis, V. (1985). La Teoria Basi di Dati, Turin, Italy: Boringhieri

Ballou, N. *et al.* (1988). Coupling an expert system shell with an object-oriented database system. *Journal of Object-Oriented Programming*, 1(2), 12-21

Bancilhon, F. (1988). Object-oriented database systems. In *Proc. of ACM Symposium on Principles of Database Systems*, Austin TX, May 1988

Bancilhon, F. (1989). A query language for the O_2 object-oriented database systems. In *Proc. 2nd International Workshop on Database Programming Languages*, Portland OR, June 1989

Banerjee, J., Kim, W., Kim, H.K. and Korth, H.F. (1987). Semantics and implementation of schema evolution in object-oriented databases. In *Proc. of ACM-SIGMOD International Conference on Management of Data*, San Francisco CA, May 1987

Banerjee, J., Kim, W., Kim, H.K. (1988). Queries in object-oriented databases. In *Proc. of Fourth IEEE International Conference on Data Engineering*, Los Angeles CA, February 1988

Banerjee, J., Kim, W., Kim, S.J. and Garza, J.F. (1988a). Clustering a DAG for CAD databases. *IEEE Trans. on Software Engineering*, 14(11), 1684-1699

Batini, C., Ceri, S. and Navathe, S. (1991). *Conceptual Database Design*. Benjamin/Cummings

Batory, D.S. (1982). Optimal file designs and reorganization points. In *ACM Trans. on Database Systems*, 7(1), 60-81

Batory, D. and Kim, W. (1985). Modelling concepts for VLSI CAD objects. In *ACM Trans. on Database Systems*, 10(3), 322-346

Batory, D., Leung, T., Wise, T.,m (1988). Implementation concepts for an extensible data model and data language. *ACM Trans. on Database Systems*, 13(3), 231-262

Bayer, R. and McCreight, E. (1972). Organization and maintenance of large ordered indexes. *Acta Informatica*, 1, 173-189

Beech, D. (1988). A foundation for evolution from relational to object databases. In *Proc. of the International Conference on Extending Database Technology (EDBT)*, Venice, Italy, March 1988

Beech, D. and Mahbod, B. (1988). Generalized version control in an object-oriented database system. In *Proc. 4th IEEE International Conference on Data Engineering*, Los Angeles CA

Benzaken, V. (1990). An evaluation model for clustering strategies in the O_2 object-oriented database system. In *Proc. of 3rd International Conference on Database Theory*, Paris, December 1990

Bertino, E., Negri, M., Pelagatti, G. and Sbattella, L. (1989). Integration of heterogeneous database applications through an object-oriented interface. *Information Systems*, 14(5), 407-420

Bertino, E. and Kim, W. (1989). Indexing techniques for queries on nested objects. *IEEE Trans. on Knowledge and Data Engineering*, 1(2), 196-214

Bertino, E., Negri, M., Pelagatti, G. and Sbattella, L. (1990). An object-oriented data model for distributed office applications. In *Proc. ACM-IEEE International Conference on Office Information Systems (COIS90)*, MIT, Cambridge MA, April 1990

Bertino, E. (1990). Query optimization using nested indices. In *Proc. of the 2nd International Conference on Extending Database Technology Conference (EDBT)*, Venice, Italy, March 1990

Bertino, E. and Martino, L. (1991). Object-oriented database management systems: concepts and issues. *Computer (IEEE Computer Society)*, 24(4), 33-47

Bertino, E. (1991). An indexing technique for object-oriented databases. In *Proc. of 7th IEEE International Conference on Data Engineering*, Kobe, Japan, April 1991

Bertino, E. and Foscoli, P.(1991). On modeling cost functions for object-oriented databases. (Submitted for publication, Dec. 1991)

Bertino, E. (1991a). On index configuration in object-oriented databases. (Submitted for publication, May 1991)

Bertino, E. (1991b). Method precomputation in object-oriented databases. In *Proc. of ACM-SIGOIS and IEEE-TC-OA International Conference on Organizational Computing Systems (COCS91)*, Atlanta GA, November 1991

Bertino, E. and Quarati, A. (1992). An approach to support method invocations in object-oriented queries. In *Proc. of International Workshop on Research Issues in Transactions and Query Processing (RIDE-TQP)*, Phoenix AZ, February 1992

Bertino, E. and Guglielmina, C. (1992a). Optimization of object-oriented queries using path indices. In *Proc. of International Workshop on Research Issues in Transactions and Query Processing (RIDE-TQP)*, Phoenix AZ, February 1992

Bertino, E. (1992). Data hiding and security in an object-oriented database system. In *Proc. of 8th IEEE International Conference on Data Engineering*, Phoenix AZ, February 1992

Bertino, E. (1992a) A view mechanism for object-oriented databases. In *Proc. 3rd International Conference on Extending Data Base Technology (EDBT)*, Vienna, Austria, March 1992

Bertino, E. and Montesi, E. (1992). Towards a logical-object oriented programming language for databases. In *Proc. of 3rd International Conference on Extending Database Technology (EDBT)*, Vienna, Austria, March 1992

Bertino, E., Damiani, M. and Randi, P. (1992). Multimedia data handling in a knowledge representation system. In *Proc. of 2nd Far-East Workshop on Future Database Systems*, Kyoto, Japan, April 1992, Advanced Database Research and Development Series – vol. 3, World Scientific

Bertino, E., Bottarelli, S., Damiani, M., Migliorati, M. and Randi, P. (1992a).

The ADKMS knowledge acquisition system. In *Proc. of 2nd Far-East Workshop on Future Database Systems*, Kyoto, Japan, April 1992, Advanced Database Research and Development Series – vol.3, World Scientific

Bertino, E., Negri, M., Pelagatti, G. and Sbattella, L. (1992b). Object-oriented query languages: the notion and the issues. *IEEE Trans. on Knowledge and Data Engineering*, 4(3), 223-237

Bertino, E. and Weigand, H. (1992). An approach to authorization modeling in object-oriented database systems, (Submitted for publication, 1992)

Bertino, E. and Foscoli, P.(1992a). Index organizations for object-oriented database systems. (Submitted for publication, 1992)

Bertino, E. and Foscoli, P.(1992b). A model of cost functions for object-oriented queries. In *Proc. of 5th International Workshop on Persistent Object Systems*, San Miniato, Pisa, Italy, September 1992

Bertino, E. and Guglielmina, C.(1992b). Path-index: an approach to the efficient execution of object-oriented queries. Accepted for publication in *Data and Knowledge Engineering* (North-Holland), 1992 (to appear)

Bertino, E., Martelli, M. and Montesi, D.(1992). CLP(AD) as a deductive database language with updates. (Submitted for publication, 1992)

Black, A. *et al.* (1987). Distribution and abstract types in Emerald. *IEEE Trans. on Software Engineering*, SE-13(1), 65-76

Borgida, A., Brachman, R., McGuinness, D. and Resnick, L.(1989). CLASSIC: a structural data model for objects. In *Proc. of ACM-SIGMOD International Conference on Management of Data*, Portland OR, May/June 1989

Breitl, R. *et al.*(1989) The GemStone data management system. In *Object-Oriented Concepts, Databases, and Applications* W. Kim, and F. Lochovsky, eds., pp. 283-308. Reading MA: Addison-Wesley

Bruce, K. (1992). *A paradigmatic object-oriented programming language: design, static typing and semantics*. Technical Report No. CS-92-01, Williams College, Williamstown MA

Cacace, F., Ceri, S., Crespi-Reghizzi, S., Tanca, L. and Zicari, R. (1990). Integrating object-oriented data modeling with a rule-based programming paradigm. In *Proc. of ACM-SIGMOD International Conference on Management of Data*, Atlantic City NJ, May 1990

Campbell, D.M. and Embley, D.W.(1985). A relationally complete query language for an ER model. In *Proc. Entity Relationship Model Conference*, Chigago IL, October 1985

Carey, M. *et al.* (1988). A data model and query language for EXODUS. In *Proc. of ACM-SIGMOD International Conference on Management of Data*, Chicago IL, May 1988

Cattell, R.G.G. (1991). *Object Data Management – Object-Oriented and Extended Relational Database Systems*. Reading MA: Addison-Wesley

Cattell, R.G.G. and Skeen, J.(1992). Object operations benchmarks. *ACM Trans. on Database Systems*, 17(1), 1-31

Ceri, S.(1992). A declarative approach to active databases. In *Proc. of 8th IEEE International Conference on Data Engineering*, Phoenix AZ, February 1992

Chamberlin, D.D. *et al.* (1976). SEQUEL 2: a unified approach to data definition, manipulation, and control. *IBM J. Research and Development*, 20(6), 560-575

Chen, P. (1976). The entity-relationship model – toward a unified view of data. *ACM Trans. on Database Systems*, 1(1), 9-36

Chen, J.R. and Hurson, A.R. (1991). Effective clustering on complex objects in object-oriented databases. In *ACM Proc. of ACM-SIGMOD International Conference on Management of Data*, Denver CO, May 1991

Chimenti, D. *et al.* (1990). The LDL system prototype. *IEEE Trans. on Knowledge and Data Engineering*, 2(1) 76-90

Chou, H.T. *et al.*(1985). Design and implementation of the Wisconsin Storage Subsystem. *Software – Practice and Experience*, 15(10), 943-962

Chou, H.T. and Kim, W. (1986) A unifying framework for versions in CAD environment. In *Proc. of International Conference on Very Large Databases (VLDB)*, Kyoto , Japan, August 1986

Chou, H.-T. and Kim, W.(1988). Versions and change notification in an object-oriented database system. In *Proc. of 25th Design Automation Conference*, June 1988

Clifford, J. and Ariav, G. (1986). Temporal data management: models and systems. In *New Directions for Database Systems* (G. Ariav and J. Clifford, eds.), pp. 168-186. Norwood NJ: Ablex Publishing Co

Cluet, S. *et al.* (1989). Reloop, an algebra based query language for an object-oriented database system. In *Proc. of 1st International Conference on Deductive and Object Oriented Databases (DOOD)*, Kyoto, Japan, December 1989

Cluet, S. and Delobel, C. (1992). A framework for query optimization in an object-oriented database. In *Proc. of ACM-SIGMOD International Conference on Management of Data*, San Diego CA, May 1992

Codd, E. (1970). A relational model for large shared data banks. *Comm. ACM*, 13(6), 377-387

Coen-Porisini, A., Lavazza, L. and Zicari, R.(1992). The ESSE project: an overview. *In Proc. of 2nd Far-East Workshop on Future Database Systems*, Kyoto, Japan, April 1992. Advanced Database Research and Development Series – vol.3, World Scientific

Comer, D. (1979). The ubiquitous B-tree. In *ACM Comput. Surveys*, 11(2), 121-137

Dahl, O.J. and Nygaard, K. (1966). SIMULA – An Algol-based Simulation Language. In *Comm. ACM*, 9(9)

Date, C.J. (1987). *A Guide to the SQL Standard*, Reading MA: Addison-Wesley

Date, C.J. (1990). *Introduction to Database Systems*, vol. 1, 5th ed., Reading MA: Addison-Wesley

Dayal, U. (1989). Queries and views in an object-oriented data model. In *Proc. of 2nd International Workshop on Database Programming Languages*, Portland OR, June 1989

Deutsch, P.L. (1991). Object-oriented software technology. *Computer (IEEE Computer Society)*, 24(9), 112-113

Deux, O. *et al.* (1990) The story of O_2. *IEEE Trans. on Knowledge and Data Engineering*, 2(1), 91-108

Dittrich, K. and Lorie, R. (1988). Version support for engineering database systems. *IEEE Trans. on Software Engineering*, 14(4), 429-437

Fernandez, E.B., Summers, R.C. and Wood, C. (1981). *Database security and integrity*. Reading MA: Addison-Wesley

Fikes, R. and Kehler, T. (1985). The role of frame-based representation in reasoning. *Comm. ACM*, 28(9), 904-920

Fishman, D. *et al.*, Overview of the Iris DBMS. In *Object-Oriented Concepts, Databases, and Applications* (Kim, W., and F. Lochovsky, eds.) Addison-Wesley (1989), pp. 219-250

Gardarin, G. and Lanzelotte, R. (1992). Optimizing object-oriented database queries using cost-controlled rewriting. In *Proc. 3rd International Conference on Extending Data Base Technology (EDBT)*, Vienna, Austria, March 1992

Goldberg, A. and Robson, D. (1983). *Smalltalk-80: the language and its implementation*. Reading MA: Addison-Wesley

Griffiths, P.P. and Wade B.W. (1976). An authorization mechanism for a relational database system. *ACM Trans. on Database Systems*, 1(3), 242-255

Guttag, J. (1977). Abstract data types and the development of data structures. *Comm. ACM*, 20(6)

Hailpern, B. and Ossher, B. (1990). Extending objects to support multiple interfaces and access control. *IEEE Trans. on Software Engineering*, 16,(11), 1247-1257

Haskin, R. and Lorie, R.A. (1982). On extending the functions of a relational database system. In *Proc. of the ACM SIGMOD International Conference on Management of Data*, New York 1982

Hornick, M.F. and Zdonik, S.B. (1987). A shared, segmented memory system for an object-oriented database. *ACM Trans. on Office Information Systems*, 5(1), 70-95

Jajodia, S., Kogan, B. and Sandhu, R. (1990). *A multilevel-secure object-oriented data model*. George Mason University, Tech. Report

Jenq, P., Woelk, D., Kim, W. and Lee, W. L. E. (1990). Query processing in distributed ORION. In *Proc. of the 2nd International Conference on Extending Database Technology Conference (EDBT)*, Venice, Italy, March 1990

Jhingram, A. (1991). Precomputation in a complex object environment. In *Proc. of 7th IEEE International Conference on Data Engineering*, Kobe, Japan, April 1991

Joseph, J., Thatte, S., Thompson, C. and Wells, D. (1991). Object-oriented databases: design and implementation. *IEEE Proceedings*, 79(1), 42-64

Katz, R. (1990). Toward a unified framework for version modelling in engineering databases. *ACM Computing Surveys*, 22(4), 375-408

Kemper, A. and Moerkotte, G. (1990). Access support in object bases. In *Proc. of ACM-SIGMOD International Conference on Management of Data*, Atlantic City NJ, May 1990

Kemper, A. and Moerkotte, G. (1990a). Advanced query processing in object bases using access support relations. In *Proc. of 16th International Conference on Very Large Databases (VLDB)*, Brisbane, Australia, August 1990

Kemper, A., Kilger, C. and Moerkotte, G. (1991). Function materialization in object bases. In *Proc. of ACM-SIGMOD International Conference on Management of Data*, Denver CO, 1991

Ketabachi, M.V. and Berzins, V. (1987). Modeling and managing CAD databases. *IEEE Computer Magazine*, 20(2), 93-102

Khoshafian, S. and Copeland, G. (1986). Object Identity. In *Proc. Conference on Object-Oriented Programming Systems and Languages (OOPSLA)*, Portland OR

Kim, W. *et al.* (1987). Composite object support in an object-oriented database systems. In *Proc. of the 2nd International Conference on Object-Oriented Programming Systems, Languages, and Applications (OOPSLA)*, Orlando FL, October 1987

Kim, W., Chou, H.T. and Banerjee J. (1987a). Operations and implementation of complex objects. In *Proc. of 3rd IEEE International Conference on Data Engineering*, Los Angeles CA, February 1987

Kim, K. C., Kim, W., Woelk, D. and Dale, A. (1988). *Acyclic query processing in object-oriented databases*. MCC Technical Report Number: ACA-ST-287-88

Kim, W. and Chou, H.T. (1988). Versions of schema for object-oriented databases. In *Proc. of the International Conference on Very Large Databases (VLDB)*, Los Angeles CA, August 1988

Kim, W. and Lochovsky, F., eds. (1989). *Object-Oriented Concepts, Databases, and Applications*. Reading MA: Addison-Wesley

Kim, W., Bertino, E. and Garza, J.F. (1989). Composite objects revisited. In *Proc. of ACM-SIGMOD International Conference on Management of Data*, Portland OR, May/June 1989

Kim, W., Ballou, N., Chou, H.T., Garza, J. and Woelk, D. (1989a). Features of the ORION object-oriented database system. In *Object-Oriented Concepts, Databases, and Applications* (Kim, W. and Lochovsky, F., eds.), pp. 251-282, Reading MA: Addison-Wesley

Kim, W. (1989). A model of queries for object-oriented database systems. In *Proc. of the International Conference on Very Large Databases (VLDB)*, Amsterdam, Holland, August 1989

Kim, W., Kim, K.C. and Dale, A. (1989b). Indexing techniques for object-oriented databases. In *Object-Oriented Concepts, Databases, and Applications* (Kim, W. and Lochovsky,F., eds.), pp.371-394. Reading MA: Addison-Wesley

Kim, W. (1990). *Introduction to Object-Oriented Databases*. Cambridge MA: The MIT Press

Kim, W., Ballou, N., Garza, J.F. and Woelk, D. (1991). A distributed object-oriented database system supporting shared and private databases. *ACM Trans. on Information Systems*, 9(1), 31-51

Klahold, P., Schlageter, G. and Wilkes, W. (1986). A general model for version management in databases. In *Proc. of the International Conference on Very Large Databases (VLDB)*, Kyoto, Japan, August 1986

Korth, H.K. and Silberschatz, A. (1986). *Database System Concepts*. New York: McGraw-Hill

Landis, G.S. (1986). Design evolution and history in an object-oriented CAD/CAM database. In *Proceedings of the 31st COMPCON Conference*, San Francisco CA, March 1986

Leblang, D.B. and Chase, R.P. (1984). Computer aided software engineering in a distributed workstation environment. In *Proc. of the ACM SIGPLAN/SIGSOFT Conference on Practical Software Development Environment*, New York 1984

Lecluse, C., Richard, P. and Velez, F. (1990) O_2, an object-oriented data model. In *Advances in Database Programming Languages* (Bancilhon, F. and Buneman, P. eds.), pp.257-276, Reading MA: Addison-Wesley

Lenzerini, M., Class hierarchies and their complexity. In *Advances in Database Programming Languages* (Bancilhon, F. and Buneman, P. eds.), pp. 43-65, Reading MA: Addison-Wesley

Lenzerini, M., Nardi, D. and Simi, M., eds. (1991). *Inheritance Hierarchies in Knowledge Representation and Programming Languages*, New York: Wiley

Maier, D. and Stein, J. (1986). Indexing in an object-oriented database. In *Proc. of IEEE Workshop on Object-Oriented DBMSs*, Asilomar CA, September 1986

Maier, D. and Zdonik, S. (1989). Fundamentals of object-oriented databases. In *Readings in Object-Oriented Database Management Systems* (Maier, D. and Zdonik, S., eds.), Morgan Kauffman

Maier, D. (1989). Making database systems fast enough for CAD applications. In *Object-Oriented Concepts, Databases, and Applications* (Kim, W. and Lochovsky,F., eds.), pp.573-583, Reading MA: Addison-Wesley

Maier, D. (1983). *The Theory of Relational Databases*. Computer Science Press

McLeod, D., Narayanaswamy, K. and Bapa Rao, K. (1983). An approach to information management for CAD/VLSI applications. In *Proc. of the SIGMOD Conference on Databases for Engineering Applications*, San Jose CA, June 1983

Meyer, B. (1988). *Object-oriented software construction*. Prentice-Hall

Moon, D.A. (1989). The Common Lisp object-oriented programming language standard. In *Object-Oriented Concepts, Databases, and Applications* (Kim, W. and Lochovsky,F., eds.), pp. 49-78. Reading MA: Addison-Wesley

Moss, J.E.B. (1990). *Working with persistent objects: to swizzle or not to swizzle*. COINS Technical Report 90-38, Department of Computer and Information Science, University of Massachusetts, Amherst MA

Object Design (1990). *ObjectStore Reference Manual*. Object Design Inc., Burlington MA

Omiecinsky, E. (1985). Incremental file reorganization. In *Proc. 11th International Conference on Very Large Databases (VLDB)*, Stockholm, Sweden, August 1985

Osborne, S. and Heaven, T. (1986). The design of a relational database system with abstract data types for domains. *ACM Trans. on Database Systems*, 11(3), 357-373

Jeffcoate, J. and Guilfoyle, C. (1991). *Databases for objects: the market opportunity*. Ovum Ltd.

Ozsoyoglu, M. *et al.* (1987). Extending relational algebra and calculus with set-valued attributes and aggregate functions. *ACM Trans. on Database Systems*, 12(4), 566-592

Pinson, L., Wiener, R., eds. (1990). *Applications of Object-Oriented Programming*. Reading MA: Addison-Wesley

Pistor, P. and Traunmuller, R. (1986). A database language for sets, lists, and tables. *Information Systems*, 11(4), 323-336

Purdy, A., Maier, D. and Schuchardt, B. (1987). Integrating an object server with other worlds. *ACM Trans. on Office Information Systems*, 5(1), 27-47

Rabitti, F., Bertino, E., Kim, W., Woelk, D. (1981). A model of authorization for next-generation database systems. *ACM Trans. on Database Systems*, 16(1), 88-131

Roth, M.A., Korth, H.F. and Silberschatz, A. (1988). Extended algebra and calculus for nested relational databases. *ACM Trans. on Database Systems*, 13(4), 389-417

Rumbaugh, J. (1987). Relations as semantic constructs in an object-oriented language. In *Proc. International Conference on Object-Oriented Programming Systems, Languages, and Applications (OOPSLA)*, Orlando FL, October 1987

Rumbaugh, J. (1988). Controlling propagation of operations using attributes on relations. In *Proc. International Conference on Object-Oriented Programming Systems, Languages, and Applications (OOPSLA)*, New York, 1988

Rumbaugh, J., Blaha, M., Premerlani, W., Eddy, F. and Lorensen, W. (1991). *Object-Oriented Modeling and Design*. Englewood Cliffs NJ: Prentice Hall

Schek, H.J. and Scholl, M.H. (1986). The relational model with relational-valued attributes. *Information Systems*, 11(2), 137-146

Schwarz *et al.*, (1986). Extensibility in the Straburst database system. In *Proc of the International Workshop on Object-Oriented Database Systems*, Pacific Grove CA, September 1986

Sciore, E. (1991). Using annotations to support multiple kinds of versioning in an object-oriented database system. *ACM Trans. on Database Systems*, 16(3), 417-438

Servio Logic Development Corporation (1990). *Programming in OPAL, Version 2.0*

Shaw, G.B. (1989). An object oriented query algebra. In *Proc. 2nd International Workshop on Database Programming Languages*, Portland OR, June 1989

Shipman, D.W. (1981). The functional data model and the data language DAPLEX. *ACM Trans. on Database Systems*, 6(1), 140-173

Sockut, G.H. and Goldberg, R.P. (1979). Database reorganization – principles and practice. *ACM Computing Surveys*, 11(4), 371-395

Soderlund, L. (1981). Concurrent database reorganization – assessment of a powerful technique through modelling. In *Proc. 7th International Conference on Very Large Data Bases (VLDB)*

Steele, G.L. Jr. (1984). *Common Lisp: The Language*. Digital Press

Stefik, M. and Bobrow, D. (1984). Object-oriented programming: themes and variations. *The AI Magazine*, pp. 40-62

Stonebraker, M., Wong, E., Kreps, P. and Held, G. (1976). The design and implementation of INGRES. *ACM Trans. on Database Systems*, 1(3), 189-222

Stonebraker, M., Rowe, L., Hirohama, M. (1990). The implementation of Postgres. *IEEE Trans. on Knowledge and Data Engineering*, 2(1), 125-142

Straube, D. and Oszu, T. (1990). Queries and query processing in object-oriented database systems. *ACM Trans. on Information Systems*, 18(4), 387-430

Stroustrup, B. (1986). *The C++ Programming Language*. Reading MA: Addison-Wesley

Sudkamp, N. and Linnemann, V. (1990). Elimination of views and redundant variables in an SQL-like database language for extended NF^2 structures. In *Proc. 16th International Conference on Very Large Data Bases (VLDB)*, Brisbane, Australia, August 1990

SUN Microsystems (1988). *Introduction to NSE*. SUN Part No. 800-2362-1300

Thuraisingham, M.B. (1989). Mandatory security in object-oriented database system. In *Proc. International Conference on Object-Oriented Programming Systems, Languages, and Applications (OOPSLA)*, New Orleans, October 1989

Tsichritzis, D. and Lochovsky, F. (1982). *Data Models*. Englewood Cliffs: Prentice-Hall

Ullman, J. (1989). *Principles of Database and Knowledge-Based Systems, vol. 1 and 2*. Rockville MD: Computer Science Press

Urban, S.D. and Delcambre, L. (1990). Constraint analysis: identifying design alternatives for operations on complex objects. *IEEE Trans. on Knowledge and Data Engineering*, 2(4), 391-400

Urban, S.D. and Desiderio, M. (1992). CONTEXT : a CONstrainT EXplanation Tool., to appear in *Data and Knowledge Engineering*, North-Holland

Urban, S.D. and Lim, B. (1992). An intelligent framework for active support of database semantics, to appear in *Advances in Database and AI, vol. 1: The Landscape of Intelligence in Database and Information Systems*. (Delcambre, L. and F. Petry, F., eds.), Jai Press

Valduriez, P., Khoshafian, S. and Copeland, G. (1986). Implementation techniques of complex objects. In *Proc. of the 12th International Conference on Very Large Data Bases (VLDB)*, Kyoto, Japan, August 1986

Valduriez, P. (1987). Join indices. *ACM Trans. on Database Systems*, 12(2), 218-246

Valduriez, P. (1987a). *Optimization of complex database queries using join indices*. MCC Technical Report, No. ACA-ST-265-87

Velez, F. (1985). LAMBDA: an ER based query language for the retrieval of structured documents. In *Proc. Entity Relationship Conference*, Chicago IL, October 1985

Versant Object Technology (1990). *Versant Reference Manual*. Menlo Park CA: Versant Object Technology Inc.

Vines, P., Vines, D. and King, T. (1988). *Configuration and change control in GAIA*. ACM, New York

Vossen, G. (1991). *Data Models, Database Languages and Database Management Systems*. Reading MA: Addison-Wesley

Woelk, D. and Kim, W. (1987). Multimedia information management in an object-oriented database system. In *Proc. of the International Conference on Very Large Data Bases (VLDB)*, Brighton, UK, September 1987

Wilkinson, K., Lyngbaek, P. and Hasan, W. (1990). The Iris architecture and implementation. *IEEE Trans. on Knowledge and Data Engineering*, 2(1), 63-75

Yao, S.B. (1977). Approximating block accesses in database organizations. *Comm. ACM*, 20(4), 260-261

Yao, S.B. (1979). Optimization of query evaluation algorithms. *ACM Trans. on Database Systems*, 4(2), 133-155

Zaniolo, C. (1983). The database language GEM. In *Proc. of ACM-SIGMOD International Conference on Management of Data*, Boston MA, June 1983

Zdonik, S. (1990). Object-oriented type evolution. In *Advances in Database Programming Languages* (Bancilhon, F. and Buneman, P. eds.), pp. 277-288. Reading MA: Addison-Wesley

Zdonik, S. and Mitchell, G. (1991). ENCORE: an object-oriented approach to database modeling and querying. *IEEE Data Engineering*, 14(2), 53-57; 277-288

Zicari, R. (1991). A framework for schema updates in an object-oriented database system. In *Proc. of Seventh IEEE International Conference on Data Engineering*, Kobe, Japan, April 1991

Zloof, M.M. (1978). Query-by-Example: a data base language. *IBM Systems Journal*, 16(4), 324-343.

Index